The Use of Pleasure

Books by Michel Foucault

Madness and Civilization: A History of Insanity in the Age of Reason
The Order of Things: An Archaeology of the Human Sciences
The Archaeology of Knowledge (and The Discourse on Language)
The Birth of the Clinic: An Archaeology of Medical Perception
I, Pierre Rivière, having slaughtered my mother, my sister, and my
brother....A Case of Parricide in the Nineteenth Century
Discipline and Punish: The Birth of the Prison
The History of Sexuality, Volumes 1, 2, and 3
Herculine Barbin, Being the Recently Discovered Memoirs of a Nineteenth-
Century French Hermaphrodite
Power/Knowledge: Selected Interviews and Other Writings, 1972–1977

The Use of Pleasure

Volume 2 of The History of Sexuality

Michel Foucault

Translated from the French by Robert Hurley

Vintage Books
A Division of Random House, Inc.
New York

VINTAGE BOOKS EDITION, MARCH 1990

Translation copyright © 1985 by Random House, Inc.

All rights reserved under International and Pan-American Copyright
Conventions. Published in the United States by Vintage Books, a
division of Random House, Inc., New York, and simultaneously in
Canada by Random House of Canada Limited, Toronto. Originally
published in France as *L'Usage des plaisirs* by Editions Gallimard.
Copyright © 1984 by Editions Gallimard. First American edition
published by Pantheon Books, a division of Random House, Inc., in
October 1985.

Library of Congress Cataloging-in-Publication Data
Foucault, Michel.   The history of sexuality.

Translation of Histoire de la sexualité.

Includes bibliographical references and indexes.

Contents: v. 1. An introduction—v. 2. The use of pleasure.

1. Sex customs—History—Collected works.   I. Title.
HQ 12.F6813 1980   301.41'7   79-460
ISBN 0-394-75122-1

Manufactured in the United States of America
579C864

Contents

Translator's Acknowledgments

A number of people contributed to this translation, at Berkeley and elsewhere. Out of respect for the author's work, they made an occasion of community for which I am grateful.

Peter Brown generously shared his knowledge of classical matters and his familiarity with the author's project. His critical comments were an invaluable service.

Stephen W. Foster reviewed the translation with a practiced eye and suggested many changes of phraseology, virtually all of which I incorporated into the text.

Denis Hollier answered several questions that cropped up when my reading did not quite match the sophistication of the author's prose.

James Faubion drew up a list of reliable English versions of the major Greek texts. Without his recommendations, I would have risked many inaccuracies.

Marie-Claude Perigon, my wife, helped me with various problems of micro-interpretation, that is, with the kind of difficulties every reader encounters but only translators have to resolve.

I am indebted most to Paul Rabinow. He offered advice and encouragement—moral support—at every stage.

I wish to dedicate this English version to the memory of Michel Foucault.

R.H.
May 1985

Introduction

1

Modifications

This series of studies is being published later than I had anticipated, and in a form that is altogether different. I will explain why.

It was intended to be neither a history of sexual behaviors nor a history of representations, but a history of "sexuality" —the quotation marks have a certain importance. My aim was not to write a history of sexual behaviors and practices, tracing their successive forms, their evolution, and their dissemination; nor was it to analyze the scientific, religious, or philosophical ideas through which these behaviors have been represented. I wanted first to dwell on that quite recent and banal notion of "sexuality": to stand detached from it, bracketing its familiarity, in order to analyze the theoretical and practical context with which it has been associated. The term itself did not appear until the beginning of the nineteenth century, a fact that should be neither underestimated nor overinterpreted. It does point to something other than a simple recasting of vocabulary, but obviously it does not mark the sudden emergence of that to which "sexuality" refers. The use of the word was established in connection with other phenomena: the development of diverse fields of knowledge (embracing the biological mechanisms of reproduction as well as the individual or social variants of behavior); the establishment of a set of rules and norms—in part traditional, in part new—which found support in religious, judicial, pedagogical, and medical institutions; and changes in the way individuals were led to assign meaning and value to their conduct, their duties, their pleasures, their feelings and sensations, their dreams. In short, it was a matter of seeing how an "experience" came to be constituted in modern Western societies, an experience that caused individuals to recognize themselves as subjects of a "sexuality," which was accessible to very diverse fields of knowledge and linked to a system of rules and constraints. What I planned, therefore, was a history of the experience of sexuality, where experience is understood as the correlation between fields of knowledge, types of normativity, and forms of subjectivity in a particular culture.

To speak of sexuality in this way, I had to break with a conception that was rather common. Sexuality was conceived of as a constant. The hypothesis was that where it was manifested in historically singular forms, this was through various mechanisms of repression to which it was bound to be subjected in every society. What this amounted to, in effect, was that desire and the subject of desire were withdrawn from the historical field, and interdiction as a general form was made to account for anything historical in sexuality. But rejection of this hypothesis was not sufficient by itself. To speak of "sexuality" as a historically singular experience also presupposed the availability of tools capable of analyzing the peculiar characteristics and interrelations of the three axes that constitute it: (1) the formation of sciences *(savoirs)* that refer to it, (2) the systems of power that regulate its practice, (3) the forms within which individuals are able, are obliged, to recognize themselves as subjects of this sexuality. Now, as to the first two points, the work I had undertaken previously—having to do first with medicine and psychiatry, and then with punitive power and disciplinary practices—provided me with the tools I needed. The analysis of discursive practices made it possible to trace the formation of disciplines *(savoirs)* while escaping the dilemma of science versus ideology. And the analysis of power relations and their technologies made it possible to view them as open strategies, while escaping the alternative of a power conceived of as domination or exposed as a simulacrum.

But when I came to study the modes according to which individuals are given to recognize themselves as sexual subjects, the problems were much greater. At the time the notion of desire, or of the desiring subject, constituted if not a theory, then at least a generally accepted theoretical theme. This very acceptance was odd: it was this same theme, in fact, or variations thereof, that was found not only at the very center of the traditional theory, but also in the conceptions that sought to detach themselves from it. It was this theme, too, that appeared to have been inherited, in the nineteenth and twentieth centuries, from a long Christian tradition. While the experience of sexuality, as a singular historical figure, is perhaps quite distinct from the Christian experience of the "flesh," both appear nonetheless to be dominated by the principle of "desiring man." In any case, it seemed to me that one could not very well analyze the formation and development of the experience of sexuality from the eighteenth century onward, without doing a historical and critical study dealing with desire and the desiring subject. In other words, without undertaking a "genealogy." This does not mean that I proposed to write a history of the successive conceptions of desire, of concupiscence, or of libido, but rather to analyze the practices by which individuals were led to focus their attention on themselves, to decipher, recognize, and acknowledge themselves as subjects of desire, bringing into play between themselves and themselves a certain relationship that allows them to discover, in desire, the truth of their being, be it natural or fallen. In short, with this genealogy the idea was to investigate how individuals were led to practice, on themselves and on others, a hermeneutics of desire, a hermeneutics of which their sexual behavior was doubtless the occasion, but certainly not the exclusive domain. Thus, in order to understand how the modern individual could experience himself as a subject of a "sexuality," it was essential first to determine how, for centuries, Western man had been brought to recognize himself as a subject of desire.

A theoretical shift had seemed necessary in order to analyze what was often designated as the advancement of learning; it led me to examine the forms of discursive practices that articulated the human sciences. A theoretical shift had also been required in order to analyze what is often described as the manifestations of "power"; it led me to examine, rather, the manifold relations, the open strategies, and the rational techniques that articulate the exercise of powers. It appeared that I now had to undertake a third shift, in order to analyze what is termed "the subject." It seemed appropriate to look for the forms and modalities of the relation to self by which the individual constitutes and recognizes himself *qua* subject. After first studying the games of truth *(jeux de verité)* in their interplay with one another, as exemplified by certain empirical sciences in the seventeenth and eighteenth centuries, and then studying their interaction with power relations, as exemplified by punitive practices—I felt obliged to study the games of truth in the relationship of self with self and the forming of oneself as a subject, taking as my domain of reference and field of investigation what might be called "the history of desiring man."

But it was clear that to undertake this genealogy would carry me far from my original project. I had to choose: either stick to the plan I had set, supplementing it with a brief historical survey of the theme of desire, or reorganize the whole study around the slow formation, in antiquity, of a hermeneutics of the self. I opted for the latter, reasoning that, after all, what I have held to, what I have tried to maintain for many years, is the effort to isolate some of the elements that might be useful for a history of truth. Not a history that would be concerned with what might be true in the fields of learning, but an analysis of the "games of truth," the games of truth and error through which being is historically constituted as experience; that is, as something that can and must be thought. What are the games of truth by which man proposes to think his own nature when he perceives himself to be mad; when he considers himself to be ill; when he conceives of himself as a living, speaking, laboring being; when he judges and punishes himself as a criminal? What were the games of truth by which human beings came to see themselves as desiring individuals? It seemed to me that by framing the question in this way, and by attempting to develop it for a period that was rather far from the horizons with which I was familiar, I would be going more closely into the inquiry that I have long been committed to—even if this approach were to demand a few years of additional work. This long detour carried risks, to be sure; but I was motivated, and I seemed to have discovered a certain theoretical advantage in the research that I envisaged.

The risks? First, there was the likelihood of delaying and upsetting the publication schedule that I had projected. I am grateful to those who followed the advances and detours of my work—I am thinking of my auditors at the Collège de France —and to those who had the patience to wait for its outcome —Pierre Nora in particular. As to those for whom to work hard, to begin and begin again, to attempt and be mistaken, to go back and rework everything from top to bottom, and still find reason to hesitate from one step to the next—as to those, in short, for whom to work in the midst of uncertainty and apprehension is tantamount to failure, all I can say is that clearly we are not from the same planet.

There was also the danger that I would be dealing with documents with which I was insufficiently acquainted.* I

---

*I am neither a Hellenist nor a Latinist. But it seemed to me that if I gave enough care, patience, modesty, and attention to the task, it would be possible to gain sufficient familiarity with the ancient Greek and Roman texts; that is, a familiarity that would allow me—in keeping with a practice that is doubtless fundamental to Western philosophy—to examine both the difference that keeps us at a remove from a way of thinking in which we recognize the origin of our own, and the proximity that remains in spite of that distance which we never cease to explore.

would run the risk of adapting them, without fully realizing it, to alien forms of analysis or to modes of inquiry that would scarcely suit them. In dealing with this risk, I have benefited greatly from the works of Peter Brown and those of Pierre Hadot, and I have been helped more than once by the conversations we have had and the views they have expressed. In the effort to familiarize myself with the ancient texts, I also ran the contrary risk of losing the thread of the questions I wanted to raise; Hubert Dreyfus and Paul Rabinow at Berkeley enabled me, through their comments and their rigorous questioning, to undertake a theoretical and methodological reformulation. François Wahl offered me invaluable advice.

Paul Veyne has given me constant assistance throughout these years. He knows what the true historian's search for truth is about, but he also knows the labyrinth one enters when one sets out to trace the history of the games of truth and error. He is one of those individuals (rare nowadays) who are willing to face the hazard that the history of truth poses for all thought. His influence on what I have written here is pervasive. As for what motivated me, it is quite simple; I would hope that in the eyes of some people it might be sufficient in itself. It was curiosity—the only kind of curiosity, in any case, that is worth acting upon with a degree of obstinacy: not the curiosity that seeks to assimilate what it is proper for one to know, but that which enables one to get free of oneself. After all, what would be the value of the passion for knowledge if it resulted only in a certain amount of knowledgeableness and not, in one way or another and to the extent possible, in the knower's straying afield of himself? There are times in life when the question of knowing if one can think differently than one thinks, and perceive differently than one sees, is absolutely necessary if one is to go on looking and reflecting at all. People will say, perhaps, that these games with oneself would better be left backstage; or, at best, that they might properly form part of those preliminary exercises that are forgotten once they have served their purpose. But, then, what is philosophy today—philosophical activity, I mean—if it is not the critical work that thought brings to bear on itself? In what does it consist, if not in the endeavor to know how and to what extent it might be possible to think differently, instead of legitimating what is already known? There is always something ludicrous in philosophical discourse when it tries, from the outside, to dictate to others, to tell them where their truth is and how to find it, or when it works up a case against them in the language of naive positivity. But it is entitled to explore what might be changed, in its own thought, through the practice of a knowledge that is foreign to it. The "essay"—which should be understood as the assay or test by which, in the game of truth, one undergoes changes, and not as the simplistic appropriation of others for the purpose of communication—is the living substance of philosophy, at least if we assume that philosophy is still what it was in times past, i.e., an "ascesis," *askēsis,* an exercise of oneself in the activity of thought.

The studies that follow, like the others I have done previously, are studies of "history" by reason of the domain they deal with and the references they appeal to; but they are not the work of a "historian." Which does not mean that they summarize or synthesize work done by others. Considered from the standpoint of their "pragmatics," they are the record of a long and tentative exercise that needed to be revised and corrected again and again. It was a philosophical exercise. The object was to learn to what extent the effort to think one's own history can free thought from what it silently thinks, and so enable it to think differently.

Was I right to take these risks? That is for others to say. I only know that by shifting, as I did, the theme and chronological frame of reference of my study, I obtained a certain theoretical benefit; I could go on to make two generalizations that enabled me both to widen its scope and to specify its method and its goal more precisely.

It seemed that by starting from the modern era, and proceeding back through Christianity to antiquity, one would not be able to avoid raising a question that was at the same time very simple and very general: why is sexual conduct, why are the activities and pleasures that attach to it, an object of moral solicitude? Why this ethical concern—which, at certain times, in certain societies and groups, appears more important than the moral attention that is focused on other, likewise essential, areas of individual or collective life, such as alimentary behaviors or the fulfillment of civic duties? A reply comes to mind immediately, I know: they have been the object of fundamental interdictions, and transgressing the latter is considered a serious offense. But this is to make an answer of the question itself; and further, it shows a failure to recognize that the ethical concern over sexual conduct is not, in its intensity or its forms, always directly tied to the system of interdictions. It is often the case that the moral solicitude is strong precisely where there is neither obligation nor prohibition. In other words, the interdiction is one thing, the moral problematization is another. It seemed to me, therefore, that the question that ought to guide my inquiry was the following: how, why, and in what forms was sexuality constituted as a moral domain? Why this ethical concern that was so persistent despite its varying forms and intensity? Why this "problematization"? But, after all, this was the proper task of a history of thought, as against a history of behaviors or representations: to define the conditions in which human beings "problematize" what they are, what they do, and the world in which they live.

But in raising this very general question, and in directing it to Greek and Greco-Roman culture, it occurred to me that this problematization was linked to a group of practices that have been of unquestionable importance in our societies: I am referring to what might be called the "arts of existence." What I mean by the phrase are those intentional and voluntary actions by which men not only set themselves rules of conduct, but also seek to transform themselves, to change themselves in their singular being, and to make their life into an *oeuvre* that carries certain aesthetic values and meets certain stylistic criteria. These "arts of existence," these "techniques of the self," no doubt lost some of their importance and autonomy when they were assimilated into the exercise of priestly power in early Christianity, and later, into educative, medical, and psychological types of practices. Still, I thought that the long history of these aesthetics of existence and these technologies of the self remained to be done, or resumed. It has been a long time now since Burckhardt pointed out their significance for the epoch of the Renaissance, but their perpetuation, their history, and their development do not end there.* In any case, it seemed to me that the study of the problematization of sexual behavior in antiquity could be regarded as a chapter— one of the first chapters—of that general history of the "techniques of the self."

There is irony in those efforts one makes to alter one's way of looking at things, to change the boundaries of what one knows and to venture out a ways from there. Did mine actually result in a different way of thinking? Perhaps at most they made it possible to go back through what I was already thinking, to think it differently, and to see what I had done from a new vantage point and in a clearer light. Sure of having traveled far, one finds that one is looking down on oneself from above. The journey rejuvenates things, and ages the relationship with oneself. I seem to have gained a better perspective on the way I worked—gropingly, and by means of different or successive fragments—on this project, whose goal is a history of truth. It was a matter of analyzing, not behaviors or ideas, nor societies and their "ideologies," but the *problematizations* through which being offers itself to be, necessarily, thought—and the *practices* on the basis of which these problematizations are formed. The archaeological di-

*It is not quite correct to imply that since Burckhardt the study of these arts and this aesthetics of existence has been completely neglected. One thinks of Benjamin's study on Baudelaire. There is also an interesting analysis in Stephen Greenblatt's recent book, *Renaissance Self-Fashioning* (1980).

mension of the analysis made it possible to examine the forms themselves; its genealogical dimension enabled me to analyze their formation out of the practices and the modifications undergone by the latter. There was the problematization of madness and illness arising out of social and medical practices, and defining a certain pattern of "normalization"; a problematization of life, language, and labor in discursive practices that conformed to certain "epistemic" rules; and a problematization of crime and criminal behavior emerging from certain punitive practices conforming to a "disciplinary" model. And now I would like to show how, in classical antiquity, sexual activity and sexual pleasures were problematized through practices of the self, bringing into play the criteria of an "aesthetics of existence."

These, then, are the reasons that led me to recenter my entire study on the genealogy of desiring man, from classical antiquity through the first centuries of Christianity. I have followed a simple chronological arrangement: this volume, *The Use of Pleasure,* is devoted to the manner in which sexual activity was problematized by philosophers and doctors in classical Greek culture of the fourth century B.C.; *Care of the Self* deals with the same problematization in the Greek and Latin texts of the first two centuries of our era; lastly, *The Confessions of the Flesh* deals with the formation of the doctrine and ministry concerning the flesh. The documents I will refer to are for the most part "prescriptive" texts—that is, texts whose main object, whatever their form (speech, dialogue, treatise, collection of precepts, etc.) is to suggest rules of conduct. I will appeal to the theoretical texts on the doctrine of pleasures and passions only to look for clarifications. The domain I will be analyzing is made up of texts written for the purpose of offering rules, opinions, and advice on how to behave as one should: "practical" texts, which are themselves objects of a "practice" in that they were designed to be read, learned, reflected upon, and tested out, and they were intended to constitute the eventual framework of everyday conduct. These texts thus served as functional devices that would enable individuals to question their own conduct, to watch over and give shape to it, and to shape themselves as ethical subjects; in short, their function was "etho-poetic," to transpose a word found in Plutarch.

But since this analysis of desiring man is situated at the point where an archaelogy of problematizations and a genealogy of practices of the self intersect, I would like to dwell briefly, before getting started, on those two notions—that is, to account for the forms of "problematization" that I chose to examine, to indicate what is to be understood by "practices of the self," and to explain how I was led, through certain paradoxes and difficulties, to substitute a history of ethical problematizations based on practices of the self, for a history of systems of morality based, hypothetically, on interdictions.

2

Forms of Problematization

Suppose for a moment that we accept categories as general as those of "paganism," "Christianity," "morality," and "sexual morality." Suppose that we ask on which points the "sexual morality of Christianity" contrasted most sharply with the "sexual morality of ancient paganism." Prohibition of incest, male domination, subjugation of women? These are not the replies that will be given, no doubt; the extent and constancy of those phenomena in their various forms are well known. Other points of differentiation will more likely be submitted. For example, the meaning of the sexual act itself: it will be said that Christianity associated it with evil, sin, the Fall, and death, whereas antiquity invested it with positive symbolic values. Or the definition of the legitimate partner: it would appear that, in contrast to what occurred in the Greek and Roman societies, Christianity drew the line at monogamous marriage and laid down the principle of exclusively procreative ends within that conjugal relationship. Or the disallowance of relations between individuals of the same sex: it would seem that Christianity strictly excluded such relationships, while Greece exalted them and Rome accepted them, at least between men. To these three points of major opposition might be added the high moral and spiritual value that Christianity, unlike pagan morality, accorded to strict abstinence, lifelong chastity, and virginity. In short, regarding all these points that have been considered for such a long time to be so important

—the nature of the sexual act, monogamous fidelity, homosexual relations, chastity—it would seem that men of ancient times were rather indifferent, and that none of this claimed much of their attention or constituted very serious problems as far as they were concerned.

But this picture is not accurate; moreover, it would be easy to show that it is not. One would only have to point out the direct borrowing and strict continuities between the first Christian doctrines and the moral philosophy of antiquity. The first great Christian text devoted to sexual practice in married life—Chapter X of Book II of *The Pedagogue* by Clement of Alexandria—is supported by a number of scriptural references, but it also draws on a set of principles and precepts borrowed directly from pagan philosophy. One already notes a certain association of sexual activity with evil, along with the rule of procreative monogamy, a condemnation of relations between individuals of the same sex, and a glorification of self-restraint. Furthermore, given a longer historical frame to consider, one could trace the persistence of themes, anxieties, and exigencies that no doubt marked the Christian ethic and the morality of modern European societies; but not only, since they were already present at the core of Greek and Greco-Roman thought. Below is some evidence to consider, comprising: (1) the expression of a fear, (2) a model of conduct, (3) the image of a stigmatized attitude, and (4) an example of abstinence.

1. A fear. Young people afflicted with seminal weakness "of necessity become old in the habit of their body, dull, languid, dispirited, sluggish, stupidly silent, weak, wrinkled, incapable of any exertion, sallow, wan, effeminate; they lose their appetite, feel cold, a sense of weight in their limbs, and torpor in their legs, their strength fails, and they become paralyzed in every effort, and with many the disease goes on to palsy. For how could it be otherwise, that the power of the nerves should suffer when the generative principle is chilled?"

This disease, which is "shameful in itself," is "dangerous in that it leads to stagnation; harmful to society in that it goes against the propagation of the species; and because it is in all respects the source of countless ills, it requires prompt treatment."[1]* One has no trouble recognizing in this text the obsessive worries that medicine and pedagogy nurtured on the subject of pure sexual expenditure—that unproductive and partnerless activity—from the eighteenth century onward. The gradual exhaustion of the organism, the death of the individual, the destruction of his offspring, and finally, harm to the entire human race, were regularly promised, through an endlessly garrulous literature, to those who would make illicit use of their sex. These solicited fears seem to have been the "naturalistic" and scientific legacy, in medical thought of the nineteenth century, of a Christian tradition that consigned pleasure to the realm of death and evil.

Now, this description is actually a translation—a free translation, in the style of the period—of a text written by a Greek physician, Aretaeus, in the first century of our era. And one could find many other statements from the same epoch, testifying to this fear of the sexual act, which was liable, if it got out of control, to produce the most deleterious effects on the life of the individual. Soranus, for example, thought that sexual activity was in any case less favorable to health than virginity and plain abstinence. Even prior to that, medicine had earnestly recommended prudence and economy in the use of sexual pleasures: avoid their untimely enjoyment, take into account the conditions in which they are to be experienced, fear their peculiar violence and the effects of errors of regimen.

*In his French translation, L. Renaud offers this comment on the passage from Aretaeus: "The gonorrhea in question differs essentially from the disease that goes by that name today, which is more correctly called blennorrhea. . . . Simple or true gonorrhea, of which Aretaeus is speaking here, is characterized by an involuntary discharge, outside coition, of the spermatic humor mixed with the prostatic humor. This shameful disease is often provoked by, and the result of, masturbation."[2] The French translation slightly alters the meaning of the Greek text, which can be found in the *Corpus Medicorum Graecorum.*

Some even advised to indulge only "if one wants to do harm to oneself." A very ancient fear, therefore.

2. *An ideal of conduct.* We know how Saint Francis of Sales exhorted people to conjugal virtue. He held out a mirror to married couples, recommending the example of the elephant and the good morals it manifested with its mate. It was "only a large beast, but the most worthy of all the animals on earth, and the one with the most intelligence. . . . It never changes females and it is tenderly loving with the one it has chosen, mating only every three years, and then only for five days, and so secretly that it is never seen in the act; but it can be seen again on the sixth day, when the first thing it does is go straight to the river and bathe its whole body, being unwilling to return to the herd before it is purified. Tell me if these are not good and honorable habits."[3] Now this text is itself a variation on a theme that had been handed down by a long tradition (via Aldrovandi, Gesner, Vincent of Beauvais, and the famous *Physiologus*); one finds it already formulated in Pliny, whom Saint Francis of Sales follows rather closely in the *Introduction to the Devout Life:* "Owing to their modesty, elephants never mate except in secret . . . the female at the age of ten; and mating takes place for two years, on five days, so it is said, of each year and not more; and on the sixth day they give themselves a shower-bath in the river, not returning to the herd before. Adultery is unknown among them."[4] Of course, Pliny was not proposing a schema as explicitly didactic as that of Saint Francis of Sales; he was, however, referring to a clearly recommended model of conduct. It is not the case that mutual faithfulness among marriage partners was a generally acknowledged and accepted imperative among the Greeks and Romans. But it was a lesson given emphasis in some philosophical currents such as late Stoicism; it was also a conduct that was valued as a manifestation of virtue, inner strength, and self-mastery. Thus, the younger Cato was praised because,

up to the age at which he decided to marry, he still had not had relations with any woman; or better yet, there was Laelius: "in the course of his long life, he knew but one woman, the wife of his youth."⁵ One can go back even further in the definition of this model of mutual conjugal fidelity. Nicocles, in the speech attributed to him by Isocrates, shows the moral and political importance he accorded to the achievement of not "having approached any woman but my own wife" from the time of his marriage.⁶ And in his ideal city, Aristotle would have sexual relations of a husband with another woman, or the wife with another man, considered "dishonorable . . . in any circumstances whatsoever."⁷ The sexual "fidelity" of a husband with respect to his legitimate wife was not required either by law or by custom; it was nevertheless a question that people raised and a form of austerity on which some moralists set a high value.

  3. An image. In nineteenth-century texts there is a stereotypical portrait of the homosexual or invert: not only his mannerisms, his bearing, the way he gets dolled up, his coquetry, but also his facial expressions, his anatomy, the feminine morphology of his whole body, are regularly included in this disparaging description. The image alludes both to the theme of role reversal and to the principle of a natural stigma attached to this offense against nature. It was as if "nature herself had become an accessory to sexual mendacity."⁸ One could doubtless trace the long history of this image (to which actual behaviors may have corresponded, through a complex play of inductions and attitudes of defiance). In the deeply negative intensity of this stereotype, one might read the age-old difficulty, for our societies, of integrating these two phenomena—different phenomena at that—of the inversion of sexual roles and intercourse between individuals of the same sex. Now this image, with the repulsive aura that surrounds it, has come down through the centuries. It was already clearly delineated in the Greco-Roman literature of the imperial age. One encounters it in the portrait of the *Effeminatus* drawn by the author of an anonymous treatise on physiognomy of the fourth century; in the description of the priests of Atargatis, whom Apuleius makes fun of in *The Golden Ass;* in the symbolization that Dio Chrysostom offers for the *daimōn* of immoderation in one of his lectures on monarchy; in the fleeting evocation of the petty orators, with their perfume and their curls, whom Epictetus calls on at the back of his class, asking them if they are men or women.[9] One could see it again in the portrait of decadent youth, such as Seneca the Elder notices around him, with great repugnance: "Libidinous delight in song and dance transfixes these effeminates. Braiding the hair, refining the voice till it is as caressing as a woman's, competing in bodily softness with women, beautifying themselves with filthy fineries—this is the pattern our youths set themselves. . . . Born feeble and spineless, they stay like that throughout their lives; taking others' chastity by storm, careless of their own."[10] But in its essential traits, the portrait is more ancient still. Socrates' first speech in the *Phaedrus* alludes to it, when he voices disapproval of the love that is given to soft boys, too delicate to be exposed to the sun as they are growing up, and all made up with rouge and decked out in ornaments.[11] And it is with these same traits that Agathon appears in *The Thesmophoriazusae:* pale complexion, smooth-shaven cheeks, woman's voice, so much so that his interlocutor wonders if he is in the presence of a man or a woman.[12] It would be completely incorrect to interpret this as a condemnation of love of boys, or of what we generally refer to as homosexual relations; but at the same time, one cannot fail to see in it the effect of strongly negative judgments concerning some possible aspects of relations between men, as well as a definite aversion to anything that might denote a deliberate renunciation of the signs and privileges of the masculine role. The domain of male loves may have been "free" in Greek antiquity, much more so at any rate than it has been in modern European societies; the fact remains that one sees the very early expression of intense negative reactions and of forms of stigmatization that will extend well into the future.

4. A model of abstention.   The virtuous hero who is able to turn aside from pleasure, as if from a temptation into which he knows not to fall, is a familiar figure in Christianity—as common as the idea that this renunciation can give access to a spiritual experience of truth and love that sexual activity excludes. But equally well known in pagan antiquity was the figure of those athletes of self-restraint who were sufficiently masters of themselves and their cravings to be able to renounce sexual pleasure. Long before a thaumaturge like Apollonius of Tyana, who vowed chastity once and for all, and then had no more sexual relations for the rest of his life,[13] Greece had known and honored similar models. In some people, such extreme virtue was the visible mark of the mastery they brought to bear on themselves and hence of the power they were worthy of exercising over others. Thus Xenophon's Agesilaus not only "kept at arm's length those whose intimacy he did not desire," but kept from embracing even the boy he did love; and he was careful to lodge only in temples or in a place where "all men's eyes became witnesses to his rectitude."[14] But, for others, this abstention was linked directly to a form of wisdom that brought them into direct contact with some superior element in human nature and gave them access to the very essence of truth. The Socrates of the *Symposium* was like this, the one everybody wanted to be near, everybody was enamored of; the one whose wisdom everybody sought to appropriate—a wisdom that manifested and proved itself precisely in the fact that he was himself able to keep from laying hands on the provocative beauty of Alcibiades.[15] The thematics of a relationship between sexual abstinence and access to truth was already quite prominent.

We must not ask too much of these few references, however. It would be a mistake to infer that the sexual morality of

Christianity and that of paganism form a continuity. Several themes, principles, or notions may be found in the one and the other alike, true; but for all that, they do not have the same place or the same value within them. Socrates is not a desert Father struggling against temptation, and Nicocles is not a Christian husband; Aristophanes' laughter at the expense of Agathon in drag has few traits in common with the disparagement of the invert that will be found much later in medical discourse. Moreover, one must also not lose sight of the fact that the Church and the pastoral ministry stressed the principle of a morality whose precepts were compulsory and whose scope was universal (which did not rule out differences of prescription relating to the status of individuals, or the existence of ascetic movements having their own aspirations). In classical thought, on the other hand, the demands of austerity were not organized into a unified, coherent, authoritarian moral system that was imposed on everyone in the same manner; they were more in the nature of a supplement, a "luxury" in relation to the commonly accepted morality. Further, they appeared in "scattered centers" whose origins were in different philosophical or religious movements. They developed in the midst of many separate groups. They proposed—more than they imposed—different styles of moderation or strictness, each having its specific character or "shape." Pythagorean austerity was not the same as that of the Stoics, which was very different in turn from that recommended by Epicurus. From the few similarities I have managed to point out, it should not be concluded that the Christian morality of sex was somehow "pre-formed" in ancient thought; one ought to imagine instead that very early in the moral thought of antiquity, a thematic complex—a "quadri-thematics" of sexual austerity—formed around and apropos of the life of the body, the institution of marriage, relations between men, and the existence of wisdom. And, crossing through institutions, sets of precepts, extremely diverse theoretical references, and in spite of many alterations, this thematics maintained a certain constancy as time went by: as if, starting in antiquity, there were four points of problematization on the basis of which—and according to schemas that were often very different—the concern with sexual austerity was endlessly reformulated.

Now, it should be noted that these themes of austerity did not coincide with the lines of demarcation that may have been traced by the great social, civil, and religious interdictions. One might think that, generally speaking, where prohibitions are most fundamental, and where obligations are most coercive, moral systems develop the most insistent demands for austerity. Such a situation may arise, and the history of Christianity or of modern Europe would doubtless afford examples of this.* But it seems in fact that this was not the case in antiquity. This appears very clearly in the dissymmetry that was a peculiar feature of all the moral reflection on sexual behavior of that age: women were generally subjected (excepting the liberty they could be granted by a status like that of courtesan) to extremely strict constraints, and yet this ethics was not addressed to women; it was not their duties, or obligations, that were recalled, justified, or spelled out. It was an ethics for men: an ethics thought, written, and taught by men, and addressed to men—to free men, obviously. A male ethics, consequently, in which women figured only as objects or, at most, as partners that one had best train, educate, and watch over when one had them under one's power, but stay away from when they were under the power of someone else (father, husband, tutor). This is doubtless one of the most remarkable aspects of that moral reflection: it did not try to define a field of conduct and a domain of valid rules—subject to the necessary modulations—for the two sexes in common; it was an elaboration of masculine conduct carried out from the

---

*The development of an ethics of marital relations, or more specifically, of reflections on the sexual behavior of husband and wife in the conjugal relationship (ideas that assumed such importance in the Christian pastoral ministry), can be seen as a consequence of the setting up of the Christian model of marriage—a slow, belated, and difficult occurrence, at that—in the course of the Middle Ages.[16]

viewpoint of men in order to give form to *their* behavior.

Better still: it did not speak to men concerning behaviors presumably owing to a few interdictions that were universally recognized and solemnly recalled in codes, customs, and religious prescriptions. It spoke to them concerning precisely those conducts in which they were called upon to exercise their rights, their power, their authority, and their liberty: in the practice of pleasures that were not frowned upon, in a marital life where no rule or custom prevented the husband from having extramarital sexual relations, in relationships with boys, which—at least within certain limits—were accepted, commonly maintained, and even prized. These themes of sexual austerity should be understood, not as an expression of, or commentary on, deep and essential prohibitions, but as the elaboration and stylization of an activity in the exercise of its power and the practice of its liberty.

Which does not mean that this thematics of sexual austerity represents nothing more than an inconsequential refinement and a speculation unconnected with any specific concern. On the contrary, it is easy to see that each of these great figures of sexual austerity is tied to an axis of experience and to a cluster of concrete relationships: relations to the body, with the question of health, and behind it the whole game of life and death; the relation to the other sex, with the question of the spouse as privileged partner, in the game of the family institution and the ties it creates; the relation to one's own sex, with the question of partners that one can choose within it, and the problem of the adjustment between social roles and sexual roles; and finally, the relation to truth, where the question is raised of the spiritual conditions that enable one to gain access to wisdom.

It thus seemed to me that a whole recentering was called for. Instead of looking for basic interdictions that were hidden or manifested in the demands of sexual austerity, it was necessary to locate the areas of experience and the forms in which sexual behavior was problematized, becoming an object of

concern, an element for reflection, and a material for stylization. More specifically, it was logical to ask why the four great
domains of relations in which it seemed that a free man in
classical societies was able to develop and display his activity
without encountering any major prohibition, were precisely
the locuses of an intense problematization of sexual practice.
Why was it in those areas—apropos of the body, of the wife,
of boys, and of truth—that the practice of pleasures became
a matter for debate? Why did the bringing of sexual activity
into these relations occasion anxiety, discussion, and reflection? Why did these axes of everyday experience give rise to
a way of thinking that sought to rarefy sexual behavior, to
moderate and condition it, and to define an austere style in the
practice of pleasures? How did sexual behavior, insofar as it
implied these different types of relations, come to be conceived
as a domain of moral experience?

3

Morality and Practice of the Self

In order to answer this question, some methodological considerations need to be brought in; more specifically, it is best to reflect on the object one has in view when one undertakes to study the forms and transformations of a "morality."

Everyone is aware of the word's ambiguity. By "morality," one means a set of values and rules of action that are recommended to individuals through the intermediary of various prescriptive agencies such as the family (in one of its roles), educational institutions, churches, and so forth. It is sometimes the case that these rules and values are plainly set forth in a coherent doctrine and an explicit teaching. But it also happens that they are transmitted in a diffuse manner, so that, far from constituting a systematic ensemble, they form a complex interplay of elements that counterbalance and correct one another, and cancel each other out on certain points, thus providing for compromises or loopholes. With these qualifications taken into account, we can call this prescriptive ensemble a "moral code." But "morality" also refers to the real behavior of individuals in relation to the rules and values that are recommended to them: the word thus designates the manner in which they comply more or less fully with a standard of conduct, the manner in which they obey or resist an interdiction or a prescription; the manner in which they respect or disregard a set of values. In studying this aspect of morality, one must determine how and with what margins of variation or transgression individuals or groups conduct themselves in reference to a prescriptive system that is explicitly or implicitly operative in their culture, and of which they are more or less aware. We can call this level of phenomena "the morality of behaviors."

There is more. For a rule of conduct is one thing; the conduct that may be measured by this rule is another. But another thing still is the manner in which one ought to "conduct oneself"—that is, the manner in which one ought to form oneself as an ethical subject acting in reference to the prescriptive elements that make up the code. Given a code of actions, and with regard to a specific type of actions (which can be defined by their degree of conformity with or divergence from the code), there are different ways to "conduct oneself" morally, different ways for the acting individual to operate, not just as an agent, but as an ethical subject of this action. Take, for example, a code of sexual prescriptions enjoining the two marital partners to practice a strict and symmetrical conjugal fidelity, always with a view to procreation; there will be many ways, even within such a rigid frame, to practice that austerity, many ways to "be faithful." These differences can bear on several points worth considering.

They concern what might be called the *determination of the ethical substance;* that is, the way in which the individual has to constitute this or that part of himself as the prime material of his moral conduct. Thus, one can relate the crucial aspects of the practice of fidelity to the strict observance of interdictions and obligations in the very acts one accomplishes. But one can also make the essence of fidelity consist in the mastery of desires, in the fervent combat one directs against them, in the strength with which one is able to resist temptations: what makes up the content of fidelity in this case is that vigilance and that struggle. In these conditions, the contradictory movements of the soul—much more than the carrying out of the acts themselves—will be the prime material of moral practice. Alternatively, one can have it consist in the intensity, continuity, and reciprocity of feelings that are experienced vis-à-vis the partner, and in the quality of the relationship that permanently binds the two spouses.

The differences can also have to do with the *mode of subjection (mode d'assujettissement);* that is, with the way in which the individual establishes his relation to the rule and recognizes himself as obliged to put it into practice. One can, for example, practice conjugal fidelity and comply with the precept that imposes it, because one acknowledges oneself to be a member of the group that accepts it, declares adherence to it out loud, and silently preserves it as a custom. But one can practice it, too, because one regards oneself as an heir to a spiritual tradition that one has the responsibility of maintaining or reviving; one can also practice fidelity in response to an appeal, by offering oneself as an example, or by seeking to give one's personal life a form that answers to criteria of brilliance, beauty, nobility, or perfection.

There are also possible differences in the forms of *elaboration,* of *ethical work (travail éthique)* that one performs on oneself, not only in order to bring one's conduct into compliance with a given rule, but to attempt to transform oneself into the ethical subject of one's behavior. Thus, sexual austerity can be practiced through a long effort of learning, memorization, and assimilation of a systematic ensemble of precepts, and through a regular checking of conduct aimed at measuring the exactness with which one is applying these rules. It can be practiced in the form of a sudden, all-embracing, and definitive renunciation of pleasures; it can also be practiced in the form of a relentless combat whose vicissitudes—including momentary setbacks—can have meaning and value in themselves; and it can be practiced through a decipherment as painstaking, continuous, and detailed as possible, of the movements of desire in all its hidden forms, including the most obscure.

Other differences, finally, concern what might be called the *telos* of the ethical subject: an action is not only moral in itself,

in its singularity; it is also moral in its circumstantial integra-
tion and by virtue of the place it occupies in a pattern of
conduct. It is an element and an aspect of this conduct, and
it marks a stage in its life, a possible advance in its continuity.
A moral action tends toward its own accomplishment; but it
also aims beyond the latter, to the establishing of a moral
conduct that commits an individual, not only to other actions
always in conformity with values and rules, but to a certain
mode of being, a mode of being characteristic of the ethical
subject. Many differences are possible here as well: conjugal
fidelity can be associated with a moral conduct that aspires to
an ever more complete mastery of the self; it can be a moral
conduct that manifests a sudden and radical detachment vis-à-
vis the world; it may strain toward a perfect tranquillity of
soul, a total insensitivity to the agitations of the passions, or
toward a purification that will ensure salvation after death and
blissful immortality.

In short, for an action to be "moral," it must not be reducible to an act or a series of acts conforming to a rule, a law,
or a value. Of course all moral action involves a relationship
with the reality in which it is carried out, and a relationship
with the self. The latter is not simply "self-awareness" but
self-formation as an "ethical subject," a process in which the
individual delimits that part of himself that will form the
object of his moral practice, defines his position relative to the
precept he will follow, and decides on a certain mode of being
that will serve as his moral goal. And this requires him to act
upon himself, to monitor, test, improve, and transform himself. There is no specific moral action that does not refer to a
unified moral conduct; no moral conduct that does not call for
the forming of oneself as an ethical subject; and no forming
of the ethical subject without "modes of subjectivation" and
an "ascetics" or "practices of the self" that support them.
Moral action is indissociable from these forms of self-activity,
and they do not differ any less from one morality to another
than do the systems of values, rules, and interdictions.

These distinctions are bound to have effects that are not confined to theory. They also have consequences for historical analysis. Anyone who wishes to study the history of a "morality" has to take into account the different realities that are covered by the term. A history of "moral behaviors" would study the extent to which actions of certain individuals or groups are consistent with the rules and values that are prescribed for them by various agencies. A history of "codes" would analyze the different systems of rules and values that are operative in a given society or group, the agencies or mechanisms of constraint that enforce them, the forms they take in their multifariousness, their divergences and their contradictions. And finally, a history of the way in which individuals are urged to constitute themselves as subjects of moral conduct would be concerned with the models proposed for setting up and developing relationships with the self, for self-reflection, self-knowledge, self-examination, for the decipherment of the self by oneself, for the transformations that one seeks to accomplish with oneself as object. This last is what might be called a history of "ethics" and "ascetics," understood as a history of the forms of moral subjectivation and of the practices of self that are meant to ensure it.

If it is true, in fact, that every morality, in the broad sense, comprises the two elements I have just mentioned: codes of behavior and forms of subjectivation; if it is true that they can never be entirely dissociated, though they may develop in relative independence from one another—then we should not be surprised to find that in certain moralities the main emphasis is placed on the code, on its systematicity, its richness, its capacity to adjust to every possible case and to embrace every area of behavior. With moralities of this type, the important thing is to focus on the instances of authority that enforce the code, that require it to be learned and observed, that penalize infractions; in these conditions, the subjectivation occurs basically in a quasi-juridical form, where the ethical subject refers his conduct to a law, or set of laws, to which he must submit

at the risk of committing offenses that may make him liable
to punishment. It would be quite incorrect to reduce Christian
morality—one probably should say "Christian moralities"—
to such a model; and yet it may not be wrong to think that
the organization of the penitential system at the beginning of
the thirteenth century, and its development up to the eve of
the Reformation, brought about a very strong "juridification"
—more precisely, a very strong "codification"—of the moral
experience. It was against this codification that many spiritual
movements reacted before the Reformation.

On the other hand, it is easy to conceive of moralities in
which the strong and dynamic element is to be sought in the
forms of subjectivation and the practices of the self. In this
case, the system of codes and rules of behavior may be rather
rudimentary. Their exact observance may be relatively unimportant, at least compared with what is required of the individual in the relationship he has with himself, in his different
actions, thoughts, and feelings as he endeavors to form himself
as an ethical subject. Here the emphasis is on the forms of
relations with the self, on the methods and techniques by
which he works them out, on the exercises by which he makes
of himself an object to be known, and on the practices that
enable him to transform his own mode of being. These "ethics-
oriented" moralities (which do not necessarily correspond to
those involving "ascetic denial") have been very important in
Christianity, functioning alongside the "code-oriented"
moralities. Between the two types there have been, at different times, juxtapositions, rivalries and conflicts, and compromises.

Now, it seems clear, from a first approach at least, that
moral conceptions in Greek and Greco-Roman antiquity were
much more oriented toward practices of the self and the question of *askēsis* than toward codifications of conducts and the
strict definition of what is permitted and what is forbidden. If
exception is made of the *Republic* and the *Laws,* one finds very
few references to the principle of a code that would define in

detail the right conduct to maintain, few references to the need for an authority charged with seeing to its application, few references to the possibility of punishments that would sanction infractions. Although the necessity of respecting the law and the customs—the *nomoi*—was very often underscored, more important than the content of the law and its conditions of application was the attitude that caused one to respect them. The accent was placed on the relationship with the self that enabled a person to keep from being carried away by the appetites and pleasures, to maintain a mastery and superiority over them, to keep his senses in a state of tranquillity, to remain free from interior bondage to the passions, and to achieve a mode of being that could be defined by the full enjoyment of oneself, or the perfect supremacy of oneself over oneself.

This explains the choice of method I have kept to throughout this study on the sexual morality of pagan and Christian antiquity; that is, I had to keep in mind the distinction between the code elements of a morality and the elements of ascesis, neglecting neither their coexistence, their interrelations, their relative autonomy, nor their possible differences of emphasis. I had to take into account everything, in these moralities, that seemed to have to do with the privileged status of the practices of the self and the interest that may have been accorded them; with the effort that was made to develop them, perfect them, and teach them; and with the debate that went on concerning them. Consequently, the question that is so often raised regarding the continuity (or break) between the philosophical moralities of antiquity and Christian morality had to be reformulated; instead of asking what were the code elements that Christianity may have borrowed from ancient thought, and what were those that it added in its own right, in order to define what was permitted and what forbidden within a sexuality assumed to be constant, it seemed more pertinent to ask how, given the continuity, transfer, or modification of codes, the forms of self-relationship (and the practices of the self that were associated with them) were defined, modified, recast, and diversified.

I am not supposing that the codes are unimportant. But one notices that they ultimately revolve around a rather small number of rather simple principles: perhaps men are not much more inventive when it comes to interdictions than they are when it comes to pleasures. Their stability is also rather remarkable; the notable proliferation of codifications (concerning permitted or forbidden places, partners, and acts) occurred rather late in Christianity. On the other hand, it appears—at any rate this is the hypothesis I would like to explore here—that there is a whole rich and complex field of historicity in the way the individual is summoned to recognize himself as an ethical subject of sexual conduct. This will be a matter of seeing how that subjectivation was defined and transformed, from classical Greek thought up to the formulation of the Christian doctrine and pastoral ministry regarding the flesh.

In this volume, I would like to take note of some general traits that characterized the way in which sexual behavior was considered by classical Greek thought as a domain of moral valuation and choice. I will start from the then common notion of "use of the pleasures"—*chrēsis aphrodisiōn*—and attempt to determine the modes of subjectivation to which it referred: the ethical substance, the types of subjection, the forms of elaboration of the self, and the moral teleology. Then, starting each time from a practice whose existence, status, and rules were native to Greek culture (the practice of the health regimen, that of household management, that of courtship), I will study the way in which medical and philosophical thought worked out this "use of the pleasures," formulating several recurrent themes of austerity that would center on four great axes of experience: the relation to one's body, the relation to one's wife, the relation to boys, and the relation to truth.

PART ONE

*The Moral
Problematization
of Pleasures*

One would have a difficult time finding among the Greeks (or the Romans either, for that matter) anything resembling the notion of "sexuality" or "flesh." I mean a notion that refers to a single entity and allows diverse phenomena to be grouped together, despite the apparently loose connections between them, as if they were of the same nature, derived from the same origin, or brought the same type of causal mechanisms into play: behaviors, but also sensations, images, desires, instincts, passions.[1]

Of course the Greeks had a whole stock of words available for designating different actions or acts that we call "sexual." They had a vocabulary for referring to specific practices; they had vaguer terms that referred in a general way to what we call sexual "intercourse," "union," or "relations": for example, *synousia, homilia, plēsiasmos, mixis, ocheia.* But the blanket category that covered all these actions, acts, and practices is much more difficult to grasp. The Greeks were fond of using a nominalized adjective: *ta aphrodisia,*[2] which the Romans translated roughly as *venerea.* "Things" or "pleasures of love," "sexual relations," "carnal acts," "sensual pleasures"—one renders the term as best one can, but the difference between the notional sets, theirs and ours, makes it hard to translate precisely. Our idea of "sexuality" does not just cover a wider area; it applies to a reality of another type, and it functions quite differently in our morals and knowledge. Moreover, we do not have a concept that specifies and subsumes a set analogous to that of *aphrodisia.* Perhaps I will be excused if occasionally I leave the Greek term in its original form.

I do not aim in this section to give an exhaustive account,

or even a systematic summary, of the different philosophical or medical doctrines that dealt in one way or another, from the fifth century to the beginning of the third, with pleasure in general and with sexual pleasures in particular. Preliminary to studying the four types of stylization of sexual conduct that were developed in a *dietetics* concerned with the body, an *economics* concerned with marriage, an *erotics* concerned with the subject of boys, and a *philosophy* concerned with truth, I intend simply to bring out a few general traits that served as a framework for them, seeing that these traits were common to the different reflections on the *aphrodisia*. One can grant the familiar proposition that the Greeks of that epoch accepted certain sexual behaviors much more readily than the Christians of the Middle Ages or the Europeans of the modern period; one can also grant that laxity and misconduct in this regard provoked less scandal back then and made one liable to less recrimination, especially as there was no institution—whether pastoral or medical—that claimed the right to determine what was permitted or forbidden, normal or abnormal, in this area; one can also grant that the Greeks attributed much less importance to all these questions than we do. But once all that is granted or assumed, one point still remains irreducible: they nonetheless concerned themselves with such matters, and there were Greek thinkers, moralists, philosophers, and doctors who believed that what the laws of the city prescribed or prohibited, what the general customs tolerated or rejected, could not suffice to regulate properly the sexual conduct of a man who cared about himself. The manner in which this kind of pleasure was enjoyed was considered by them to be an ethical problem.

What I would like to define in the next few pages are just those general aspects which their preoccupation with these questions shared; that is, the general form of the moral inquiry that they pursued concerning the *aphrodisia*. And for this we will need to consult texts that are radically different from one another—essentially those of Xenophon, Plato, and Aristotle.

I will attempt to restore, not the "doctrinal context" that might give each one its peculiar meaning and its differential value, but rather the "field of problematization" that they had in common and that made each of them possible. The object, therefore, will be to elicit, in its general features, the constitution of the *aphrodisia* as a domain of moral concern. I will consider four notions that are often encountered in the reflection on sexual ethics: the notion of *aphrodisia*, through which one can grasp what was recognized as the "ethical substance" in sexual behavior; the notion of "use," of *chrēsis*, which allows one to perceive the type of subjection that the practice of pleasures had to undergo in order to be morally valorized; the notion of *enkrateia*, of mastery, that defines the attitude that was required with respect to oneself in order to make oneself into an ethical subject; and lastly, the notion of "moderation," of *sōphrosynē*, that characterized the ethical subject in his fulfillment. It should thus be possible to determine what structured the moral experience of sexual pleasures—its ontology, its deontology, its ascetics, its teleology.

1

Aphrodisia

The *Suda* gives a definition of *aphrodisia* that will be repeated by Hesychius: *aphrodisia* are "the works, the acts of
Aphrodite" *(erga Aphroditēs)*. Doubtless one should not expect to see a very rigorous attempt at conceptualization in
such a work as the one mentioned, but it is a fact that the
Greeks had not evinced, either in their theoretical reflection
or in their practical thinking, a very insistent concern for
defining precisely what they meant by *aphrodisia*—whether it
was a question of determining the nature of the thing designated, of delimiting its scope, or of drawing up an inventory
of its elements. In any case, they had nothing resembling those
long lists of possible acts, such as one finds later in the penitential books, the manuals of confession, or in works on psy-
chopathology; no table that served to define what was licit,
permitted, or normal, and to describe the vast family of prohibited gestures. Nor was there anything resembling the concern—which was so characteristic of the question of the flesh
or of sexuality—for discovering the insidious presence of a
power of undetermined limits and multiple masks beneath
what appeared inoffensive or innocent. Neither classification
nor decipherment. They might take great pains to fix the
optimal age to marry and have children, and the best season
for having sexual relations, but they would never say, like a
Christian spiritual director, which gestures to make or avoid
making, which preliminary caresses were allowed, which posi-

tion to take, or in which conditions one could interrupt the act. To the insufficiently prepared, Socrates recommended to flee from the sight of a handsome boy, even if it meant a year's exile,[1] and the *Phaedrus* evokes the lover's long struggle against his own desire; but nowhere is there a statement, as there will be in Christian spirituality, of the precautions that have to be taken in order to prevent desire from entering the soul surreptitiously, or to detect its secret traces. Even stranger perhaps: the doctors who set forth, in some detail, the elements of the *aphrodisia* regimen are practically silent concerning the forms that the acts themselves may take; they say very little—aside from a few references to the "natural position"—regarding what is in accord with or contrary to the will of nature.

Was this due to modesty? Possibly. For, as much as we like to credit the Greeks with a great liberty of morals, the representation of sexual acts that they suggest in their written works—and even in their erotic literature—seems to have been characterized by a good deal of reserve,* despite the impression one gets from the entertainments they staged or from certain iconographic representations that have been rediscovered.[3] In any case, one does sense that Xenophon, Aristotle, and later Plutarch would not have thought it decent to dispense the sort of presumptive and pragmatic advice on sexual relations with one's lawful wife that the Christian authors lavishly distributed on the subject of conjugal pleasures. They were not prepared, as the directors of conscience would be, to regulate the process of demands and refusals, of first caresses, of the modalities of union, of the pleasures one experienced and the conclusion they should properly be given. But there was a positive reason for this attitude that we may perceive retrospectively as "reticence" or "reserve." It was due to their conception of the *aphrodisia*, to the kind of questioning they directed to them, which was not oriented in the

*K. J. Dover notes an accentuation of this reserve in the course of the classical age.[2]

least toward the search for their profound nature, their canonical forms, or their secret potential.

1. The *aphrodisia* are the acts, gestures, and contacts that produce a certain form of pleasure. When Saint Augustine in his *Confessions* recalls the friendships of his youth, the intensity of his affections, the pleasures of the days spent together, the conversations, the enthusiasms and good times, he wonders if, underneath its seeming innocence, all that did not pertain to the flesh, to that "glue" which attaches us to the flesh.[4] But when Aristotle in his *Nicomachean Ethics* wants to determine exactly which people deserve to be called "self-indulgent," his definition is cautiously restrictive: self-indulgence—*akolasia*—relates only to the pleasures of the body; and among these, the pleasures of sight, hearing, and smell must be excluded.[5] It is not self-indulgent to "delight in" *(charein)* colors, shapes, or paintings, nor in theater or music; one can, without self-indulgence, delight in the scent of fruit, roses, or incense; and, he says in the *Eudemian Ethics,*[6] anyone who would become so intensely absorbed in looking at a statue or in listening to a song as to lose his appetite or taste for lovemaking could not be reproached for self-indulgence, any more than could someone who let himself be seduced by the Sirens. For there is pleasure that is liable to *akolasia* only where there is touch and contact: contact with the mouth, the tongue, and the throat (for the pleasures of food and drink), or contact with other parts of the body (for the pleasure of sex). Moreover, Aristotle remarks that it would be unjust to suspect self-indulgence in the case of certain pleasures experienced on the surface of the body, such as the noble pleasures that are produced by massages and heat in the gymnasium: "for the contact characteristic of the self-indulgent man does not affect the whole body but only certain parts."[7]*

*One should, however, note the importance attributed by many Greek texts to the gaze and to the eyes in the genesis of desire or love; but it is not that the pleasure

It will be one of the characteristic traits of the Christian experience of the "flesh," and later of "sexuality," that the subject is expected to exercise suspicion often, to be able to recognize from afar the manifestations of a stealthy, resourceful, and dreadful power. Reading these signs will be all the more important as this power has the ability to cloak itself in many forms other than sexual acts. There is no similar suspicion inhabiting the experience of the *aphrodisia*. To be sure, in the teaching and the exercise of moderation, it is recommended to be wary of sounds, images, and scents; but this is not because attachment to them would be only the masked form of a desire whose essence is sexual: it is because there are musical forms capable of weakening the soul with their rhythms, and because there are sights capable of affecting the soul like a venom, and because a particular scent, a particular image, is apt to call up the "memory of the thing desired."[9] And when philosophers are laughed at for claiming to love only the beautiful souls of boys, they are not suspected of harboring murky feelings of which they may not be conscious, but simply of waiting for the *tête-à-tête* in order to slip their hand under the tunic of their heart's desire.[10]

What of the form and variety of these acts? Greek natural history gives some descriptions, at least as concerns animals: Aristotle remarks that mating is not the same among all animals and does not take place in the same manner.[11] And in the part of Book VI of the *History of Animals* that deals more specifically with viviparous animals, he describes the different forms of copulation that can be observed: they vary according to the form and location of the organs, the position taken by the partners, and the duration of the act. But he also evokes the types of behavior that characterize the mating season: wild

---

of the gaze is self-indulgent; rather, it is thought to make an opening through which the soul is reached. In this connection, see Xenophon's *Memorabilia.* As for the kiss, it was very highly valued as a physical pleasure and a communication of souls despite the danger it carried. As a matter of fact, an entire historical study could be undertaken on the "pleasure body" and its transformations.

boars preparing for battle, elephants whose frenzy extends to the destruction of their keeper's house, or stallions that group their females together by tracing a big circle around them before throwing themselves against their rivals.[12] With regard to the human animal, while the description of organs and their functioning may be detailed, the subject of sexual behavior, with its possible variants, is barely touched upon. Which does not mean, however, that there was, in Greek medicine, philosophy, or ethics, a zone of strict silence around the sexual activity of humans. It is not that people were careful to avoid talking about these pleasurable acts; but when they were the subject of questioning, what was at issue was not the form they assumed, it was the activity they manifested. Their dynamics was much more important than their morphology.

This dynamics was defined by the movement that linked the *aphrodisia* to the pleasure that was associated with them and to the desire to which they gave rise. The attraction exerted by pleasure and the force of the desire that was directed toward it constituted, together with the action of the *aphrodisia* itself, a solid unity. The dissociation—or partial dissociation at least—of this ensemble would later become one of the basic features of the ethics of the flesh and the notion of sexuality. This dissociation was to be marked, on the one hand, by a certain "elision" of pleasure (a moral devaluation through the injunction given in the preaching by the Christian clergy against the pursuit of sensual pleasure as a goal of sexual practice; a theoretical devaluation shown by the extreme difficulty of finding a place for pleasure in the conception of sexuality); it would also be marked by an increasingly intense problematization of desire (in which the primordial sign of a fallen nature or the structure characteristic of the human condition would be visible). In the experience of the *aphrodisia* on the other hand, act, desire, and pleasure formed an ensemble whose elements were distinguishable certainly, but closely bound to one another. It was precisely their close linkage that constituted one of the essential characteristics of that form of activity. Nature intended (for reasons we shall consider) that the performance of the act be associated with a pleasure, and it was this pleasure that gave rise to *epithumia,* to desire, in a movement that was naturally directed toward what "gives pleasure," according to a principle that Aristotle cites: desire is always "desire for the agreeable thing" *(hē gar epithumia tou hēdeos estin).* [13] It is true—Plato always comes back to the idea—that for the Greeks there could not be desire without privation, without the want of the thing desired and without a certain amount of suffering mixed in; but the appetite, Plato explains in the *Philebus,* can be aroused only by the representation, the image or the memory of the thing that gives pleasure; he concludes that there can be no desire except in the soul, for while the body is affected by privation, it is the soul and only the soul that can, through memory, make present the thing that is to be desired and thereby arouse the *epithumia.* [14] Thus, what seems in fact to have formed the object of moral reflection for the Greeks in matters of sexual conduct was not exactly the act itself (considered in its different modalities), or desire (viewed from the standpoint of its origin or its aim), or even pleasure (evaluated according to the different objects or practices that can cause it); it was more the dynamics that joined all three in a circular fashion (the desire that leads to the act, the act that is linked to pleasure, and the pleasure that occasions desire). The ethical question that was raised was not: which desires? which acts? which pleasures? but rather: with what force is one transported "by the pleasures and desires"? The ontology to which this ethics of sexual behavior referred was not, at least not in its general form, an ontology of deficiency and desire; it was not that of a nature setting the standard for acts; it was an ontology of a force that linked together acts, pleasures, and desires. It was this dynamic relationship that constituted what might be called the texture of the ethical experience of the *aphrodisia.* *

*The frequency of expressions that link pleasures and desires very closely together should be noted. These expressions show that what is at stake in the ethical system

This dynamics is analyzed in terms of two major variables. The first is quantitative; it has to do with the degree of activity that is shown by the number and frequency of acts. What differentiates men from one another, for medicine and moral philosophy alike, is not so much the type of objects toward which they are oriented, nor the mode of sexual practice they prefer; above all, it is the intensity of that practice. The division is between lesser and greater: moderation or excess. It is rather rare, when a notable personage is depicted, for his preference for one form of sexual practice or another to be pointed up.* On the other hand, it is always important for his moral characterization to note whether he has been able to show moderation in his involvement with women or boys, like Agesilaus, who carried moderation to the point that he refused to kiss the young man that he loved; or whether he surrendered, like Alcibiades or Arcesilaus, to the appetite for the pleasures that one can enjoy with both sexes.[18] This point is supported by the famous passage of the first book of the *Laws:* it is true that Plato draws a sharp opposition in this passage between the relationship "according to nature" that joins man and woman for procreative ends, and relations "against nature" of male with male and female with female.[19] But this opposition, as marked as it is from the standpoint of naturalness, is referred by Plato to the more basic distinction between self-restraint and self-indulgence. The practices that contravene nature and the principle of procreation are not explained as the effect of an abnormal nature or of a peculiar form of desire; they are merely the result of immoderation: "a lack of

of the *aphrodisia* is the dynamic ensemble consisting of desire and pleasure associated with the act. The *epithumiai-hēdonai* pair occurs quite commonly in Plato.[15] Frequent, too, are expressions that speak of pleasure as a force that persuades, transports, triumphs, as in Xenophon's *Memorabilia.*[16]

*It sometimes happens that a man's particular fondness for boys will be mentioned for narrative purposes. Xenophon does this in the *Anabasis,* in regard to a certain Episthenes. But when he draws a negative portrait of Menon, he does not reproach him for this kind of taste, but for misusing such pleasures: obtaining a command too young, or loving an overage boy while still being beardless himself.[17]

self-restraint with regard to pleasure" *(akrateia hēdonēs)* is their source.[20] And when, in the *Timaeus,* Plato declares that lust should be considered as the effect, not of a bad volition of the soul, but of a sickness of the body, this disorder is described in terms of a grand pathology of excess: the sperm, instead of remaining enclosed in the marrow and its bony casing, overflows and starts to stream through the whole body, so that the latter becomes like a tree whose vegetative power exceeds all limits; the individual is thus driven to distraction for a large part of his existence by "pleasures and pains in excess."[21] This idea that immorality in the pleasures of sex is always connected with exaggeration, surplus, and excess is found again in the third book of the *Nicomachean Ethics:* Aristotle explains that for the natural desires that are common to everyone, the only offenses that one can commit are quantitative in nature: they pertain to "the more" *(to pleion);* so that natural desire only consists in satisfying needs, "to eat or drink whatever offers itself till one is surfeited is to exceed the natural amount [*tōi plēthei*]." It is true that Aristotle also makes allowance for the particular pleasures of individuals. It happens that people commit different types of offenses, either by not taking their pleasure "where they should," or by behaving "like the crowd," or again, by not taking their pleasure "as they ought." But, Aristotle adds, "self-indulgent individuals exceed [*hyperballousi*] in all these ways; they both delight in some things that they ought not to delight in, and if one ought to delight in some of the things they delight in, they do so more than one ought and than most men do." What constitutes self-indulgence in this sphere is excess, "and that is culpable."[22]* It appears, then, that the primary dividing line laid down by moral judgment in the area of sexual behavior was not prescribed by the nature of the act, with its possible variations, but by the activity and its quantitative gradations.

*It should be noted, however, that Aristotle gives his attention on several occasions to the question of the "disgraceful pleasures" that some individuals tend to seek.[23]

The practice of the pleasures was also related to another variable that might be labeled "role or polarity specific." Corresponding to the term *aphrodisia* was the verb *aphrodisiazein*. It refers to sexual activity in general: people thus spoke of the moment when animals reached an age at which they were capable of *aphrodisiazein.*[24] It also denotes the accomplishment of a sexual act of any kind: thus, in Xenophon, Antisthenes mentions the desire to *aphrodisiazein,* which he sometimes has.[25] But the verb can also be employed in its active sense, in which case it relates specifically to the so-called "masculine" role in intercourse, and to the active function defined by penetration. And inversely, one can use it in its passive form—*aphrodisiasthēnai*—designating in this case the other role in sexual union: the "passive" role of the object partner. This role is the one that nature had set aside for women—Aristotle speaks of the age at which girls become capable of *aphrodisiasthēnai;*[26] it is the role that could be imposed by force on someone who was thus reduced to being the object of the other's pleasure;[27] it is also the role accepted by the boy or man who let himself be penetrated by his partner —the author of the *Problems* thus speculates about what causes some men to take pleasure in *aphrodisiazeisthai.*[28]

It is doubtless correct to say that there is no noun in the Greek vocabulary that would consolidate, into a common notion, whatever might be specific to male sexuality and female sexuality.[29] But it should be remarked that in the practice of sexual pleasures two roles and two poles can be clearly distinguished, just as they can be distinguished in the reproductive function; these consisted of two positional values: that of the subject and that of the object, that of the agent and that of the "patient"—as Aristotle says, "the female, as female, is passive, and the male, as male, is active."[30] Whereas the experience of the "flesh" would be considered as an experience common to men and women, even if it did not take the same form in both, and while "sexuality" would be marked by the great caesura between male and female sexuality, the *aphrodi-*

sia were thought of as an activity involving two actors, each having its role and function—the one who performs the activity and the one on whom it is performed.

From this viewpoint, and in this ethics (always bearing in mind that it was a male ethics, made by and for men), it can be said that the dividing line fell mainly between men and women, for the simple reason that there was a strong differentiation between the world of men and that of women in many ancient societies. But more generally, it fell between what might be called the "active actors" in the drama of pleasures, and the "passive actors": on one side, those who were the subjects of sexual activity (and who were expected to carry it out in a measured and opportune manner); and on the other, those who were the object-partners, the supporting players with whom it was carried out. The first were men, naturally, but more specifically they were adult free men; the second included women of course, but women made up only one element of a much larger group that was sometimes referred to as a way of designating the objects of possible pleasure: "women, boys, slaves." In the text known as the Hippocratic Oath, the doctor pledges to refrain from *erga aphrodisia* in every house he enters, with any person whatsoever, whether a woman, a free man, or a slave.[31]

Hence the second major variable that engaged moral valuation, in addition to the "quantity of activity" criterion, was the question of remaining in one's role or abandoning it, being the subject of the activity or its object, joining those who underwent it—even if one was a man—or remaining with those who actively performed it. For a man, excess and passivity were the two main forms of immorality in the practice of the *aphrodisia.*

2.   While sexual activity had thus to become an object of moral differentiation and valuation, the reason for this was not that the sexual act was bad in itself, nor that it bore the mark of a primordial fall from grace. Even when the current form

of sexual relations and love was referred back, as it was by Aristophanes in the *Symposium,* to an original tragedy involving the pride of humans and punishment by the gods, neither the act nor pleasure was considered bad for all that; on the contrary, they tended toward the restoration of the highest state of being that man had achieved.[32] In general, sexual activity was perceived as natural (natural and indispensable) since it was through this activity that living creatures were able to reproduce, the species as a whole was able to escape extinction,[33] and cities, families, names, and religions were able to endure far longer than individuals, who were destined to pass away. The desires that led to the *aphrodisia* were classed by Plato among the most natural and necessary; and the pleasures that could be obtained from the *aphrodisia* had their cause, according to Aristotle, in necessary things that concerned the body and the life of the body in general.[34] In short, as Rufus of Ephesus was to point out, seeing that sexual activity was deeply and harmoniously grounded in nature, there was no way that it could be considered bad.[35] In this respect, the moral experience of the *aphrodisia* was of course radically different from the experience of the flesh that would develop later.

But as natural and even necessary as it may have been considered, it was nonetheless the object of a moral concern. It called for a delimitation that would enable one to determine the proper degree and extent to which it could be practiced. And yet, if it could pose questions of good and evil, this was not in spite of its naturalness, or because the latter might have been altered; it was precisely because of the way in which it had been organized by nature. Two traits marked the pleasure with which it was associated. First, there was its inferior character: bearing in mind that for Aristippus and the Cyrenaics "pleasure does not differ from pleasure,"[36] sexual pleasure was generally characterized as being, not a bearer of evil, but ontologically or qualitatively inferior—for several reasons: it was common to animals and men (and thus did not constitute a specifically human trait); it was mixed with privation and suffering (in contrast to the pleasures of sight and hearing); it depended on the body and its necessities and it was aimed at restoring the organism to its state prior to need.[37] But there was also the fact that this conditioned, subordinate, and inferior pleasure was extremely acute; as Plato explains at the beginning of the *Laws*, if nature arranged for men and women to be attracted to one another, it was in order that procreation might be possible and the survival of the species might be ensured.[38] Now, this purpose was so important and it was so essential that humans produce descendants, that nature attached an extremely intense pleasure to the act of procreation. Just as animals are reminded of the need to nourish themselves, thus assuring their individual survival, by the natural pleasure that is associated with eating and drinking, so the necessity of begetting offspring, of leaving a progeny behind, is constantly recalled by the pleasure and the desire that accompany the mating of the sexes. The *Laws* thus refers to the existence of three basic appetites, relating to food, drink, and reproduction. All three are strong, imperative, and intense, but the third one in particular, although "the latest to emerge," is "the keenest lust."[39] Socrates asks his interlocutor in the *Republic* whether he knows of "a greater and sharper pleasure than the sexual."[40]

It was just this natural acuteness of pleasure, together with the attraction it exerted on desire, that caused sexual activity to go beyond the limits that were set by nature when she made the pleasure of the *aphrodisia* an inferior, subordinate, and conditioned pleasure. Because of this intensity, people were induced to overturn the hierarchy, placing these appetites and their satisfaction uppermost, and giving them absolute power over the soul. Also because of it, people were led to go beyond the satisfaction of needs and to continue looking for pleasure even after the body had been restored. The tendency to rebellion and riotousness was the "stasiastic" potential of the sexual appetite; and the tendency to exaggeration, to excess, was

its "hyperbolic" potential.[41] Nature had invested human beings with this necessary and redoubtable force, which was
always on the point of overshooting the objective that was set
for it. One understands why, in these conditions, sexual activity required a moral discrimination that was, as we have seen,
more dynamic than morphological. If it was necessary, as
Plato said, to bridle it with the three strongest restraints: fear,
law, and true reason; if it was necessary, as Aristotle thought,
for desire to obey reason the way a child obeyed his tutor; if
Aristippus himself advised that, while it was all right to "use"
pleasures, one had to be careful not to be carried away by
them[42]—the reason was not that sexual activity was a vice, nor
that it might deviate from a canonical model; it was because
sexual activity was associated with a force, an *energeia,* that
was itself liable to be excessive. In the Christian doctrine of
the flesh, the excessive force of pleasure had its principle in the
Fall and in the weakness that had marked human nature ever
since. For classical Greek thought, this force was potentially
excessive by nature, and the moral question was how to confront this force, how to control it and regulate its economy in
a suitable way.

The fact that sexual activity appeared in the form of a play
of forces established by nature, but subject to abuse, related
it to eating and the moral problems the latter tended to pose.
This association between the ethics of sex and the ethics of the
table was a constant factor in ancient culture. One could find
countless examples of it. When, in the first book of the
Memorabilia, he wants to show how useful Socrates was to his
disciples, by his example and his observations, Xenophon sets
forth the precepts and conduct of his master "concerning
eating and drinking and the pleasures of love."[43] The interlocutors of the *Republic,* when they deal with the education
of guardians, come to agree that moderation *(sōphrosynē)*
demands the threefold mastery of the pleasures of drink, sex,
and food *(potoi, aphrodisia, edōdai).* [44] And Aristotle follows

suit: in the *Nicomachean Ethics,* the three examples he gives
of "common pleasures" are those of eating, drinking, and, for
youths and vigorous men, the "pleasures of the bed."[45] In
these three forms of pleasure, he recognizes the same type of
danger: that of exceeding what is necessary; he even identifies
a physiological principle that they hold in common, noting
pleasures of contact and touch in all three (according to him,
food and drink do not cause their particular pleasure except
by coming in contact with the tongue and especially the
throat).[46] When he speaks in the *Symposium,* the doctor Eryximachus claims for his art the prerogative of advising on the
manner in which one must make use of the pleasures of the
bed and the table; according to him, it is doctors who ought
to say how to enjoy rich food without making oneself sick; it
also rests with them to prescribe, to those who practice physical love—Eros Pandemos—how to have an orgasm without
any resulting ill effects.[44]

It would be interesting, surely, to trace the long history of
the connections between alimentary ethics and sexual ethics,
as manifested in doctrines, but also in religious rituals and
dietary rules; one would need to discover how, over a long
period of time, the play of alimentary prescriptions became
uncoupled from that of sexual morals, by following the evolution of their respective importance (with the rather belated
moment, no doubt, when the problem of sexual conduct became more worrisome than that of alimentary behaviors) and
the gradual differentiation of their specific structure (the moment when sexual desire began to be questioned in terms other
than alimentary appetite). In any case, in the reflection of the
Greeks in the classical period, it does seem that the moral
problematization of food, drink, and sexual activity was carried out in a rather similar manner. Foods, wines, and relations with women and boys constituted analogous ethical
material; they brought forces into play that were natural, but
that always tended to be excessive; and they all raised the

same question: how could one, how must one "make use"
(chrēsthai) of this dynamics of pleasures, desires, and acts?
A question of right use. As Aristotle expresses it, "all men
enjoy in some way or another both savoury foods and wines
and sexual intercourse, but not all men do so as they ought
[ouch' hōs dei]."[48]

2

Chrēsis

How does a man enjoy his pleasure "as one ought"? To what principles does he refer in order to moderate, limit, regulate that activity? What sort of validity might these principles have that would enable a man to justify his having to obey them? Or, in other words, what is the mode of subjection that is implied in this moral problematization of sexual conduct?

The goal of moral reflection on the *aphrodisia* was much less to establish a systematic code that would determine the canonical form of sexual acts, trace out the boundary of the prohibitions, and assign practices to one side or the other of a dividing line, than to work out the conditions and modalities of a "use"; that is, to define a style for what the Greeks called *chrēsis aphrodisiōn,* the use of pleasures. The common expression *chrēsis aphrodisiōn* related, in a general way, to sexual activity (for example, people would speak of times of the year or the age in one's life when it was good to *chrēsthai aphrodisiois*).[1] But the term also referred to the manner in which an individual managed his sexual activity, his way of conducting himself in such matters, the regimen he allowed himself or imposed on himself, the conditions in which he accomplished sexual acts, the share he allotted them in his life.* It was not

---

*Plato talks about the right "possession and practice" *(ktēsis te kai chreia)* of women and children, so that what was at issue was the whole range of relationships and forms of relations that one could have with them.[2] Polybius speaks of the *chreia aphrodisiōn* which, along with indulgence in luxurious clothes and food, characterized the habits of hereditary rulers and provoked discontent and revolution.[3]

a question of what was permitted or forbidden among the desires that one felt or the acts that one committed, but of prudence, reflection, and calculation in the way one distributed and controlled his acts. In the use of pleasures, while it was necessary to respect the laws and customs of the land, to keep from offending the gods, and to heed the will of nature, the moral rules to which one conformed were far removed from anything that might form a clearly defined code.* It was much more a question of a variable adjustment in which one had to take different factors into account: the element of want and natural necessity; that of opportuneness, which was temporal and circumstantial; that of the status of the individual himself. *Chrēsis* had to be decided on the basis of these different considerations. Thus, one can see a threefold strategy at work in this reflection on the use of pleasures: that of need, timeliness, and status.

1. The strategy of need.   The scandalous gesture of Diogenes is well known: when he needed to satisfy his sexual appetite, he would relieve himself in the marketplace.[5] Like many of the Cynics' provocations, this one had a double meaning. It owed its impact to the public character of the act, of course, which went against every convention in Greece; it was customary to assert the need for privacy as a reason for making love only at night, and the care one took not to let oneself be seen engaging in this kind of activity was regarded as a sign that the practice of *aphrodisia* was not something that honored the most noble qualities of mankind. It was against this rule of privacy that Diogenes directed his "performance" criticism. Diogenes Laertius reports that in fact he was in the habit of "doing everything in public, the works of Demeter and Aphrodite alike," reasoning as follows: "If breakfast be not absurd, neither is it absurd to breakfast in the market-place."[6] But this parallel with food gave Diogenes' action an additional

---

*Aristotle's *Rhetoric* defines moderation as that which makes us conduct ourselves with regard to the pleasures of the body "as the *nomos* requires."[4]

meaning: the practice of the *aphrodisia,* which could not be shameful since it was natural, was nothing more or less than the satisfaction of a need; and just as the Cynic looked for the simplest food that might gratify his stomach (it seems that he tried eating raw meat), he likewise found in masturbation the most direct means of appeasing his sexual appetite. He even regretted that it was not possible to satisfy hunger and thirst in so simple a manner: "Would to heaven that it were enough to rub one's stomach in order to allay one's hunger."

In this, Diogenes was only pushing to its logical extreme one of the great precepts of the *chrēsis aphrodisiōn.* He was reducing to a minimum the behavior that Antisthenes had already advocated in Xenophon's *Symposium:* "If I ever feel a natural desire to have sex with women, I am so well satisfied with whatever chance puts in my way that those to whom I make my advances are more than glad to welcome me because they have no one else to consort with them. In a word, all these items appeal to me as being so conducive to enjoyment that I could not pray for greater pleasure in performing any one of them, but could pray rather for less—so much more pleasurable do I regard some of them than is good for one."[7] Antisthenes' regimen is not very far removed in principle (even if the practical consequences are quite different) from several precepts or examples that Socrates, according to Xenophon, gave to his disciples. For if he recommended that those who were insufficiently fortified against the pleasures of love flee from the sight of beautiful boys, and go into exile if necessary, he did not in any case advocate a total, definitive, and unconditional abstention. The Socratic lesson, at least as Xenophon presents it, was that people should "limit themselves to such indulgence as the soul would reject unless the need of the body were pressing, and such as would do no harm when the need was there."[8]

But in this need-regulated use of the *aphrodisia,* the objective was not to reduce pleasure to nothing; on the contrary, what was wanted was to maintain it and to do so through the

need that awakened desire. Everyone knew that pleasure was
dulled if it offered no satisfaction to the keenness of a desire:
"To my friends, meat and drink bring sweet and simple enjoyment [hēdeia . . . apolausis apragmōn]," says Virtue in Prodicus' speech as reported by Socrates, "for they wait till they
crave them."⁹ And in a discussion with Euthydemus, Socrates
remarks that "hunger or thirst or desire [aphrodisiōn epi-
thumia] or lack of sleep are the sole causes of pleasure in
eating and drinking and sexual indulgence, and in resting or
sleeping, after a time of waiting and resistance until the moment comes when these will give the greatest possible satisfaction [hōs eni hēdista]."¹⁰ But if pleasure must be sustained
through desire, this did not mean that, conversely, desires
must be increased by recourse to pleasures that were not of a
natural kind. It is fatigue, says Prodicus, and not continuous
idleness, that ought to make one feel like sleeping; and if it was
proper to satisfy sexual desires when they appeared, it was not
good to create desires that went beyond needs. Need ought to
serve as a guiding principle in this strategy, which clearly
could never take the form of a precise codification or a law
applicable to everyone alike in every circumstance. The strategy made possible an equilibrium in the dynamics of pleasure
and desire: it kept this dynamics from "running away," from
becoming excessive, by setting the satisfaction of a need as its
internal limit; and it prevented this natural force from revolt-
ing, from usurping a place that was not its own, because it
provided only for what was necessary to the body and was
intended by nature, and nothing more.

At the same time it enabled one to avoid immoderation,
which was, strictly speaking, a behavior that did not have its
basis in nature. It was for this reason that it could assume two
forms against which the ethical regimen of pleasures had to
struggle. There was an immoderation that might be called an
immoderation of "plethora" or "fulfillment."¹¹ There was also
what might be called an immoderation of "artifice," which
was a product of the first type of immoderation: it consisted

in seeking sensual pleasures in the gratification of unnatural desires; it was this type that led people to "get three cooks to give zest to eating, to buy costly wines, and to run to and fro in search of snow in the summer"; it was this type, too, that "used men as women"[12] in order to find new pleasures in the *aphrodisia*. Understood in this way, moderation could not take the form of an obedience to a system of laws or a codification of behaviors; nor could it serve as a principle for nullifying pleasures; it was an art, a practice of pleasures that was capable of self-limitation through the "use" of those pleasures that were based on need: "Self-control alone," says Socrates, "causes them to endure the sufferings I have named, and therefore she alone causes them to experience any pleasure worth mentioning in such enjoyments."[13] And this is how Socrates himself experienced them in everyday life, according to Xenophon: "He ate just sufficient food to make eating a pleasure, and he was so ready for his food that he found appetite the best sauce; and any kind of drink he found pleasant, because he drank only when he was thirsty."[14]

2. The strategy of timeliness.   Another strategy consisted in determining the opportune time, the *kairos.* This was one of the most important objectives, and one of the most delicate, in the art of making use of the pleasures. Plato emphasizes the point in the *Laws:* fortunate was the one (whether an individual or a state) who knew what needed to be done in this sphere, "at the right time and in the right amount"; whoever, on the contrary, acted "without knowledge [*anepistēmonōs*] and at the wrong time [*ektos tōn kairōn*]" would "live a life that is just the opposite."[15]

One has to keep in mind that this theme of the "right time" had always had considerable importance for the Greeks, not only as a moral problem, but also as a question of science and technique. The exercise of practical skills as in medicine, government, and navigation (a grouping that was quite traditional for them) implied that one was not content with knowing general principles but that one was able to determine the moment when it was necessary to act and the precise manner in which to do so in terms of existing circumstances. And in fact it was one of the essential aspects of the virtue of prudence that it made one capable of practicing the "politics of timeliness" in the different domains—whether this involved the city or the individual, the body or the soul—where it was important to seize the *kairos*. In the use of pleasures, morality was also an art of the "right time."

That time could be decided according to several scales. There was the scale of a person's entire life. Doctors thought that it was not good to begin the practice of pleasures too young; they also thought that it could be harmful if one extended it to an advanced age; it had its season in life. In general, the latter was limited to a period characterized not only as the span during which procreation was possible, but also that in which the offspring would be healthy, well formed, and robust.* There was also the scale of the year, with its seasons: as we shall see in Part Two, dietary regimens attached great importance to the correlation between sexual activity and climatic variation, between cold and heat, humidity and dryness. It was also recommended to choose the right time of day: one of Plutarch's "table talks" deals with this problem, and proposes a solution that appears to have been traditional; dietary reasons, but also reasons of decency and religious considerations, argued for the evening, for this was the time most favorable to the body, the moment when darkness blotted out unseemly images, and when it was possible to insert the space of a night between that activity and the next morning's religious observances.[17] The choice of moment—of the *kairos*—ought to depend on other activities as well. If Xenophon could point to Cyrus as an example of moderation, this

---

*This period was thought to begin late; for Aristotle, sperm remained sterile up to the age of twenty-one. But the age a man had to wait for before he could expect fine offspring was later still: "After the age of twenty-one, women are fully ripe for child-bearing, but men go on increasing in vigor."[16]

was not because he had renounced pleasures; it was because he knew how to distribute them properly over the course of his existence, not permitting them to divert him from his occupations, and allowing them only after a prior period of work had cleared the way for honorable recreation.[18]

The importance of the "right time" in sexual ethics appears rather clearly in a passage of the *Memorabilia* dealing with incest. Socrates states unequivocally that the precept that "parents shall not have sexual intercourse with their children nor children with their parents" constitutes a universal dictum, laid down by the gods. He sees the proof of this in the fact that those who break the rule receive a punishment. Now, the punishment consists in this: regardless of the intrinsic qualities that the incestuous parents might possess, their off-spring will come to no good. And why is this? Because the parents failed to respect the principle of the "right time," mixing their seed unseasonably, since one of them was necessarily much older than the other: for people to procreate when they were no longer "in full vigor" was always "to beget badly."[19] Xenophon and Socrates do not say that incest is reprehensible only in the form of an "inopportune" action; but it is remarkable that the evil of incest is manifested in the same way and with the same consequences as the lack of regard for the proper time.

3. The strategy of status.   The art of making use of pleasure also had to be adapted to suit the user and his personal status. The author of the *Erotic Essay* (attributed to Demosthenes) restates this principle, taking his cue from the *Symposium:* every sensible person knows very well that love relations with a boy are not "absolutely either honorable or shameful but for the most part vary according to the persons concerned," so that it would be "unreasonable to adopt the same attitude" in every case.[20]

It may well be a trait common to all societies that the rules of sexual conduct vary according to age, sex, and the condition of individuals, and that obligations and prohibitions are not imposed on everyone in the same manner. But, restricting ourselves to the case of Christian morality, this specification occurs within the framework of an overall system that defines the value of the sexual act in terms of general principles, indicates the conditions in which it may be legitimate or not, according to whether one is married or not, bound by vows or not, etc.; this is an instance of modulated universality. It seems, on the other hand, that in the classical ethics, with the exception of a few precepts that applied to everyone, standards of sexual morality were always tailored to one's way of life, which was itself determined by the status one had inherited and the purposes one had chosen. The same Demosthenes of the *Erotic Essay* addresses Epicrates in order to "counsel him on the means of rendering his life still more worthy of esteem"; he does not want to see the young man make decisions that are not based on "the right advice on the conduct of life"; and this good advice is not given in order to review the general principles of behavior, but to point up the legitimate difference that exists among moral criteria: "we do not reproach men of humble and insignificant natural gifts even when they commit a dishonorable act"; on the other hand, if they are someone like Epicrates himself, who has "attained distinction, even a bit of negligence in some matter of high honor brings disgrace."[21] It was a generally accepted principle of government that the more one was in the public eye, the more authority one had or wanted to have over others, and the more one sought to make one's life into a brilliant work whose reputation would spread far and last long—the more necessary it was to adopt and maintain, freely and deliberately, rigorous standards of sexual conduct. Such was the counsel given by Simonides to Hiero concerning "meat and drink and sleep and love": these were pleasures that all creatures alike seemed to enjoy, whereas the love of honor and praise was peculiar to humans, and it was that love which enabled one to endure dangers and privations.[22] And this was also the manner in which Agesilaus conducted himself, again according to Xeno-phon, with regard to the pleasures "that prove too strong for many men"; indeed, he thought that "a ruler's superiority over ordinary men should be shown not by weakness but by endurance."[23]

Moderation was quite regularly represented among the qualities that belonged—or at least should belong—not just to anyone but particularly to those who had rank, status, and responsibility in the city. When the Socrates of the *Memorabilia* describes for Critobulus the gentleman whose friendship is worth seeking, he places moderation on the list of qualities that characterize a man worthy of social esteem—a list that includes being ready to render a service to a friend, being disposed to return kindnesses received, and being accom-modating in business matters.[24] In order to show the advan-tages of moderation to his disciple Aristippus, who "was rather intemperate in such matters," Socrates, still according to Xenophon, asks the question: if he had to educate two youths, one of whom would go on to lead an ordinary life and the other would be destined to command, which of the two would he teach to "control his passions" so that they would not hinder him from doing what he would have to do?[25] Else-where in the *Memorabilia,* Socrates submits that since people prefer to have slaves who are not intemperate, all the more when it comes to choosing a leader, "should we choose one whom we know to be the slave of the belly, or of wine, or lust, or sleep?"[26] It is true that Plato would give the entire state the virtue of moderation; but he does not mean by this that all would be equally self-controlled: *sōphrosynē* would character-ize the city in which those who ought to be ruled would obey, and those who were destined to rule would in fact rule: hence there would be a multitude of "appetites and pleasures and pains" in children, women, and slaves, as well as in the inferior majority; "but those desires that are simple and measured and directed by reasoning with intelligence and right belief" would be found "in but few people who are the best by nature and the best educated." In the moderate state, the passions of the unprincipled multitude would be controlled by "the desires and the knowledge of the fewer and the better."[27]

We are a long way from a form of austerity that would tend to govern all individuals in the same way, from the proudest to the most humble, under a universal law whose application alone would be subject to modulation by means of casuistry. On the contrary, here everything was a matter of adjustment, circumstance, and personal position. The few great common laws—of the city, religion, nature—remained present, but it was as if they traced a very wide circle in the distance, inside of which practical thought had to define what could rightfully be done. And for this there was no need of anything resembling a text that would have the force of law, but rather, of a *technē* or "practice," a *savoir-faire* that by taking general principles into account would guide action in its time, according to its context, and in view of its ends. Therefore, in this form of morality, the individual did not make himself into an ethical subject by universalizing the principles that informed his action; on the contrary, he did so by means of an attitude and a quest that individualized his action, modulated it, and perhaps even gave him a special brilliance by virtue of the rational and deliberate structure his action manifested.

3

Enkrateia

The interiority of Christian morality is often contrasted with the exteriority of a pagan morality that would consider acts only in their concrete realization, in their visible and manifest form, in their degree of conformity with rules, and in the light of opinion or with a view to the memory they leave behind them. But this traditionally accepted opposition may well miss the essential elements of both. What is called Christian interiority is a particular mode of relationship with oneself, comprising precise forms of attention, concern, decipherment, verbalization, confession, self-accusation, struggle against temptation, renunciation, spiritual combat, and so on. And what is designated as the "exteriority" of ancient morality also implies the principle of an elaboration of self, albeit in a very different form. The evolution that occurred—quite slowly at that—between paganism and Christianity did not consist in a gradual interiorization of rules, acts, and transgressions; rather, it carried out a restructuration of the forms of self-relationship and a transformation of the practices and techniques on which this relationship was based.

Classical language had a term for designating this form of relationship with oneself, this "attitude" which was necessary to the ethics of pleasures and which was manifested through the proper use one made of them: *enkrateia*. As a matter of fact, for a long time the word remained rather close to *sōphrosynē:* one often finds them employed together or alternatively, with very similar meanings. When Xenophon speaks of moderation—which, together with piety, wisdom, courage, and justice, was among the five virtues he usually recognized—he employs the words *sōphrosynē* and *enkrateia* interchangeably.[1] Plato refers to this proximity of the two words when Socrates, questioned by Callicles concerning what he meant by "ruling himself" *(auton heauton archein),* replies that it consists in "being temperate, master of himself [*sōphrona onta kai enkratē auton heautou*], ruling the pleasures and appetites within him [*archein tōn hēdonōn kai epithumiōn*]."[2] And when, in the *Republic,* he considers the four cardinal virtues in turn—wisdom, courage, justice, and moderation *(sōphrosynē)*—he defines the latter by *enkrateia:* "Moderation [*sōphrosynē*] is a certain orderliness and mastery [*kosmos kai enkrateia*] over certain pleasures and appetites."[3]*

We may note, however, that while the meanings of these two words are very close, they stop short of being exact synonyms. Each refers to a somewhat different mode of relationship to self. The virtue of *sōphrosynē* is described rather as a very general state that ensures that one will do "what is fitting as regards both gods and men"[4]—that is, one will be not only moderate but righteous and just, and courageous as well.† In contrast, *enkrateia* is characterized more by an active form of self-mastery, which enables one to resist or struggle, and to achieve domination in the area of desires and pleasures. According to Helen North, Aristotle was the first to distinguish systematically between *sōphrosynē* and *enkrateia.*[6] The former is characterized in the *Nicomachean Ethics* by the fact that the subject deliberately chooses reasonable principles of action, that he is capable of following and applying them, that he holds to the "right mean" between insensitivity and excess (a middle course that is not equidistant between the two, because

---

*Aristotle says that some people believe that one who is *sōphrōn* is *enkratēs* and *karterikos.*

†Compare: "The correct apportionment is one which honors most the good things pertaining to the soul, provided it has moderation."[5]

moderation is actually much further away from excess than from insensitivity), and that he derives pleasure from the moderation he displays. The opposite of *sōphrosynē* is the immoderation *(akolasia)* that is expressed by deliberately choosing bad principles, following them of one's own accord, surrendering even to the weakest desires, and taking pleasure in bad conduct: the immoderate individual is shameless and incorrigible. *Enkrateia*, with its opposite, *akrasia*, is located on the axis of struggle, resistance, and combat; it is self-control, tension, "continence"; *enkrateia* rules over pleasures and desires, but has to struggle to maintain control. Unlike the "moderate" man, the "continent" one experiences pleasures that are not in accord with reason, but he no longer allows himself to be carried away by them, and his merit will be greater in proportion as his desires are strong. As an opposite, *akrasia* is not, like immoderation, a deliberate choosing of bad principles; it invites comparison, rather, with those cities that have good laws but are incapable of enforcing them; the incontinent individual lets himself be overcome in spite of himself, and despite the reasonable principles he embraces, either because he does not have the strength to put them into practice or because he has not given them sufficient thought: this explains why the incontinent person can come to his senses and achieve self-mastery.[7] Thus, *enkrateia* can be regarded as the prerequisite of *sōphrosynē*, as the form of effort and control that the individual must apply to himself in order to become moderate *(sōphrōn)*.

In any case, the term *enkrateia* in the classical vocabulary seems to refer in general to the dynamics of a domination of oneself by oneself and to the effort that this demands.

1. To begin with, this exercise of domination implies an agonistic relation. The Athenian of the *Laws* reminds Cleinias of this: if it is true that the man who is blessed with courage will attain "only half his potential" without "experience and training" in actual combat, it stands to reason that he will not be able to become moderate *(sōphrōn)* "if he has not fought triumphantly against the many pleasures and desires [*pollais hēdonais kai epithumiais diamemachēmenos*] using the help of speech, deed, and art [*logos, ergon, technē*] in games and in serious pursuits."[8] These are almost the same words that Antiphon the Sophist employed on his own account: "He is not wise [*sōphrōn*] who has not tried the ugly and the bad; for then there is nothing he has conquered [*kratein*] and nothing that would enable him to assert that he is virtuous [*kosmios*]."[9] One could behave ethically only by adopting a combative attitude toward the pleasures. As we have seen, the *aphrodisia* were made not only possible but desirable by an interplay of forces whose origin and finality were natural, but whose potential, by the fact that they had their own energy, was for revolt and excess. These forces could not be used in the moderate way that was fitting unless one was capable of opposing, resisting, and subduing them. Of course, if it was necessary to confront them, this was because they were inferior appetites that humans happen to share—like hunger and thirst—with the animals;[10] but this natural inferiority would not of itself be a reason for having to combat them, if there was not the danger that, winning out over all else, they would extend their rule over the whole individual, eventually reducing him to slavery. In other words, it was not their intrinsic nature, their disqualification on principle, that necessitated this "polemical" attitude toward oneself, but their possible ascendancy and dominion. Ethical conduct in matters of pleasure was contingent on a battle for power. This perception of the *hēdonai* and *epithumiai* as a formidable enemy force, and the correlative constitution of oneself as a vigilant adversary who confronts them, struggles against them, and tries to subdue them, is revealed in a whole series of expressions traditionally employed to characterize moderation and immoderation: setting oneself against the pleasures and desires, not giving in to them, resisting their assaults, or on the contrary, letting oneself be overcome by them,[11] defeating them or being defeated by them,[12] being armed or equipped against them.[13] It is also revealed in metaphors such as that of the battle that has to be fought against armed adversaries, or that of the acropolis-soul assaulted by a hostile band and needing a solid garrison for its defense, or that of hornets that set upon reasonable and moderate desires, killing them or driving them out unless one manages to rid oneself of these attackers.[14] It is expressed, too, by such themes as that of the untamed forces of desire that invade the soul during its slumber if it has not had the foresight to take the necessary precautions.[15] The relationship to desires and pleasures is conceived as a pugnacious one: a man must take the position and role of the adversary with respect to them, either according to the model of the fighting soldier or the model of the wrestler in a match. One should keep in mind that the Athenian of the *Laws,* when he speaks of the need to restrain the three basic appetites, invokes the aid of "the Muses and the gods of contests [*theoi agōnioi*]."[16] The long tradition of spiritual combat, which was to take so many diverse forms, was already clearly delineated in classical Greek thought.

2. This combative relationship with adversaries was also an agonistic relationship with oneself. The battle to be fought, the victory to be won, the defeat that one risked suffering—these were processes and events that took place between oneself and oneself. The adversaries the individual had to combat were not just within him or close by; they were part of him. To be sure, we would need to account for the various theoretical formulations that were proposed concerning this differentiation between the part of oneself that was supposed to fight and the part that was supposed to be defeated. Parts of the soul that ought to maintain a certain hierarchical relationship among themselves? Body and soul understood as two realities with different origins? Forces straining toward different goals and working against one another like the two horses of a team? But in any case, the thing to remember in trying to define the

general style of this ascetics is that the adversary that was to be fought, however far removed it might be by nature from any conception of the soul, reason, or virtue, did not represent a different, ontologically alien power. The conceptual link between the movement of concupiscence, in its most insidious and most secret forms, and the presence of the Other, with its ruses and its power of illusion, was to be one of the essential traits of the Christian ethics of the flesh. In the ethics of the *aphrodisia,* the inevitability and difficulty of the combat derived, on the contrary, from the fact that it unfolded as a solo contest: to struggle against "the desires and the pleasures" was to cross swords with oneself.

In the *Republic,* Plato stresses how strange, and at the same time somewhat ludicrous and outmoded, is a familiar expression that he himself had resorted to several times: it is the one that consists in saying that a person is "stronger" or "weaker" than himself *(kreittōn, hēttōn heautou).* [17] Indeed, there is paradox in claiming that one is stronger than oneself, since this implies that one is also, by the same token, weaker than oneself. But according to Plato, the expression is supported by the fact of a prior distinction between two parts of the soul, a better part and a worse, and that with regard to the victory or the defeat of oneself over oneself, the speaker places himself on the side of the first: "The expression self-control seems to want to indicate that in the soul of the man himself there is a better part and a worse part; whenever what is by nature the better part is in control of the worse, this is expressed by saying that the man is self-controlled or master of himself, and this is a term of praise. When, on the other hand, the smaller and better part, because of poor upbringing or bad company, is overpowered by the larger and worse, this is made a reproach and called being defeated by oneself, and a man in that situation is called uncontrolled." [18] And it is made clear at the beginning of the *Laws* that this antagonism of oneself toward oneself is meant to structure the ethical attitude of the individual vis-à-vis desires and pleasures: the reason that is given for the need of a ruling authority and a legislative authority in every state is that even in peacetime all states are at war with one another; in the same way one must assume that if "all are enemies of all in public," then "in private each is an enemy of himself"; and of all the victories it is possible to win, "the first and best" is the victory "of oneself over oneself," whereas "being defeated by oneself is the most shameful and at the same time the worst of all defeats."[19]

3. Such a "polemical" attitude with respect to oneself tended toward a result that was quite naturally expressed as victory—a victory much more impressive, says the *Laws,* than those won in wrestling and running contests.[20] This victory was sometimes characterized by the complete extirpation or expulsion of desires.[21]* But much more often, it was defined by the setting up of a solid and stable state of rule of the self over the self; the intensity of the desires and pleasures did not disappear, but the moderate subject controlled it well enough so as never to give way to violence. The famous test of Socrates, in which he proves capable of resisting seduction by Alcibiades, does not show him "purified" of all desire for boys: it reveals his ability to resist whenever and however he chooses. Such a test would meet with disapproval from Christians because it would testify to the abiding presence—for them immoral—of desire. But long before them, Bion the Borysthenite made light of it, declaring that if Socrates felt desire for Alcibiades, he was foolish to abstain, and if he felt none, his conduct was entirely unremarkable.[23] Similarly, in Aristotle's analysis, *enkrateia,* defined as mastery and victory, presupposes the presence of desires, and is all the more valuable as it manages to control those that are violent.[24] *Sōphrosynē* itself, although defined by Aristotle as a state of virtue, did not imply the suppression of desires but rather their control: Aristotle places it in an intermediary position between a self-

---

*In the *Nicomachean Ethics,* it is a question of "bidding pleasure be gone," as the old people of Troy wanted to do with Helen.[22]

indulgence *(akolasia)* in which one gladly abandons oneself to one's pleasures, and an insensitivity *(anaisthēsia)*—extremely rare, it should be added—in which one feels no pleasure; the moderate individual is not one who has no desires but one who desires "only to a moderate degree, not more than he should, nor when he should not."[25]

In the domain of pleasures, virtue was not conceived as a state of integrity, but as a relationship of domination, a relation of mastery. This is shown by the terms that are used—whether in Plato, Xenophon, Diogenes, Antiphon, or Aristotle—to define moderation: "rule the desires and the pleasures," "exercise power over them," "govern them" *(kratein, archein)*. There is an aphorism that captures this general conception of pleasure; interestingly, it is attributed to Aristippus, who had a rather different theory of pleasure from that of Socrates: "It is not abstinence from pleasures that is best, but mastery over them without ever being worsted" *(to kratein kai mē hēttasthai hēdonōn ariston, ou to mē chrēsthai).*[26] In other words, to form oneself as a virtuous and moderate subject in the use he makes of pleasures, the individual has to construct a relationship with the self that is of the "domination-submission," "command-obedience," "mastery-docility" type (and not, as will be the case in Christian spirituality, a relationship of the "elucidation-renunciation," "decipherment-purification" type). This is what could be called the "heautocratic" structure of the subject in the ethical practice of the pleasures.

4. The development of this heautocratic form was patterned after several models: for example, in Plato there is the model of the team with its driver, and in Aristotle, that of the child with the adult (our desiring faculty ought to comply with the prescriptions of reason "as the child should live according to the direction of his tutor").[27] But it was related to two great schemas in particular. That of domestic life, first of all: just as a household could not be in good order unless the rank and authority of the master was respected within it, so a man

would be moderate only insofar as he was able to rule his desires as if they were his servants. Conversely, immoderation could be likened to a household that was mismanaged. At the beginning of the *Oeconomicus*—which deals precisely with the role of the master of the house and the art of ruling one's wife, one's estate, and one's servants—Xenophon describes the disorganized soul. It is at once a counter-example of what a well-ordered household should be, and a portrait of those bad masters who, incapable of governing themselves, bring ruin to their estates; in the soul of the immoderate man, "harsh" masters (gluttony, drunkenness, lust, ambition) enslave the man who should be governing, and after exploiting him in his youth, abandon him to grow old in misery.[28] The model of civic life is also called on in order to define the moderate attitude. It is a familiar theme in Plato that desires can be likened to a low-born populace that will grow agitated and rebellious unless it is kept in check;[29] but the strict correlation between the individual and the city, which is the mainstay of Plato's thinking in the *Republic,* enables him to elaborate on the "civic" model of moderation and its opposite, page after page. There, the ethics of pleasure is of the same order of reality as the political structure: "If the individual is like the city, the same structure must prevail in him"; and he will be self-indulgent when he lacks the power structure, the *archē,* that would allow him to defeat, to rule over *(kratein)* the inferior powers; then "his soul must be full of servitude and lack freedom"; the soul's "best parts" will be enslaved and "a small part, the most wicked and mad, is master."[30] At the end of the next to last book of the *Republic,* after having set up the model of the city, Plato acknowledges that the philosopher will have little chance of encountering a state so perfect in this world or of serving his function within it; but he goes on to say that, nevertheless, the "paradigm" of the city is laid up in heaven for him who wants to contemplate it; looking upon it, the philosopher will be able to "set up the government of his soul" *(heauton kratoikizein):* "It makes no difference whether it exists anywhere or will exist. He would take part in the public affairs of that city only, not of any other."[31] Individual virtue needed to be structured like a city.

5.   A struggle of this kind required training. The metaphor of the match, of athletic competition and battle, did not serve merely to designate the nature of the relationship one had with desires and pleasures, with their force that was always liable to turn seditious or rebellious; it also related to the preparation that enabled one to withstand such a confrontation. As Plato says, a man will not be able to oppose or defeat them if he is *agymnastos*.[32] Exercise was no less indispensable in this order of things than in the case of other techniques one acquired: *mathēsis* alone was not sufficient; it had to be backed up by a training, an *askēsis*. This was one of the great Socratic lessons; it did not contradict the principle that said one could not willfully do wrong, knowing that it was wrong; it gave this knowledge a form that was not reducible to the mere awareness of a principle. Speaking in reference to the accusations brought against Socrates, Xenophon takes care to distinguish his teaching from that of the philosophers—or "self-styled lovers of wisdom"—for whom once man has learned what it is to be just or moderate *(sōphrōn),* he can become unjust or dissolute. Like Socrates, Xenophon objects to this theory: if one does not exercise one's body, one cannot sustain the functions of the body *(ta tou sōmatos erga);* similarly, if one does not exercise the soul, one cannot sustain the functions of the soul, so that one will not be able to "do what one ought to do nor avoid what one ought not to do."[33] It is for this reason that Xenophon thinks that Socrates cannot be held accountable for Alcibiades' misbehavior: the latter was not a victim of the teaching he received, but rather, after all his successes with men, women, and a whole populace made him a champion, he acted like many athletes: once victory was won, he thought he could "neglect his training" *(amelein tēs askēseōs).*[34]

Plato returns often to this Socratic principle of *askēsis.* He

represents Socrates showing Alcibiades or Callicles that they
have no right to involve themselves with the affairs of the city
or to govern others if they have not first learned what is
necessary and trained accordingly: "And then, when we have
practiced it [*askēsantes*] together this way, then finally, if you
think we ought to, we'll undertake political business."[35] And
he associates this requirement of practice with the need to
attend to oneself. This *epimeleia heautou,* care of the self,
which was a precondition that had to be met before one was
qualified to attend to the affairs of others or lead them, included not only the need to know (to know the things one does
not know, to know that one is ignorant, to know one's own
nature), but to attend effectively to the self, and to exercise and
transform oneself.[36] The doctrine and practice of the Cynics
also accorded a good deal of importance to *askēsis;* indeed, the
Cynic life as a whole could be seen as a sort of continuous
exercise. Diogenes advocated training the body and the soul
at the same time: each of the two exercises "was worthless
without the other, good health and strength being no less
useful than the rest, since what concerns the body concerns
the soul as well." The object of this twofold training was both
to enable the individual to face privations without suffering,
as they occurred, and to reduce every pleasure to nothing
more than the elementary satisfaction of needs. Considered as
a whole, this exercise implied a reduction to nature, a victory
over self, and a natural economy that would produce a life of
real satisfactions: "Nothing in life," Diogenes maintained,
"has any chance of succeeding without strenuous practice;
and this is capable of overcoming anything [*pan eknikēsai*].
. . . Instead of useless toils men should choose such as nature
recommends, whereby they might have lived happily. . . . For
even the despising of pleasure is itself most pleasurable, when
we are habituated to it; and just as those accustomed to a life
of pleasure feel disgust when they pass over to the opposite
experience, so those whose training has been of the opposite
kind derive more pleasure from despising pleasure than from

the pleasures themselves [*hēdion autōn tōn hēdonōn kataphro-nousi*]."[37]

The importance of exercise would not be neglected in the subsequent philosophical tradition. In fact it was considerably amplified: new exercises were added, and procedures, objectives, and possible variants were defined; their effectiveness was debated; *askēsis* in its different forms (training, meditation, tests of thinking, examination of conscience, control of representations) eventually became a subject matter for teaching and constituted one of the basic instruments used in the direction of souls. By contrast, in the texts of the classical period one finds relatively few details on the concrete form that the ethical *askēsis* could take. Doubtless the Pythagorean tradition recognized many exercises: dietary regimens, reviewing of one's misdeeds at the end of the day, or meditation practices that ought to precede sleep so as to ward off bad dreams and encourage the visions that might come from the gods. Plato makes a precise reference to these evening spiritual preparations in a passage of the *Republic* in which he evokes the danger of desires that are always apt to invade the soul.[38] But, apart from these Pythagorean practices, one finds few instances—whether in Xenophon, Plato, Diogenes, or Aristotle—where *askēsis* is specified as an exercise in self-control. There are two likely reasons for this: first, exercise was regarded as the actual practice of what one needed to train for; it was not something distinct from the goal to be reached. Through training, one became accustomed to the behavior that one would eventually have to manifest.* Thus Xenophon praises Spartan education for teaching children to endure hunger by rationing their food, to endure cold by giving them only one garment, and to endure suffering by exposing them to physical punishments, just as they were taught to practice self-control by being made to show the strictest modesty in

---

*Compare Plato in the *Laws*: "Whatever a man intends to become good at, this he must practice [*meletēan*] from childhood; whether he's playing or being serious, he should spend his time with each of the things that pertain to the activity."[39]

demeanor (walking in the streets in silence, with downcast eyes and with hands hidden beneath their cloaks).[40] Similarly, Plato proposes subjecting young people to tests of courage that would expose them to simulated dangers; this would be a means of training and improving them, and a means of gauging their merit at the same time: just as one leads "colts into noise and tumult to see if they are fearful, so we must expose our young to fears and pleasures to test them, much more thoroughly than one tests gold in fire, and see whether a guardian is hard to bewitch and behaves well in all circumstances as a good guardian of himself and of the cultural education he has received."[41] In the *Laws,* Plato goes so far as to imagine a drug that has not yet been invented: it would make everything look frightening to anyone who ingested it, and it could be used for trying one's courage: either in private "out of a sense of shame at being seen before he was in what he considered good condition," or in a group and even in public "in the company of many fellow drinkers," to show that one was able to overcome "the power of the necessary transformation effected by the drink."[42] In the same way, banquets could be planned and accepted as tests of self-control, so to speak, based on this artificial and ideal model. Aristotle expresses this circularity of ethical apprenticeship and learnable virtue in a simple phrase: "By abstaining from pleasures we become temperate and it is when we have become so that we are most able to abstain from them."[43]

As for the other reason that may explain the absence of a specific art for exercising the soul, it has to do with the fact that self-mastery and the mastery of others were regarded as having the same form; since one was expected to govern oneself in the same manner as one governed one's household and played one's role in the city, it followed that the development of personal virtues, of *enkrateia* in particular, was not essentially different from the development that enabled one to rise above other citizens to a position of leadership. The same apprenticeship ought to make a man both capable of virtue and capable of exercising power. Governing oneself, managing one's estate, and participating in the administration of the city were three practices of the same type. Xenophon's *Oeconomicus* shows the continuity and isomorphism between these three "arts," as well as the chronological sequence by which they were to be practiced in the life of an individual. The young Critobulus declares that he is now capable of ruling himself, that he will no longer allow himself to be dominated by his desires and pleasures (Socrates reminds him that the latter are like servants who are best kept under supervision); therefore it is time for him to marry and with the help of his wife to administer his household; and, as Xenophon points out several times, this domestic government—understood as the management of a household and the cultivation of a domain, the maintenance or development of an estate—constituted, when given the right amount of dedication, a remarkable physical and moral training for anyone who aimed to fulfill his civic obligations, establish his public authority, and assume leadership functions. Generally speaking, anything that would contribute to the political education of a man as a citizen would also contribute to his training in virtue; and conversely, the two endeavors went hand in hand. Moral *askēsis* formed part of the *paideia* of the free man who had a role to play in the city and in dealings with others; it had no need of separate methods; gymnastics and endurance trials, music and the learning of vigorous and manly rhythms, practice in hunting and warfare, concern with one's demeanor in public, acquiring the *aidōs* that would lead to self-respect through the respect one showed for others—all this was a means of educating the man who would be of service to his city, and it was also moral training for anyone who intended to master himself. Commenting on the tests of contrived fear that he recommends, Plato speaks of them as a means of identifying those boys who are most likely to be "the best men for themselves and for the city"; those will be the ones recruited to govern: "The one who is thus tested as a child, as a youth, and as an adult, and comes out of it untainted [*akēratos*] is to be made a ruler as well as a guardian."[44] And in the *Laws,* when the Athenian wants to define what he means by *paideia,* he characterizes it as what trains "from childhood in virtue" and makes one "desire and love to become a perfect citizen who knows how to rule and be ruled with justice."[45]

In a word, we can say that the theme of an *askēsis,* as a practical training that was indispensable in order for an individual to form himself as a moral subject, was important—emphasized even—in classical Greek thought, especially in the tradition issuing from Socrates. And yet, this "ascetics" was not organized or conceived as a corpus of separate practices that would constitute a kind of specific art of the soul, with its techniques, procedures, and prescriptions. It was not distinct from the practice of virtue itself; it was the rehearsal that anticipated that practice. Further, it made use of the same exercises as those that molded the citizen: the master of himself and the master of others received the same training. It would not be long before this ascetics would begin to have an independent status, or at least a partial and relative autonomy. In two ways: there was to be a differentiation between the exercises that enabled one to govern oneself and the learning of what was necessary in order to govern others; there was also to be a differentiation between the exercises themselves and the virtue, moderation, and temperance for which they were meant to serve as training: their procedures (trials, examinations, self-control) tended to form a particular technique that was more complex than the mere rehearsal of the moral behavior they anticipated. The time would come when the art of the self would assume its own shape, distinct from the ethical conduct that was its objective. But in classical Greek thought, the "ascetics" that enabled one to make oneself into an ethical subject was an integral part—down to its very form —of the practice of a virtuous life, which was also the life of a "free" man in the full, positive and political sense of the word.

4

Freedom and
Truth

1. "Tell me, Euthydemus, do you think that freedom is a
noble and splendid possession both for individuals and for
communities?" "Yes, I think it is, in the highest degree."
"Then do you think that the man is free who is ruled by bodily
pleasures and is unable to do what is best because of them?"
"By no means."[1]

Sōphrosynē was a state that could be approached through
the exercise of self-mastery and through restraint in the practice of pleasures; it was characterized as a freedom. If it was
so important to govern desires and pleasures, if the use one
made of them constituted such a crucial ethical problem, this
was not because the Greeks hoped to preserve or regain an
original innocence; nor was it in general—except of course in
the Pythagorean tradition—because they wanted to maintain
a purity;* it was because they wanted to be free and to be able
to remain so. This could be regarded as further proof, if such
were needed, that freedom in classical Greek thought was not
considered simply as the independence of the city as a whole,
while the citizens themselves would be only constituent ele-

*Obviously I am not suggesting that the theme of purity was absent from the Greek
ethics of pleasures in the classical period. It occupied a place of considerable importance among the Pythagoreans, and it was very important for Plato. However, it does
seem that on the whole, as regards desires and pleasures, ethical conduct was conceived as a matter of domination. The emergence and development of an ethics of
purity, with its correlative practices of the self, was a historical phenomenon that was
to have far-reaching consequences.

ments, devoid of individuality or interiority. The freedom that needed establishing and preserving was that of the citizens of a collectivity of course, but it was also, for each of them, a certain form of relationship of the individual with himself. The organization of the city, the nature of its laws, the forms of education, and the manner in which the leaders conducted themselves obviously were important factors for the behavior of citizens; but conversely, the freedom of individuals, understood as the mastery they were capable of exercising over themselves, was indispensable to the entire state. Consider this passage from Aristotle's *Politics:* "A state is good in virtue of the goodness of the citizens who have a share in the government. In our state all the citizens have a share in the government. We have therefore to consider how a man can become a good man. True, it is possible for all to be good collectively, without each being good individually. But the better thing is that each individual citizen should be good. The goodness of all is necessarily involved in the goodness of each."[2] The individual's attitude toward himself, the way in which he ensured his own freedom with regard to himself, and the form of supremacy he maintained over himself were a contributing element to the well-being and good order of the city.

This individual freedom should not, however, be understood as the independence of a free will. Its polar opposite was not a natural determinism, nor was it the will of an all-powerful agency: it was an enslavement—the enslavement of the self by oneself. To be free in relation to pleasures was to be free of their authority; it was not to be their slave.

Of the dangers carried by the *aphrodisia,* dishonor was not the most serious; the greatest danger was bondage to them. Diogenes was in the habit of saying that servants were slaves of their masters, and that immoral people were slaves of their desires *(tous de phaulous tais epithumiais douleuein).*[3] Socrates cautions Critobulus against this kind of servitude at the beginning of the *Oeconomicus,* and Euthydemus is similarly cautioned in a dialogue of the *Memorabilia* that is a hymn to self-control considered as freedom: "To do what is best appears to you to be freedom, and so you think that to have masters who will prevent such activity is bondage." "I am sure of it." "You feel sure then that the incontinent are bond slaves. . . . And what sort of slavery do you believe to be the worst?" "Slavery to the worst masters, I think." "The worst slavery, therefore, is the slavery endured by the incontinent. . . ." "Socrates, I think you mean that he who is at the mercy of the bodily pleasures has no concern whatever with virtue in any form." "Yes, Euthydemus; for how can an incontinent man be any better than the dullest beast?"[4]

But this freedom was more than a nonenslavement, more than an emancipation that would make the individual independent of any exterior or interior constraint; in its full, positive form, it was a power that one brought to bear on oneself in the power that one exercised over others. In fact, the person who, owing to his status, was under the authority of others was not expected to find the principle of his moderation within himself; it would be enough for him to obey the orders and instructions he was given. This is what Plato explains in regard to the craftsman: what is degrading in his case is that the best part of the soul "is naturally weak and cannot rule the animals within but pampers them and can learn nothing but ways to flatter them"; now, what should be done so that this man might be governed by a reasonable principle, "similar to that which rules the best man"? The only solution is to place him under the authority of this superior man: "he must be enslaved to the best man, who has a divine ruler within himself."[5] On the other hand, the man who ought to lead others was one who had to be completely in command of himself: both because, given his position and the power he wielded, it would be easy for him to satisfy all his desires, and hence to give way to them, but also because disorderly behavior on his part would have its effects on everyone and in the collective life of the city. In order not to be excessive, not to do violence, in order to avoid the trap of tyrannical authority (over others) coupled with a soul tyrannized by desires, the exercise of political power required, as its own principle of internal regulation, power over oneself. Moderation, understood as an aspect of dominion over the self, was on an equal footing with justice, courage, or prudence; that is, it was a virtue that qualified a man to exercise his mastery over others. The most kingly man was king of himself *(basilikos, basileuōn heautou).* [6]

Hence the importance given in the ethics of pleasures to two exemplary moral figures. On the one hand, there was the vicious tyrant; he was incapable of mastering his own passions and was therefore always prone to abuse his power and to do violence *(hubrizein)* to his subjects. He provoked disturbances in his state and caused the citizens to rebel against him. The sexual abuses of the despot, when he undertook to dishonor the citizens' children (boys or girls), were often invoked as an initial justification for plots aimed at overthrowing tyrannies and restoring liberty: this was the case with Pisistratus at Athens, Periander in Ambracia, and others mentioned by Aristotle in Book V of the *Politics.* [7] Opposite the tyrant, there was the positive image of the leader who was capable of exercising a strict control over himself in the authority he exercised over others. His self-rule moderated his rule over others. A case in point is Xenophon's Cyrus, who was in a better position than anyone else to abuse power, but who let it be known in his court that he had mastered his emotions: "He secured at court great correctness of conduct on the part of his subordinates, who gave precedence to their superiors; and thus he also secured from them a great degree of respect and politeness toward one another." [8] Similarly, when Isocrates' Nicocles praises the moderation and marital fidelity that he himself practices, he refers to the demands of his political office: how can a man expect to obtain the obedience of others if he is unable to subdue his own desires? [9] It is in terms of prudence that Aristotle advises the absolute ruler not to succumb to any debauchery; he ought to take into consideration the attachment of gentlemen for their honor; for this reason, it would be imprudent for him to subject them to the humiliation of corporal punishment; for the same reason, he ought to refrain from "outrage of the young." "When he indulges himself with the young, he is doing so not in the license of power but because he is generally in love. In all such cases, too, he should atone for the dishonors which he appears to inflict by the gift of still greater honors."[10] And we may recall that this was the question that was debated by Socrates and Callicles: should those who rule others be thought of as "rulers or ruled" *(archontas ē archomenous)* as concerns themselves?— this self-rule being defined by the fact of being *sōphrōn* and *enkratēs;* that is, "ruling the pleasures and appetites that are in himself."[11]

The day would come when the paradigm most often used for illustrating sexual virtue would be that of the woman, or girl, who defended herself from the assaults of a man who had every advantage over her; the safeguarding of purity and virginity, and faithfulness to commitments and vows, were to constitute the standard test of virtue. This figure was not unknown in antiquity, certainly; but it does seem that, for Greek thought, a more representative model of the virtue of moderation, one more expressive of the latter's specific nature, was that of the man, the leader, the master who was capable of curbing his own appetite even when his power over others allowed him to indulge it as he pleased.

2. What was affirmed through this conception of mastery as active freedom was the "virile" character of moderation. Just as in the household it was the man who ruled, and in the city it was right that only men should exercise power, and not slaves, children, or women, so each man was supposed to make his manly qualities prevail within himself. Self-mastery was a way of being a man with respect to oneself; that is, a way of commanding what needed commanding, of coercing what was not capable of self-direction, of imposing principles of

reason on what was wanting in reason; in short, it was a way of being active in relation to what was by nature passive and ought to remain so. In this ethics of men made for men, the development of the self as an ethical subject consisted in setting up a structure of virility that related oneself to oneself. It was by being a man with respect to oneself that one would be able to control and master the manly activity that one directed toward others in sexual practice. What one must aim for in the agonistic contest with oneself and in the struggle to control the desires was the point where the relationship with oneself would become isomorphic with the relationship of domination, hierarchy, and authority that one expected, as a man, a free man, to establish over his inferiors; and it was this prior condition of "ethical virility" that provided one with the right sense of proportion for the exercise of "sexual virility," according to a model of "social virility." In the use of male pleasures, one had to be virile with regard to oneself, just as one was masculine in one's social role. In the full meaning of the word, moderation was a man's virtue.

This does not mean of course that women were not expected to be moderate, that they were not capable of *enkrateia,* or that the virtue of *sōphrosynē* was unknown to them. But where women were concerned, this virtue was always referred in some way to virility. An institutional reference, since moderation was imposed on them by their condition of dependence in relation to their families, their husbands, and their procreative function, which ensured the perpetuation of the family name, the transmission of wealth, and the survival of the city. But there was also a structural reference, since in order for a woman to be moderate, she had to establish a relationship of superiority and domination over herself that was virile by definition. It is significant that Socrates, in Xenophon's *Oeconomicus,* after hearing Ischomachus praise the merits of the wife he has himself educated, declares (not without first invoking the goddess of austere matrimony): "By Hera, Ischomachus, you display your wife's masculine understanding

[*andrikē dianoia*]." To which, in order to introduce the lesson
in fastidious deportment he has given his wife, Ischomachus
gives a reply that reveals the two essential elements of this
virtuous virility of women—strength of character and dependence on the man: "There are other instances of her high-
mindedness [*megalophrōn*] that I am willing to relate to you,
instances of her obeying me quickly in some matter after
hearing it only once."[12]

We know that Aristotle explicitly rejected the Socratic argument for a basic unity of virtue, which implied that this was
identical in men and women. And yet, he does not describe
feminine virtues that would be exclusively feminine; those he
attributes to women are defined with reference to one essential
virtue, which achieves its full and complete form in men. And
he sees the reason for this in the fact that the relation between
men and women is "political"; it is the relation of ruler to
ruled. For the relation to be in good order, both partners must
have a share in the same virtues; but each will possess them
in his own way. The one who rules—i.e., the man—"possesses
moral goodness in its full and perfect form," whereas the
ruled, including women, need only have "moral goodness to
the extent required of them." As concerns the man, therefore,
moderation and courage are a full and complete "ruling"
virtue; as for the moderation or courage of the woman, they
are "serving" virtues; in other words, the man stands both as
a complete and finished model of these virtues and as the
principle motivating their practice.[13]

That moderation is given an essentially masculine structure
has another consequence, which is symmetrical and opposite
to the one just discussed: immoderation derives from a passivity that relates it to femininity. To be immoderate was to be
in a state of nonresistance with regard to the force of pleasures,
and in a position of weakness and submission; it meant being
incapable of that virile stance with respect to oneself that
enabled one to be stronger than oneself. In this sense, the man
of pleasures and desires, the man of nonmastery *(akrasia)* or

self-indulgence *(akolasia)* was a man who could be called feminine, but more essentially with respect to himself than with respect to others. In the experience of sexuality such as ours, where a basic scansion maintains an opposition between masculine and feminine, the femininity of men is perceived in the actual or virtual transgression of his sexual role. No one would be tempted to label as effeminate a man whose love for women leads to immoderation on his part; that is, short of doing a whole job of decipherment that would uncover the "latent homosexuality" that secretly inhabits his unstable and promiscuous relation to them. In contrast, for the Greeks it was the opposition between activity and passivity that was essential, pervading the domain of sexual behaviors and that of moral attitudes as well; thus, it was not hard to see how a man might prefer males without anyone even suspecting him of effeminacy, provided he was active in the sexual relation and active in the moral mastering of himself. On the other hand, a man who was not sufficiently in control of his pleasures—whatever his choice of object—was regarded as "feminine." The dividing line between a virile man and an effeminate man did not coincide with our opposition between hetero- and homosexuality; nor was it confined to the opposition between active and passive homosexuality. It marked the difference in people's attitudes toward the pleasures; and the traditional signs of effeminacy—idleness, indolence, refusal to engage in the somewhat rough activities of sports, a fondness for perfumes and adornments, softness *(malakia)*—were not necessarily associated with the individual who in the nineteenth century would be called an "invert," but with the one who yielded to the pleasures that enticed him: he was under the power of his own appetites and those of others. On seeing a boy who was too dressed-up, Diogenes would get annoyed, but he allowed for the fact that such a feminine appearance could just as well betray a taste for women as for men.[14] In the eyes of the Greeks, what constituted ethical negativity par excellence was clearly not the loving of both sexes, nor was it the preferring of one's own sex over the other; it consisted in being passive with regard to the pleasures.

3.   This freedom-power combination that characterized the mode of being of the moderate man could not be conceived without a relation to truth. To rule one's pleasures and to bring them under the authority of the *logos* formed one and the same enterprise: moderation, says Aristotle, desires only "what the rational principle [*orthos logos*] directs."[15] We are familiar with the long debate that developed concerning the role of knowledge in the practice of virtue in general and moderation in particular. Xenophon, in the *Memorabilia*, calls attention to Socrates' argument to the effect that wisdom and moderation cannot be separated: to those who raise the possibility of one's knowing what ought to be done and yet proceeding to do the contrary, Socrates replies that immoderate individuals are always ignorant as well, for in any case men "choose and follow the course which they judge most advantageous."[16] These principles are discussed at length by Aristotle, without his critique ending a debate that would continue in and around Stoicism. But whether or not one granted the possibility of doing wrong while knowing it to be wrong, and whatever the mode of knowledge that one assumed in those who acted in defiance of the principles that they knew, there was one point that was not contested: one could not practice moderation without a certain form of knowledge that was at least one of its essential conditions. One could not form oneself as an ethical subject in the use of pleasures without forming oneself at the same time as a subject of knowledge.

The relationship to the *logos* in the practice of pleasures was described by Greek philosophy of the fourth century in terms of three principal forms. First, there was a structural form: moderation implied that the *logos* be placed in a position of supremacy in the human being and that it be able to subdue the desires and regulate behavior. Whereas in the immoderate individual, the force that desires usurps the highest place and rules tyrannically, in the individual who is *sōphrōn,* it is reason that commands and prescribes, in consonance with the structure of the human being: "it is fitting that the reasonable part should rule," Socrates says, "it being wise and exercising foresight on behalf of the whole soul"; and he proceeds to define the *sōphrōn* as the man in whom the different parts of the soul are in agreement and harmony, when the part that commands and the part that obeys are at one in their recognition that it is proper for reason to rule and that they should not contend for its authority.[17] And in spite of all the differences that opposed the Platonic tripartition of the soul and the Aristotelian conception at the time of the *Nicomachean Ethics,* it is still in terms of the superiority of reason over desire that *sōphrosynē* is characterized in that text: "in an irrational being the desire for pleasure is insatiable even if it tries every source of gratification," so that desire will grow excessive if one is not "chastened and made obedient to authority"; and this authority is that of the *logos* to which "the appetitive element" *(to epithumētikon)* must submit.[18]

But the exercise of the *logos* in the practice of moderation is also described in terms of an instrumental form. In fact, since one's domination of the pleasures ensures a use that is adaptable to needs, times, and circumstances, a practical reason is necessary in order to determine, as Aristotle says, "the things he ought, as he ought, and when he ought."[19] Plato emphasizes that it is important for the individual and for the city not to use the pleasures "without knowledge [*anepistēmonōs*] and at the wrong time [*ektos tōn kairōn*]."[20] And from a similar viewpoint, Xenophon shows that the man of moderation is also the man of dialectics—competent to command and discuss, capable of being the best—for, as Socrates explains in the *Memorabilia,* "only the self-controlled have power to consider things that matter most, and sorting them out after their kind, by word and deed alike to prefer the good and reject the evil."[21]

In Plato the exercise of the *logos* in the practice of moderation appears in a third form: that of the ontological recognition of the self by the self. The need to know oneself in order to practice virtue and subdue the desires is a Socratic theme. But a text like the great speech in the *Phaedrus,* telling of the voyage of souls and the birth of love, fills in the details. This text is doubtless the first description in ancient literature of what will later be known as "spiritual combat." Here one is far from the impassiveness and the feats of endurance and abstinence of the sort that Socrates was able to display according to Alcibiades of the *Symposium,* for the *Phaedrus* presents a whole drama of the soul struggling with itself and against the violence of its desires. These different elements were destined to have a long career in the history of spirituality: the distress that takes hold of the soul, so alien that the latter cannot even give it a name; the anxiety that keeps the soul on the alert; the mysterious seething; the suffering and pleasure that alternate and intermix; the movement that transports one's being; the struggle between opposing powers; the lapses, the wounds, the pains, the reward and the final appeasement. Now, throughout this narrative that claims to reveal the true nature of the human and divine soul, the relation to truth plays a fundamental role. When the soul is caught up in a frenzy of love, driven wild and deprived of self-control, it is indeed because it had beheld "the realities that are outside the heavens" and perceived their reflection in an earthly beauty; but it is also because its memories carry it "towards the reality of Beauty," and because it "sees her again enthroned in her holy place attended by Chastity," that it holds back, that it undertakes to restrain physical desire and seeks to rid itself of everything that might burden it down and prevent it from rediscovering the truth that it has seen.[22] The relation of the soul to truth is at the same time what founds Eros in its movement, its force, and its intensity, and what helps it to become detached from all physical enjoyment, enabling it to become true love.

The point is obvious: be it in the form of a hierarchical

structure of the human being, in the form of a practice of prudence or of the soul's recognition of its own being, the relation to truth constituted an essential element of moderation. It was necessary for the measured use of pleasures, necessary for controlling their violence. But it is important to note that this relation to truth never took the form of a decipherment of the self by the self, never that of a hermeneutics of desire. It was a factor constituting the mode of being of the moderate subject; it was not equivalent to an obligation for the subject to speak truthfully concerning himself; it never opened up the soul as a domain of potential knowledge where barely discernible traces of desire needed to be read and interpreted. The relation to truth was a structural, instrumental, and ontological condition for establishing the individual as a moderate subject leading a life of moderation; it was not an epistemological condition enabling the individual to recognize himself in his singularity as a desiring subject and to purify himself of the desire that was thus brought to light.

4. Now, while this relation to truth, constitutive of the moderate subject, did not lead to a hermeneutics of desire, it did on the other hand open onto an aesthetics of existence. And what I mean by this is a way of life whose moral value did not depend either on one's being in conformity with a code of behavior, or on an effort of purification, but on certain formal principles in the use of pleasures, in the way one distributed them, in the limits one observed, in the hierarchy one respected. Through the *logos,* through reason and the relation to truth that governed it, such a life was committed to the maintenance and reproduction of an ontological order; moreover, it took on the brilliance of a beauty that was revealed to those able to behold it or keep its memory present in mind. Xenophon, Plato, and Aristotle often provide glimpses of this moderate existence whose hallmark, grounded in truth, was both its regard for an ontological structure and its visibly beautiful shape. For example, this is the way Socrates de-

scribes it in the *Gorgias*, supplying his own answers to the questions he puts to a silent Callicles: "The virtue of each thing, a tool, a body, and, further, a soul and a whole animal, doesn't come to be present in the best way just at random, but by some structure and correctness and craft [*taxis, orthotēs, technē*], the one that is assigned to each of them. Is this so? I say so. Then the virtue of each thing is something structured and ordered by a structure? I would say so myself. Then it is some order [*kosmos tis*]—the proper order for each of the things that are—which makes the thing good by coming to be present in it? I myself think so. Then a soul with its proper order is better than a disordered soul? It must be. But now the soul which has order is orderly? Of course it is. And the orderly soul is temperate? It certainly must be. Then the temperate soul is good. . . . And so I set these things down this way, and say that these things are true. And if they are true, then apparently the man who wants to be happy must pursue and practice temperance [*diōkteon kai askēteon*]."[23]

As if echoing this text that links moderation with the beauty of a soul whose order corresponds to its real nature, the *Republic* will show, conversely, how the brilliance of a soul and that of a body are incompatible with the excess and violence of the pleasures: "When a man's soul has a beautiful character [*kala ēthē*], and his body matches it in beauty and is thus in harmony with it, that harmonizing combination, sharing the same mould, is the most beautiful spectacle for anyone who has eyes to see." "It certainly is." "And that which is most beautiful is most lovable [*erasmiōtaton*]." "Of course. . . ." "Tell me this, however, is excessive pleasure compatible with moderation?" "How can it be since it drives one to frenzy?" "Or with the other virtues?" "In no way." "Well then, is it compatible with violence and lack of restraint [*hubris, akolasia*]?" "Very much so." "Can you think of a greater and sharper pleasure than the sexual?" "No, nor a madder one." "But the right kind of love [*ho orthos erōs*] is to love a well-behaved and beautiful person with moderation and restraint?"

"Certainly." "The right kind of love has nothing frenzied or licentious about it?" "Nothing."[24]

We may also recall Xenophon's idealized description of Cyrus' court, which presented a vision of beauty for its own enjoyment, due to the perfect dominion that each individual exercised over himself; the ruler publicly exhibited a mastery and a restraint that spread to everyone, issuing out from them, according to the rank they held, in the form of a moderate conduct, a respect for oneself and for others, a careful supervision of the soul and the body, and a frugal economy of acts, so that no involuntary and violent movement disturbed the beautiful order that seemed to be present in everyone's mind: "Among them you would never have detected any one raising his voice in anger or giving vent to his delight in boisterous laughter; but on seeing them you would have judged that they were in truth making a noble life their aim."[25] The individual fulfilled himself as an ethical subject by shaping a precisely measured conduct that was plainly visible to all and deserving to be long remembered.

The foregoing is only a rough sketch for preliminary purposes; a few general traits that characterized the way in which, in classical Greek thought, sexual practice was conceptualized and made into an ethical domain. The elements of this domain —the "ethical substance"—were formed by the *aphrodisia;* that is, by acts intended by nature, associated by nature with an intense pleasure, and naturally motivated by a force that was always liable to excess and rebellion. The principle according to which this activity was meant to be regulated, the "mode of subjection," was not defined by a universal legislation determining permitted and forbidden acts; but rather by a *savoir-faire,* an art that prescribed the modalities of a use that depended on different variables (need, time, status). The effort that the individual was urged to bring to bear on himself, the necessary ascesis, had the form of a battle to be fought, a victory to be won in establishing a dominion of self over self, modeled after domestic or political authority. Finally, the mode of being to which this self-mastery gave access was characterized as an active freedom, a freedom that was indissociable from a structural, instrumental, and ontological relation to truth.

As we shall see, this moral reflection developed themes of austerity—concerning the body, marriage, and love of boys— that show a resemblance to the precepts and interdictions that were to appear later on. But we must not let this apparent continuity obscure the fact that the ethical subject would no longer be constituted in the same manner. In the Christian morality of sexual behavior, the ethical substance was to be defined not by the *aphrodisia,* but by a domain of desires that lie hidden among the mysteries of the heart, and by a set of acts that are carefully specified as to their form and their conditions. Subjection was to take the form not of a *savoir-faire,* but of a recognition of the law and an obedience to pastoral authority. Hence the ethical subject was to be characterized not so much by the perfect rule of the self by the self in the exercise of a virile type of activity, as by self-renunciation and a purity whose model was to be sought in virginity. This being the case, one can understand the significance that was attached, in Christian morality, to two opposite yet complementary practices: a codification of sexual acts that would become more and more specific, and the development of a hermeneutics of desire together with procedures of self-decipherment.

Putting it schematically, we could say that classical antiquity's moral reflection concerning the pleasures was not directed toward a codification of acts, nor toward a hermeneutics of the subject, but toward a stylization of attitudes and an aesthetics of existence. A stylization, because the rarefaction of sexual activity presented itself as a sort of open-ended requirement. The textual record is clear in this regard: neither the doctors who made recommendations about the regimen one should follow, nor the moralists who demanded that husbands respect their wives, nor those who gave advice concerning the right conduct to manifest in the love of boys, ever say exactly what ought or ought not to be done in the way of sexual acts or practices. And it is very unlikely that this was owing to the authors' reticence or sense of shame; rather, it was because the problem was elsewhere: sexual moderation was an exercise of freedom that took form in self-mastery; and the latter was shown in the manner in which the subject behaved, in the self-restraint he displayed in his virile activity, in the way he related to himself in the relationship he had with others. It was this attitude—much more than the acts one committed or the desires one concealed—that made one liable to value judgments. A moral value that was also an aesthetic value and a truth value since it was by aiming at the satisfaction of real needs, by respecting the true hierarchy of the human being, and by never forgetting where one stood in regard to truth, that one would be able to give one's conduct the form that would assure one of a name meriting remembrance.

Now we will see how some of the great themes of sexual austerity—themes that would have a historical destiny extending well beyond Greek culture—were formed and elaborated in the thought of the fourth century. I will not start from the general theories of pleasure and virtue; rather, I will take as my source material the existing and recognized practices by which men sought to shape their conduct: their dietary practice, their practice of domestic government, their courtship practice as expressed in amorous behavior. I will try to show how these three practices were conceptualized in medicine or philosophy and how these reflections resulted in various recommendations, not for codifying sexual conduct in a precise way, but for "stylizing" it: stylizations within dietetics, understood as an art of the everyday relationship of the individual with his body; in economics as an art of a man's behavior as head of a family; and in erotics as an art of the reciprocal conduct of a man and a boy in a love relationship.*

*Henri Joly's work *Le Renversement platonicien* offers an example of how Greek thought can be analyzed from the standpoint of the relationships that existed between the field of practices and philosophical reflection.

PART TWO

Dietetics

The moral reflection of the Greeks on sexual behavior did not seek to justify interdictions, but to stylize a freedom—that freedom which the "free" man exercised in his activity. This produced a state of affairs that might well seem paradoxical at first glance: the Greeks practiced, accepted, and valued relations between men and boys; and yet their philosophers dealt with the subject by conceiving and elaborating an ethics of abstention. They were quite willing to grant that a married man might go in search of sexual pleasures outside of marriage, and yet their moralists conceived the principle of a matrimonial life in which the husband would have relations only with his own wife. They never imagined that sexual pleasure was in itself an evil or that it could be counted among the natural stigmata of a transgression; and yet their doctors worried over the relationship between sexual activity and health, and they developed an entire theory concerning the dangers of sexual practice.

Let us begin by considering this last point. First of all, it should be noted that for the most part their reflection was not concerned with analyzing the different pathological effects of sexual activity; nor did they seek to organize this behavior as a domain in which normal behavior might be distinguished from abnormal and pathological practices. These themes were not totally absent of course. But this was not what constituted the general theme of the inquiry into the relationships between the *aphrodisia,* health, life, and death. The main objective of this reflection was to define the use of pleasures—which conditions were favorable, which practice was recommended, which rarefaction was necessary—in terms of a certain way of caring for one's body. The preoccupation was much more "dietetic" than "therapeutic": a matter of regimen aimed at regulating an activity that was recognized as being important for health. The medical problematization of sexual behavior was accomplished less out of a concern for eliminating pathological forms than out of a desire to integrate it as fully as possible into the management of health and the life of the body.

1

Regimen in
General

In order to appreciate the importance the Greeks ascribed
to regimen, and to understand the general interpretation they
gave to "dietetics" and the way in which they linked its practice to medicine, we can refer to two origin stories: one is
found in the Hippocratic collection, the other in Plato.

The author of the treatise on *Ancient Medicine,* far from
considering regimen as an adjacent practice associated with
the medical art—one of its applications or extensions—attributes the birth of medicine to a primordial and essential preoccupation with regimen.[1] According to him, mankind set itself
apart from animal life by means of sort of dietary disjunction.
In the beginning, the story goes, men did eat the same kind
of food as animals: meat and raw plants. This type of nourishment was apt to toughen the most vigorous individuals, but
it was hard on the weaker ones; in a word, people died young
or old. Consequently, men sought a diet that was better suited
"to their nature": it was this regimen that still characterized
the present way of life. But with this milder diet, illness had
become less immediately fatal, and it was realized that the
food healthy people ate was not suited to people who were ill:
they needed other nourishment. Medicine thus came into
being as an appropriate "diet" for the sick, emerging from a
search for the specific regimen for their condition. In this tale
of genesis, it is dietetics that appears to be initial; it gives rise
to medicine as one of its particular applications.

Plato—being rather suspicious of dietetic practice, or at least fearful of the excesses he associates with it, for political and ethical reasons we shall consider below—thinks, on the contrary, that the concern with regimen was born of a change in medical practices:[2] in the beginning, the god Asclepius taught men how to cure illnesses and heal wounds by means of drastic and effective remedies. According to Plato, Homer provides evidence of this practice of simple treatments in the account he gives of the cures of Menelaus and Eurypylus beneath the walls of Troy: the blood of the wounded was sucked, emollients were poured over their wounds, and they were made to drink wine sprinkled with barley meal and grated cheese.* It was later, when men had forsaken the rough, healthy life of former times, that one would attempt to follow illnesses "step by step" and, by means of a protracted regimen, to sustain those who were in bad health precisely because, no longer living as they should, they were victims of lasting sicknesses. According to this genesis, dietetics came into existence as a kind of medicine for soft times; it was designed for mismanaged lives that sought to prolong themselves. But it is clear that if, for Plato, dietetics was not an original art, this was not because regimen *(diaitē)* was unimportant; the reason people did not concern themselves with dietetics in the time of Asclepius or his first successors was that the "regimen" that men actually followed, the manner in which they nourished themselves and exercised their bodies, was in accord with nature.[4] Viewed from this perspective, dietetics did represent one modality in medicine, but it did not become an extension of the art of healing until the day when regimen as a way of life became separated from nature; and while it always constituted a necessary accompaniment of medicine, this was simply because one could not treat a person without rectifying the lifestyle that made him sick in the first place.[5]

*Actually the details given by Plato are not exactly those that one finds in the *Iliad.*[3]

In any case, whether dietetic knowledge was considered an original art or seen as a later derivation, it is clear that "diet" itself—regimen—was a fundamental category through which human behavior could be conceptualized. It characterized the way in which one managed one's existence, and it enabled a set of rules to be affixed to conduct; it was a mode of problematization of behavior that was indexed to a nature which had to be preserved and to which it was right to conform. Regimen was a whole art of living.

1. The area that a properly designed regimen ought to cover was defined by a list that became almost conventional as time went on. It is the list found in Book VI of the *Epidemics;* it included "exercises [*ponoi*], foods [*sitia*], drinks [*pota*], sleep [*hypnoi*], and sexual relations [*aphrodisia*]"—everything that needed to be "measured."[6] Among the exercises, those that were natural (walking, strolling) were distinguished from those that were violent (foot races, wrestling); and it was determined which ones ought to be practiced and with what intensity, depending on the time of day, the season of the year, the age of the subject, the food he had consumed. Exercises might be combined with baths—hot or cold, and also depending on season, age, activities, and meals already eaten or to be prepared. The alimentary regimen—food and drink—had to take into consideration the nature and quantity of what one ingested, the general condition of the body, the climate, and the activities one engaged in. Evacuations—purges and vomiting—served to correct alimentary practice and its excesses. Sleep, too, comprised different components, which could be made to vary according to the regimen: the time allotted to it, the hours one chose, the quality of the bed, its hardness, its warmth. Hence regimen had to take account of numerous elements in the physical life of a man, or at least that of a free man, and this meant day by day, all day long, from getting up in the morning to going to bed at night. When broken down into its component parts, regimen looks like a real daily routine: thus the regimen suggested by Diocles follows the course of an ordinary day, moment by moment, from waking up on through to the evening meal and the onset of sleep, with attention given along the way to the very first exercises, the ablutions and massagings of the body and the head, the walks, the private activities and the gymnasium, lunch, napping, and another round of walking and gymnasium activities, oiling and massage, dinner. At all times, and encompassing all of a man's activities, regimen problematized the relation to the body and developed a way of living whose forms, options, and variables were determined by a concern with the body. But the body was not the only thing in question.

2.　In the different areas where it was required, regimen needed to establish a measure: "even a pig would know," says one of the interlocutors in the Platonic dialogue *The Lovers:* "in everything connected with the body," what is useful is "the right measure," and not what is large or small in quantity.[7] Now, this measure is to be understood as referring not only to the corporal realm but to the moral realm as well. The Pythagoreans, who doubtless played an important part in the development of dietetics, strongly emphasized the correlation between the care given the body and the concern for preserving the purity and harmony of the soul. While it is true that they expected medicine to purge the body and music to cleanse the soul, they also credited song and instruments with beneficial effects on the equilibrium of the organism.[8] The many alimentary taboos they set for themselves had cultural and religious significance; and the criticism they directed against every abuse connected with eating, drinking, exercises, and sexual activities had both the authority of a moral precept and the utility of sound advice for health.*

*"For bodily ailments, he had curative tunes which he sang that got sick people on their feet again. Others made one forget pain, calmed fits of anger, drove out immoderate desires. Now for his diet: for lunch honey, for dinner a biscuit and vegetables, meat infrequently. . . . In this way his body kept the same condition, as if on a straight line, without being sometimes healthy, sometimes sick, and without growing heavier

Even outside the strictly Pythagorean context, regimen was regularly defined with reference to these two associated dimensions of good health maintenance and proper care of the soul. This was because the one implied the other, but also because the resolve to follow a measured and reasonable regimen and the diligence one manifested in the actual task were themselves evidence of an indispensable moral fortitude. Xenophon's Socrates calls attention to this correlation when he advises young people to exercise their bodies regularly by practicing gymnastics. He sees this as a means of ensuring that they will be able to defend themselves better in warfare, to avoid earning a coward's reputation as a soldier, to best serve their native land, and to obtain high rewards (and hence to bequeath wealth and status to their descendants). He believes the practice will provide protection against illnesses and infirmities of the body; but he also points up the good effects of gymnastics that accrue, he says, where one would least expect to see them: in the mind, for an unhealthy body causes forgetfulness, loss of courage, bad temper, and madness, so that in the end the knowledge one has acquired may even be dislodged from the soul.[10]

But it was also the case that the severity of a physical regimen, with the determination that was required in order to keep to it, called for an essential moral firmness, which made its observance possible. Moreover, as Plato saw it, this was the real justification for these practices by which one sought to acquire strength, beauty, and physical health. Not only will the judicious man, says Socrates in Book IX of the *Republic,* "not abandon his body to the irrational pleasure of the beast"; not only will he not "turn himself that way"; he will do more: "It is not even health he aims at, nor does he consider it important that he should be strong, healthy, or beautiful, unless he acquires moderation as a result." The physical regi-

---

and stouter, then thinner and leaner; and by his expression, his soul always showed the same character [*to homoion ēthos*]." It seems that Pythagoras also gave advice on regimen to athletes.[9]

men ought to accord with the principle of a general aesthetics of existence in which the equilibrium of the body was one of the conditions of the proper hierarchy of the soul: "He will cultivate harmony in his body for the sake of consonance in his soul"—which will enable him to conduct himself like a true musician *(mousikos)*. [11] Physical regimen must not, therefore, be too intensely cultivated for its own sake.

The possibility of a danger in the very practice of "diet" was readily acknowledged. For if the aim of regimen was to prevent excesses, one might exaggerate the importance one lent to it and the autonomy one permitted it to assume. This risk was generally perceived as having two forms. There was the danger of what might be called "athletic" excess; this was due to repeated workouts that overdeveloped the body and ended by making the soul sluggish, enveloped as it was within a too-powerful musculature; on several occasions Plato finds fault with this athletic forcing, declaring that he would want nothing of the sort for the young people of his city.*

But there was also the danger of what could be called "valetudinary" excess; that is, the constant vigilance that one applied to one's body, one's health, to the least ailment. The best example of this excess was furnished, according to Plato, by an individual held to be one of the founders of dietetics, Herodicus the trainer; entirely taken up in the effort to avoid breaking the least rule of the regimen he had imposed on himself, he "trained" away for years, while living the life of a dying man. This attitude drew two reproaches from Plato. It was characteristic of idle men who were of no use to the city; there was a telling comparison that could be made with those serious craftsmen who would not stop to swathe their heads on account of a migraine, for they had no time to lose in petty medical treatments. But it was also characteristic of those who, in order to keep from losing their hold on life, tried their

---

*Aristotle also criticizes the excesses of the athletic regimen and of certain kinds of training. [12]

utmost to delay the term that had been appointed by nature. The practice carried the danger—moral but political as well —of exaggerating one's care of the body *(peritte epimeleia tou somatos).* [13] Asclepius, whose treatment was confined to potions and surgery, was politically astute: he knew that in a well-governed state, no one had the leisure to spend his life being sick and having himself treated.*

3. The distrust of excessive regimens shows that the purpose of diet was not to extend life as far as possible in time nor as high as possible in performance, but rather to make it useful and happy within the limits that had been set for it. Nor was diet supposed to determine the conditions of existence once and for all. A regimen was not good if it only permitted one to live in one place, with one type of food, and if it did not allow one to be open to any change. The usefulness of a regimen lay precisely in the possibility it gave individuals to face different situations. It is in these terms that Plato contrasts the regimen of athletes, which is so strict that they cannot depart from it without becoming "seriously and violently ill," with the regimen he would like to see adopted for his warriors. They need to be like dogs always on the alert; in their campaigns they will "endure frequent changes of drinking water and food, of summer and winter weather" and still maintain an "unvarying health."[15] Plato's warriors would have special responsibilities no doubt. But more general regimens also obeyed this same principle. The author of the *Regimen* in the Hippocratic collection is careful to emphasize that his advice is not addressed to a privileged minority of idle individuals, but to the great majority of people, to "those who work, those who travel, go on sea voyages, expose themselves to sun and cold."[16] This passage has sometimes been interpreted as indicating a particular interest in the forms of active and professional life. The thing to

*In the *Timaeus,* Plato asserts that the life span of every living creature is determined by fate.[14]

note, however, is the concern it shows—one that was shared by ethics and medicine—with preparing the individual for a multitude of possible circumstances. One could not and one should not expect regimen to circumvent fate or to alter nature. What could be expected of it was that it would enable one to react, with some degree of readiness, to unforeseen events as they occurred. Dietetics was a strategic art in the sense that it ought to permit one to respond to circumstances in a reasonable, hence useful, manner.

In the vigilance it brought to bear on the body and its activities, dietetics necessitated two quite particular forms of attention on the part of the individual. It required what might be called a "serial" attention; that is, an attention to sequences: activities were not simply good or bad in themselves; their value was determined in part by those that preceded them or those that followed, and the same thing (a certain food, a type of exercise, a hot or cold bath) would be recommended or advised against according to whether one had engaged in or was about to engage in such or such other activity (the practices that followed one after the other ought to counterbalance one another in their effects, but the contrast between them must not be too extreme). The practice of regimen also implied a "circumstantial" vigilance, a sharply focused yet wide-ranging attention that must be directed toward the external world, its elements, its sensations: the climate of course, the seasons, the hours of the day, the degree of humidity and dryness, of heat or cold, the winds, the characteristic features of a region, the layout of a city. And the relatively detailed instructions that are given by the Hippocratic regimen were meant to help the individual who familiarized himself with them to modulate his way of living according to all these variables. Regimen should not be understood as a corpus of universal and uniform rules; it was more in the nature of a manual for reacting to situations in which one might find oneself, a treatise for adjusting one's behavior to fit the circumstances.

4. Lastly, dietetics was a technique of existence in the sense that it was not content to transmit the advice of a doctor to an individual, who would then be expected to apply it passively. Without going into the history of the dispute between medicine and gymnastics over the issue of their respective competence to determine the proper regimen, we must keep in mind that diet was not thought of as an unquestioning obedience to the authority of another; it was intended to be a deliberate practice on the part of an individual, involving himself and his body. In order to follow the right regimen, it was of course necessary to listen to those who knew, but this relationship was supposed to take the form of persuasion. If it was to be reasonable, properly adjusting itself to time and circumstances, the diet of the body had also to be a matter of thought, deliberation, and prudence. Whereas medications and operations acted upon the body, and the body submitted to that action, regimen addressed itself to the soul, and inculcated principles in the soul. Thus, in the *Laws,* Plato distinguishes between two kinds of doctors: those who are good for slaves (they are usually slaves themselves) and who confine themselves to giving prescriptions without offering any explanation; and the freeborn doctors who attend to free men.[17] Not contenting themselves with prescriptions, they enter into conversation with the patient and gather information from him and his friends; they instruct him, exhort him, and persuade him with arguments that, once he is convinced, are likely to cause him to lead the right kind of life. From the expert doctor, the free man could expect more than the means for a cure in the strict sense of the term; he ought to receive a rational framework for the whole of his existence.* A brief passage in the *Memorabilia* shows a clear perception of regimen as a concrete and active practice of the relation to self.

*See Plato's *Timaeus,* where the author sums up what he has just said concerning regimen as follows: "Let this suffice for the treatment of the living creature as a whole and of its bodily part, and the way in which a man may best lead a rational life, both governing and being governed by himself."[18]

In this text, one sees Socrates absorbed in the effort to make
his disciples "independent," irrespective of their social position. To this end he urges them to learn (either from him or
from another teacher) whatever a gentleman should know,
within the fixed limits of what is useful, and nothing beyond
that: they should learn the essentials in the fields of geometry,
astronomy, and arithmetic. But he also recommends that they
"take care of their health." And this "care," which should be
supported by accepted knowledge, should also develop into a
vigilant attentiveness to themselves: self-observation, accompanied—significantly—by taking notes: "Everyone should
watch himself throughout his life, and notice what sort of
meat and drink and what form of exercise suit his constitution,
and how he should regulate them in order to enjoy good
health." To become an art of existence, good management of
the body ought to include a setting down in writing carried out
by the subject concerning himself; with the help of this note-
taking, the individual would be able to gain his independence
and choose judiciously between what was good and bad for
him: "For by such attention to yourselves you can discover
better than any doctor what suits your constitution."[19]

In short, the practice of regimen as an art of living was
something more than a set of precautions designed to prevent
illnesses or complete their cure. It was a whole manner of
forming oneself as a subject who had the proper, necessary,
and sufficient concern for his body. A concern that permeated
everyday life, making the major or common activities of existence a matter both of health and of ethics. It defined a circumstantial strategy involving the body and the elements that
surrounded it; and finally, it proposed to equip the individual
himself for a rational mode of behavior. What place was it
agreed that the *aphrodisia* should have in this reasonable and
natural management of life?

2

The Diet of
Pleasures

Two treatises of dietetics have come down to us. Both belong to the Hippocratic collection. The older of the two, also
the shorter, is the *Peri diaitēs hygiainēs (A Regimen for
Health);* it was long regarded as constituting the last part of
the treatise *The Nature of Man.*[1] The other, the *Peri diaitēs,*
is also the more developed. In addition, Oribasius included in
his *Medical Collection* a text on hygiene by Diocles, which
gives a meticulously detailed set of rules for everyday life.[2]
And lastly, this same Diocles, who lived at the end of the
fourth century, has been credited with a very brief text that
was collected in the works of Paul of Aegina; in this text, the
author tells how to recognize the first signs of illness in oneself
and offers a few general rules of seasonal regimen.[3]

Whereas *A Regimen for Health* does not say a word on the
subject of the *aphrodisia,* the *Peri diaitēs* includes a series of
recommendations and prescriptions relating to the question.
The first part of the work is presented as a reflection on the
general principles that should determine the organization of
the regimen. The author acknowledges that some of his many
predecessors have managed to give good advice on various
particular points; however, none of them was able to present
an adequate treatment of the subject matter they proposed to
discuss, the reason being that in order to "treat correctly
concerning human diet," it is necessary to "acquire knowledge
and discernment" of human nature in general, of man's origi-

nal constitution *(hē ex archēs systasis)*, and of the principle
that ought to have control within the body *(to epicrateon en
tōi sōmati)*. ⁴ The author considers the two fundamental elements of regimen to be alimentation and exercise; the latter
causes expenditures that food and drink serve to compensate.

The second part of the text discusses the practice of dietetics
from the standpoint of the properties and effects of the elements that go into the regimen. After some remarks on places
—high or low, dry or wet, exposed to such and such a wind
—the author undertakes a review of foods (barley or wheat,
considered in terms of the fineness of grinding, the time at
which the dough was kneaded, the quantity of water that was
mixed with the flour; meats, differentiated in terms of their
varied origins; fruits and vegetables, evaluated according to
their different varieties), then baths (hot, cold, taken before or
after meals), vomitings, sleep, natural exercises (like those of
hearing, voice, thought, or walking) and violent exercises
(such as running, arm motions, wrestling, and punchball, performed in the dust or with an oiled body). In this enumeration
of the elements of regimen, sexual activity *(lagneiē)* is barely
mentioned—between baths and oilings on one side, and vomitings on the other—and such mention as it does get is only
owing to its three effects. Two of these are qualitative: a warming due to the violence of the exercise *(ponos)*, and to the
elimination of a humid element; but also a moistening because
the exercise has caused some of the flesh-parts to melt. A third
effect is quantitative: the evacuation causes weight loss. "Sexual intercourse reduces, moistens, and warms. It warms owing
to the fatigue and the excretion of moisture; it reduces owing
to the evacuation; it moistens because of the remnant in the
body of matters melted by the fatigue."⁵

On the other hand, in the third part of this *Regimen*, one
does find a certain number of prescriptions concerning the
aphrodisia. In its first pages, this part resembles a sort of great
calendar of health, a permanent almanac of the seasons and
the regimens appropriate to them. But the author notes that

it is not possible to give a general formula for determining the correct balance between exercises and foods. He stresses the need to take account of the differences among things, individuals, places, and times;⁶ the almanac is thus not to be read as a set of imperative recipes but as strategic principles that one must know how to adapt to circumstances. In short, whereas the second part of the text dealt more with the elements of regimen in themselves, with a view to their intrinsic properties (and the *aphrodisia* are mentioned only in passing), the third part, in its beginning, is especially concerned with situational variables.

The year is divided into four seasons, of course. But these in turn are subdivided into shorter periods of a few weeks or even a few days. This is because the peculiar characteristics of each season often develop in stages; and further, it is always risky to alter one's regimen abruptly; like excesses, sudden changes have harmful consequences—" 'Little by little' [*to kata mikron*] is a safe rule, especially in cases of change from one thing to another." Which means that "in each season the various items of regimen should be changed gradually [*kata mikron*]."⁷ Thus, the winter regimen should be subdivided as the season itself demands, into a period of forty-four days that extend from the setting of the Pleiades to the solstice, then into an exactly equivalent period followed by a relaxation of the regimen. Spring begins with a period of thirty-two days, from the rising of Arcturus and the arrival of the swallows to the equinox; within this time span, the season should be divided into six periods of eight days. Then comes the summer season, which comprises two phases: from the rising of the Pleiades to the solstice, and from the solstice to the equinox. From that time to the setting of the Pleiades, one should spend forty-eight hours preparing for the "winter regimen."

The author does not provide a complete regimen for these small subdivisions. Rather, he defines, more or less in detail, an overall strategy that depends on the qualities that are characteristic of each of these times of the year. This strategy is based on a principle of compensation, if not opposition or resistance: the cold of one season should be counterbalanced by a warming regimen lest the body become chilled; inversely, extreme heat calls for a soothing, cooling regimen. But it should also obey the principle of imitation and conformity: a mild season that progresses gradually needs a mild and graduated regimen; in the period when plants prepare for their growth, humans should do likewise, preparing to develop their bodies; similarly, just as trees harden and brace themselves against the harsh days of winter, men should toughen themselves by not fleeing the cold but by exposing themselves to it "courageously."[8]

This is the general context in which the *aphrodisia* are to be regulated, taking account of the effects they may have on the interaction of heat and cold, of dryness and moisture, according to the general notions that one finds in the second part of the text. Recommendations concerning them are placed for the most part between alimentary prescriptions and advice on exercises and evacuations. Winter, from the setting of the Pleiades to the spring equinox, is a season in which regimen should have a drying and warming effect, considering the coldness and wetness of the season: hence, roasted rather than boiled meats, whole-wheat bread, small portions of dry vegetables, slightly diluted wine, but in small amounts; numerous exercises of every sort (running, wrestling, walking); baths that should be cold after running workouts, which always heat up the body, and hot after all the other exercises; more frequent sexual relations, especially for older men whose bodies tend to become chilled; emetics three times per month for those with moist constitutions, two times per month for those who are dry.[9] During the spring period, when the air is warmer and dryer, and when one must prepare for the growth of the body, one should eat as many boiled meats as roasted, together with moist vegetables; take baths; decrease the quantity of sexual relations and emetics; vomit only two times per month, then even less frequently, so that the body will maintain "a pure flesh." After the rising of the Pleiades, with the coming of summer, dryness is what regimen must fight against: drink light wines, white and diluted; eat barley cakes, boiled or raw vegetables, if they can be eaten without over-heating the body; abstain from emetics and reduce sexual activity to a minimum *(toisi de aphrodisioisin hōs hēkista);* exercise less; avoid running, which dessicates the body, as well as walking in the sun, giving preference instead to wrestling in the dust.[10] As one gets nearer to the rising of Arcturus and the autumn equinox, the regimen must be made milder and more moist; nothing specific is said about sexual regimen.

Diocles' *Regimen* is much less developed than that of Hippocrates. However, it is quite detailed in its treatment of daily routine, which takes up a large part of the text: from the massages that should immediately follow getting up from bed, in order to reduce the stiffness of the body, to the positions to take in bed when it is time to lie down ("neither too extended nor too bent," and never on one's back), all the important moments of the day are examined, with the baths, the rub-downs, the oilings, the evacuations, the walks, and the foods that ought to accompany them.[11] The question of sexual pleasures and their modulation is considered only in connection with seasonal variations, and only after some general principles of balance are called to mind: "It is a very important point for health that our body's potency not be diminished by another potency." But the author restricts himself to brief generalities: first, no one should "make frequent and continual use of sexual intercourse"; the latter is more suitable for "cold, moist, atrabilious, and flatulent persons," and least suitable for thin ones; there are periods in life when it is more harmful, as in the case of old people or for those who are "in the period that extends from childhood to adolescence."[12] As for the presumably later text, taken to be a letter from Diocles to King Antigonus, the economy of pleasures it sets forth is very close in its general outline to that of Hippocrates: at winter solstice, which is the time when one is most susceptible to catarrh, sexual practice should not be restricted. During the time of the Pleiades' ascent, a period in which bitter bile is dominant in the body, one must indulge in sexual acts with a good deal of moderation. One should even forgo them completely at summer solstice time, when black bile takes over in the organism; and it is necessary to abstain from sexual activity, as well as from any vomiting, till the autumn equinox.[13]*

Several aspects of this regimen of pleasures merit our attention. First, there is the limited space given to the problem of sexual relations compared with that accorded to exercises, and especially to food. As far as the thinking on dietetics was concerned, the question of foods—considered in terms of their peculiar qualities, and of the circumstances in which they were consumed (whether the seasons of the year or the particular state of the organism)—was a good deal more important than sexual activity. In addition, it should be noted that the preoccupation with regimen was never focused on the *form* of the acts: nothing was said about the types of sexual relations, nothing about the "natural" position or about unseemly practices, nothing about masturbation, nor anything about the questions—which would later become so important—of coitus interruptus and methods of contraception.† The *aphrodisia* were considered in the aggregate, as an activity whose significance was not determined by the various forms it could take; one needed to ask oneself only whether the activity ought to take place, how frequently, and in what context. The problematization was carried out primarily in terms of quantity and circumstances.

Moreover, this quantity was not evaluated in the form of a precise numerical determination. One always remained within the compass of a general assessment: use pleasures "more amply" *(pleon),* or in smaller amounts *(elasson),* or as little as

---

*This seasonal rhythm for sexual regimen was accepted for a long time. One encounters it again in imperial times in the writings of Celsus.
†See, however, Diocles' remarks about sleeping in the dorsal position, which induces nocturnal emissions.[14]

possible *(hōs hēkista)*. Which did not mean that it was useless to concentrate one's attention on the problem, but rather that it was not possible to determine in advance and for everyone, the rhythm of an activity that engaged an interplay of qualities —dryness, heat, moisture, cold—between the body and its milieu. If in fact sexual acts were a proper concern of regimen, and if they required "moderation," this was because they produced—through the motions of the body and the ejaculation of semen—warming, cooling, drying, and moistening effects. They raised or lowered the level of each of the elements that were responsible for the body's equilibrium. Hence they also altered the relationship between this equilibrium and the interaction of these elements in the outside world: heating or drying, which might be good for a cold, moist body, would be less so if the season and the climate were themselves hot and dry. It was not the function of regimen to prescribe quantities and determine rhythms: given relations that could only be defined in terms of their general characteristics, the role of regimen was to negotiate qualitative changes and make such readjustments as were necessitated by circumstances. We may note in passing that the author of the Aristotelian *Problems* seems to have been the only one to draw from one of the best-known principles of this qualitative psychology (namely, that women are generally cold and moist while men are hot and dry) the inference that the active season for sexual relations was not the same for both sexes: summer was when women were most disposed to sexual intercourse, whereas men felt the strongest inclination in winter.[15]

Thus, dietetics problematized sexual practice not as a set of acts to be differentiated according to their forms and according to the value of each of them, but as an "activity" the whole of which should be given free rein or curtailed depending on chronological considerations. A point that allows us to draw a parallel between this regimen and certain regulations found later, in the Christian pastoral ministry. There too, in fact, some of the criteria used for delimiting sexual activity are temporal in nature. But those criteria are not only more precise; they operate in a completely different way: they determine times when sexual practice is permitted and other times when it is forbidden; and this strict partition is established in reference to different variables: the liturgical year, menstrual cycles, the period of pregnancy, or the time subsequent to childbirth.* In the ancient medical regimens, on the other hand, the variations were gradual; and instead of being organized according to the binary form of permitted and forbidden, they suggest a constant oscillation between more and less. The sexual act was not considered as a licit or an illicit practice according to the temporal boundaries within which it was inscribed: situated at the point of intersection between the individual and the world, temperament and climate, the qualities of the body and those of the seasons, it was viewed as an activity that could be more or less pernicious in its consequences and should therefore be subjected to a more or less restrictive economy. It was a practice that demanded reflection and prudence. So it was not a question of determining the "working days" of sexual pleasures, uniformly and for everyone, but of how best to calculate the opportune times and the appropriate frequencies.

*On this point, J. L. Flandrin's book *Un Temps pour embrasser* (1983) should be consulted. Citing sources from the seventh century, it shows the importance of the divisions between permitted times and forbidden times, together with the many forms taken by that rhythmic ordering. One sees how this distribution of time was different from the circumstantial strategies of Greek dietetics.

3

Risks and Dangers

The regimen of the *aphrodisia,* with the need to moderate their practice, did not operate on the assumption that sexual acts in themselves and by nature were bad. They were not the object of any disqualification based on principle. The question that was raised concerning them had to do with use, a use that was to be modulated according to the condition of the body and external circumstances. However, the need to have recourse to a careful regimen and to bring vigilant attention to bear on sexual practice was justified by two sets of reasons that reveal a certain anxiety about the effects of this activity.

1. The first set of reasons concerns the effects of the sexual act on the individual's body. Granted there were constitutions for which sexual activity was beneficial on the whole: this was the case for those suffering from an abundance of phlegm— for intercourse facilitated the elimination of fluids which would otherwise become corrupt, giving rise to that humor— or for those whose digestion was bad, whose body consumed itself, and whose belly was cold and dry.[1] But for others, whose bodies and heads were congested with humors, its effects were largely detrimental.[2]

Yet, despite this neutral valuation, this contextual ambivalence, sexual activity was the object of a rather constant suspicion. Diogenes Laertius reports a phrase by Pythagoras in which the general requirements of a seasonal regimen are

117

directly associated with a need for continuous rarefaction and a conviction that the *aphrodisia* are intrinsically harmful: "Keep to the winter for sexual pleasures, in summer abstain; they are less harmful in autumn and spring, but they are always harmful and not conducive to health." And he goes on to cite this response from Pythagoras to the person who asked him when the best time was for making love: "When you want to lose what strength you have."[3] But the Pythagoreans were not the only ones by any means to manifest this sort of apprehension; the rule of "as little as possible" and the pursuit of the "lesser evil" are also invoked in texts whose aims are purely medical or hygienic: Diocles' *Regimen* proposes to establish the conditions in which the use of pleasures would cause "the least harm" *(hēkista enochlei);* and the Aristotelian *Problems,* where the effects of the sexual act are compared to those of pulling a plant from the ground, which always damages the roots, advises one to have relations only in case of a pressing need.[4] In this dietetics, whose business it was to determine when it was beneficial and when it was harmful to practice the pleasures, one perceives the emergence of a general tendency toward a restrictive economy.

This distrust is apparent in the idea that several of the most important organs are affected by sexual activity and may suffer from its abuses. Aristotle remarks that the brain is the first organ to feel the consequences of the sexual act, for it is the "coldest part" of the whole body; by withdrawing a "pure natural heat" from the organism, the emission of semen induces a general cooling effect.[5] Diocles places the gall bladder, kidneys, lungs, eyes, and spinal cord among the organs that are particularly exposed to the effects of pleasure's excesses.[6] According to the *Problems,* it is especially the eyes and the loins that are affected, either because they contribute to the act more than the other organs, or because the excessive heat produces a liquefaction within them.[7]

These manifold organic correlations explain the various pathological consequences that were associated with sexual activity when it did not obey the rules of an indispensable economy. It should be remarked that one finds little mention —in the case of men at least*—of the troubles that might be caused by total abstinence. Illnesses due to a poor distribution of sexual activity were much more often illnesses of excess. Such as the famous "dorsal phthisis" defined by Hippocrates in the treatise *Diseases* and redescribed with the same etiology over a very long span of Western medicine: it was a disease that "attacks young married people in particular" and "people fond of sexual intercourse" *(philolagnoi);* its point of origin was the marrow (considered to be the part of the body where the sperm is located, as we shall see); it gave a tingling sensation that descended the length of the spinal column; the sperm discharged spontaneously during sleep, in the urine and the stools; the patient became sterile. When the disease was accompanied by breathing difficulties and headaches, he could die from it. A regimen of softening food and evacuation might bring about a cure, but only after a whole year of abstention from wine, exercise, and *aphrodisia*. [9] The *Epidemics* also mention subjects in whom an abuse of pleasures brought on serious illnesses: in the case of a resident of Abdera, sexual relations and drinking had resulted in a fever, accompanied at the start by nausea, heart pain, thirst, dark urine, and a parched tongue; the cure was finally obtained on the twenty-fourth day, after several remissions and recurrences of fever; but a young man from Meliboea died in the midst of a delirium after a twenty-four-day illness, which had begun with intestinal and respiratory troubles, subsequent to repeated abuses of alcohol and sexual pleasures. [10]

By contrast, the regimen of athletes, often criticized for its exaggerations, was cited as an example of the beneficial effects that could result from sexual abstinence. Plato calls attention

---

*But we shall see further on that sexual intercourse was regarded as a health factor where women were concerned. The author of the *Problems* observes, however, that healthy, well-nourished men experience bile attacks if they do not engage in sexual activity. [8]

to this in the *Laws,* in regard to Iccus of Tarentum, a winner at Olympia: he was so set on victory, and "possessed in his soul such art, and such courage mixed with moderation that he never touched a woman—or a boy, for that matter—during the entire time of his intensive training." Tradition said that the same was true of Crison, Astylus, and Diopompus.[11] Several related themes converged on this practice no doubt: that of a ritual abstention which, in contests and battles alike, formed one of the conditions for success; that of a moral victory which the athlete needed to win over himself if he wished to be capable and worthy of assuring his superiority over others; but also that of an economy necessary for his body in order to conserve strength, which the sexual act would waste on the outside. Whereas women needed sexual relations so that the discharge necessary to their organism might occur in a regular manner, men could—in certain cases at least—retain all their semen; far from causing them harm, strict abstinence on their part would preserve their force in its entirety, accumulate it, concentrate it, and carry it finally to a higher level.

Hence a paradox resides in this preoccupation with a regimen by which one sought both an equitable distribution of an activity that could not in itself be regarded as a vice, and a restrictive economy in which "less" seemed almost always preferable to "more." While it was natural that the body produce a vigorous substance having the capacity to procreate, the very act that roused the organism and cast it out into the world actually risked being as dangerous in its effects as it was harmonious with nature in its principle. The whole body, with its most important or most fragile organs, risked paying a high price for an expenditure that nature had nonetheless willed; and to retain that substance which sought by its own power to escape, could be a means of charging the body with its most intense energy.

2.   A concern about progeny also motivated the vigilance that one needed to display in the use of pleasures. For while

it was granted that nature had organized the union of the sexes in order to provide people with a lineage and to ensure the survival of the species; and also granted that, for the same reason, she had associated the sexual relation with such a keen pleasure, this lineage was recognized as being fragile, at least in terms of its quality and worth. It was dangerous for the individual to take his pleasure at random; but if he procreated at random and no matter how, the future of his family would be placed in jeopardy. In the *Laws,* Plato solemnly underscores the importance of the precautions that had to be taken for this purpose that concerned parents and the city as a whole. There were measures to be taken at the time of the first sexual act between the two partners on the occasion of marriage: all the values and all the dangers traditionally associated with inaugural acts were present here: on that day and night, it was necessary to refrain from any misdeed with respect to the matter at hand, "for the beginning, which among human beings is established as a god, is the saviour of all things—if She receives the proper honor from each of those who make use of Her." But it was also necessary to be cautious each day during the whole life of the marriage: indeed, no one knew "what day or night" the deity would assist in a conception; hence "throughout the whole year and all one's life," especially during the period of procreation, one must "be careful and avoid doing anything that voluntarily brings on sickness or involves insolence or injustice. Otherwise, one will necessarily stamp these effects on the souls and bodies of the embryos"; one ran the risk of "begetting offspring who are irregular, untrustworthy, and not at all straight in character or body."[12]

The dangers that were suspected and hence the precautions that were recommended related to three important questions. The age of the parents, first of all. The age at which a man was thought to be capable of producing the finest offspring was relatively late: from thirty to thirty-five, according to Plato; whereas in the case of girls he limited the age for marriage to the years between sixteen and twenty.[13]* The same chronological disparity appears in Aristotle; he holds it to be absolutely necessary in order to ensure a vigorous progeny, and he calculates that with this age gap the husband and wife will arrive together at the age when fertility declines and when in any case it will hardly be desirable for procreation to take place. Moreover, children who are conceived during this period of life will offer the advantage of reaching the right age in time to relieve their parents' burden in their declining years: "Women should therefore marry about the age of eighteen, and men at thirty-seven or thereabouts. If those ages are observed, union will begin while the bodies of both partners are still in their prime."[15]

Another important question was the "diet" of parents: avoid excesses of course, be careful not to procreate in a state of drunkenness, but also follow a general and continuous regimen. Xenophon praises Lycurgus' legislation and measures that were taken to assure healthy offspring by providing for vigorous parents; girls who were destined to be mothers were not to drink wine, or if they did, only when it was diluted with water; bread and meats were carefully measured out to them; like men, they were supposed to do physical exercises; Lycurgus even instituted "races and trials of strength for women competitors and for men, believing that if both parents are strong they produce more vigorous offspring."[16]† Aristotle, on the other hand, was against a strenuous athletic regimen; he preferred a regimen suitable for a citizen, one that ensured the disposition the citizen needed for his activity (euexia politikē): "The best habit is one which comes midway between the athletic and the valetudinarian, some amount of exertion must therefore go to its making. But the exertion must not be violent or specialized, as is the case with the athlete; it should

---

*In the Republic, the period is specified as twenty-five to fifty years old for men, and twenty to forty years old for women.[14]

†In the Laws, Plato dwells on the effects of parents' drunkenness at the time of conception.[17]

rather be a general exertion, directed to all the activities of a free man."[18] For women, he was in favor of a regimen that would give them the same kind of qualities.*

As for the time of year or season that was most conducive to obtaining a fine progeny, it was seen as depending on a whole cluster of complex elements; it was no doubt precautions of this sort, among other things, that would occupy the attention of the women inspectors—in Plato's scheme—who were to oversee the good conduct of married couples during the ten years within which they were required or allowed to procreate.[20] Aristotle mentions briefly the knowledge that the doctors of his day and the naturalists were capable of imparting on this subject. According to him, the husband and wife ought to acquaint themselves with all these lessons: "doctors can tell them all they need to know about the times of good physical condition" (according to convention, winter is best); as for the "physicists," they "hold that the north wind is better than the south."[21]

In view of all these obligatory precautions, it is clear that procreative practice required a great deal of attention, indeed a whole moral attitude, if one wished to avert all the dangers that threatened it and to achieve the desired results. Plato insists that both spouses must keep in mind *(dianoeisthai)* that they are expected to present the city with "the noblest and best children possible." They should earnestly reflect on the task, guided by the principle that human beings accomplish what they set out to do "if they reflect intelligently upon themselves and the deed itself," whereas they fail "if they don't apply their intelligence to it, or if they lack intelligence." Therefore, "the groom should reflect intelligently [*prosechetō ton noun*] on the bride and the making of children and the bride should do likewise—especially during the time when they don't yet

---

*According to Xenophon, it was so that they might have vigorous offspring that the young married couples of Sparta were not supposed to have relations very often: "With this restriction on intercourse the desire of the one for the other must necessarily be increased, and their offspring was bound to be more vigorous than if they were surfeited with one another."[19]

have children."[22] We may recall in this connection an observation that appears in the Aristotelian *Problems:* if it is so often the case that the children of human beings do not resemble their parents, the reason is that the latter, at the time of the sexual act, had many other things on their minds instead of thinking only of what they were doing at that moment.[23] Later on, in the world of the flesh, it would be a rule necessary for justifying the sexual act, that it must be performed with a single purpose in mind, that of procreation. Here, however, such an intention was not necessary in order for sexual intercourse to avoid being a mortal sin. Yet, in order for it to achieve its aim, enabling the individual to live on in his children and to contribute to the security of the city, a whole mental endeavor was necessary: an unfailing concern for the dangers that surrounded the use of pleasures, threatening the purpose that nature gave them.*

---

*Plato, in the *Laws*, would have women lead a life sheltered from overly intense pleasures and pains.[24]

4

Act, Expenditure, Death

And yet, while the use of pleasures constituted a problem
in the individual's relationship with his own body, and made
it difficult to define a regimen for him, the reason lay not
simply in the fact that this use was suspected of being the
source of certain illnesses or that people feared its consequences for their offspring. The sexual act was certainly not
perceived by the Greeks as an evil; for them it was not the
object of a moral disqualification. But the texts bear witness
to an anxiety concerning the activity itself. And this anxiety
revolved around three focal points: the very form of the act,
the cost it entailed, and the death to which it was linked. It
would be a mistake to see in Greek thought only a positive
valuation of the sexual act. Medical and philosophical reflection describes it as posing a threat, through its violence, to the
control and mastery that one ought to exercise over oneself;
as sapping the strength the individual should conserve and
maintain, through the exhaustion it caused; and as prefiguring
the death of the individual while assuring the survival of the
species. If the regimen of pleasures was important, this was
not simply because excess might lead to an illness; it was
because in sexual activity in general man's mastery, strength,
and life were at stake. To give this activity the rarefied and
stylized form of a regimen was to ensure oneself against future
ills; it was also to form, exercise, and prove oneself an individual capable of controlling his violence and of allowing it to

operate within appropriate limits, of keeping the source of his energy within himself, and of accepting his death while providing for the birth of his descendants. The physical regimen of the *aphrodisia* was a health precaution; at the same time, it was an exercise—an *askēsis*—of existence.

1. The violence of the act.   Plato was thinking about the *aphrodisia* when, in the *Philebus,* he described the effects of pleasure when it is mixed with a little distress: pleasure "takes possession of a man, sometimes making him leap about in ecstasy, so that he changes complexion, takes up all kinds of strange positions, pants in strange ways, and is driven completely out of his senses with mad cries and shouts. . . . He feels bound to say to himself, as do others, that he is almost dying with enjoyment when he indulges in these delights. The more unrestrained and intemperate [*akolastoteros, aphronesteros*] he is, the more fervently he goes after them in wholehearted pursuit."[1]

Hippocrates has been credited with the statement that orgasm has the form of a brief epileptic seizure: at any rate, that is what Aulus Gellius reports: "Hippocrates, a man of divine wisdom, believed of venery [*coitus venereus*] that it was part of the horrible disease which our countrymen call *comitalis,* or the 'election disease'; for these are his very words as they have come down to us: 'coition is a brief epilepsy' [*tēn synousian einai mikran epilepsian*]."[2] Actually the phrase comes from Democritus. The Hippocratic treatise *The Seed,* which in its first pages gives a detailed description of the sexual act, accords with another tradition, that of Diogenes of Apollonia; the model this tradition (also represented by Clement of Alexandria) referred to was not the pathological model of epilepsy, but the mechanical model of a heated, foaming fluid: "Some people," reports *The Pedagogue,* "suppose that the semen of living creatures is the foamy substance of the blood. The blood being greatly agitated during the intertwining of bodies, and heated by the natural warmth of the male, forms a froth and spreads through the spermatic veins. According to Diogenes of Apollonia, this phenomenon would explain the term *aphrodisia.* "[3] This general theme of fluids, agitation, and spreading foam is treated in *The Seed* from the Hippocratic collection, in the form of a description organized entirely around what might be called the "ejaculatory schema"; it is this schema that is carried over unchanged from man to woman, and used to decipher the relationships between male and female roles in terms of confrontation and contest, but also domination and regulation of the one by the other.

The sexual act is analyzed, from start to finish, as a violent mechanical action that is directed toward the emission of sperm.[4] First, the rubbing of the genitals and the movement given to the whole body produce a general warming effect; the latter, combined with agitation, gives the humor, diffused into the whole body, a greater fluidity, so that it begins to "foam" *(aphrein),* "in the same way as all other fluids produce foam when they are agitated." At this stage a phenomenon of "separation" *(apokrisis)* occurs; the most vigorous part of this foaming fluid, "the most potent and the richest" *(to ischyrotaton kai piotaton)* is carried to the brain and the spinal marrow, descending its length to the loins. Then the warm foam passes to the kidneys and from there through the testicles to the penis, from which it is expelled by means of a violent spasm *(tarachē).* This process, which is voluntary at the beginning when there is sexual union and "rubbing of the genitals," can also unfold in an entirely involuntary manner. This is what occurs in the case of nocturnal emission, an occurrence mentioned by the author of *The Seed:* when work or another activity has caused the body to be heated, the fluid starts to produce foam spontaneously; it "behaves as in coition," and ejaculation takes place, accompanied by dream images, no doubt following the frequently invoked principle that dreams, or at least some of them, reveal the current state of the body.[5]

The Hippocratic description establishes a general isomorphism between the man's sexual act and that of the woman.

The process is the same, except that in the case of the woman the heating starts in the womb stimulated by the male sex organ during intercourse: "In the case of women, it is my contention that when during intercourse the vagina is rubbed and the womb is disturbed, an irritation is set up in the womb which produces pleasure and heat in the rest of the body. A woman also releases something from her body, sometimes into the womb, and sometimes externally as well."[6] There is the same type of substance and the same formation (sperm formed from blood through warming and separation); there is also the same mechanism and the same terminal act of ejaculation. The author does bring out certain differences, however, relating not to the nature of the act but to its peculiar violence, and to the intensity and duration of the pleasure that accompanies it. In the act itself, the woman's pleasure is much less intense than that of the man, because in the case of the latter the excretion of fluid occurs abruptly and with much greater violence. In the case of the woman, on the other hand, the pleasure begins at the start of the act and lasts as long as intercourse itself. Throughout intercourse her pleasure depends on the man; it does not cease until "the man releases the woman"; and if she happens to reach orgasm before him, this does not mean her pleasure ends—it is only experienced in a different way.[7]

Between these two acts having the same form in the man and in the woman, the Hippocratic text posits a relation that is causal and competitive at the same time: a contest, as it were, where the male plays the role of instigator and where he should always have the final victory. In order to explain the effects of the man's pleasure on that of the woman, the text appeals—as do other, no doubt ancient passages from the Hippocratic collection—to the two elements of water and fire, and to the reciprocal effects of heat and cold; the male liquor sometimes acts as the stimulant, sometimes as the dampener; as for the female element, always hot, it is sometimes represented by flame and sometimes by a liquid. If the woman's pleasure intensifies "at the moment the sperm arrives in the womb," this happens in the way a flame suddenly flares up when one pours wine on it; if, on the other hand, the man's ejaculation puts an end to the woman's pleasure, it is like pouring a cold liquid on very hot water: the boiling stops immediately.[8] Two similar acts, therefore, bringing analogous substances into play, but substances endowed with opposing qualities that confront one another in sexual union: force against force, cold water against boiling, alcohol on a flame. But, in any case, it is the male act that determines, regulates, stimulates, dominates. It is the male act, too, that ensures the health of the female organs by ensuring that they function properly: "If women have intercourse with men their health is better than if they do not. For in the first place, the womb is moistened by intercourse, whereas when the womb is drier than it should be it becomes extremely contracted, and this extreme contraction causes pain to the body. In the second place, intercourse by heating the blood and rendering it more fluid gives an easier passage to the menses; whereas if the menses do not flow, women's bodies become prone to sickness."[9] For the woman's body, penetration by the man and absorption of sperm are the primary source of the equilibrium of its qualities and the key stimulus for the necessary flow of its humors.

This "ejaculatory schema," through which sexual activity as a whole—and in both sexes—was always perceived, shows unmistakably the near-exclusive domination of the virile model. The female act was not exactly the complement of the male act; it was more in the nature of a duplicate, but in the form of a weakened version that depended on the male act both for health and for pleasure. By focusing entirely on this moment of emission—of foamy excretion, seen as the essential part of the act—one placed at the core of sexual activity a process that was characterized by its violence, an all but irrepressible mechanics, and a force that escaped control. But one also raised—as an important problem in the use of pleasures—a question of economy and expenditure.

2. Expenditure. The sexual act extracted from the body a substance that was capable of imparting life, but only because it was itself tied to the existence of the individual and claimed a portion of that existence. By expelling their semen, living creatures did not just evacuate a surplus fluid, they deprived themselves of elements that were valuable for their own existence.

All the various authors do not give the same explanation for this preciousness of the sperm. *The Seed* seems to refer to two conceptions of the origin of sperm. According to one of these, it originates in the head: formed in the brain, it descends via the marrow to the lower parts of the body. By Diogenes Laertius' account, this was the general principle of the Pythagorean conception: the sperm was held to be "a clot of brain containing hot vapor within it"; from that fragment of matter the whole body would subsequently be formed, with its "flesh, sinews, bones, hairs"; from the hot ether that it contained, the soul of the embryo would be born, along with sensation.[10] This privileging of the head in the formation of semen is echoed in the Hippocratic text, where there is the statement that for men who have had an incision made next to the ear, while they remain capable of sexual intercourse, they have a semen that is small in quantity, weak, and sterile: "For the greater part of the sperm travels from the head past the ears into the spinal marrow: now when the incision has formed a scar, this passage becomes obstructed."[11] But this importance given to the head is not incompatible, in the treatise *The Seed*, with the general principle that semen issues from the body as a whole: a man's sperm "comes from all the fluid in the body" through "veins and nerves which extend from every part of the body through the penis"; it is secreted "from the whole body—from the hard parts as well as the soft, and from the total bodily fluid" in its four forms.[12] A woman also "ejaculates from the entire body"; and if boys and girls are not able to secrete semen before puberty, this is because at that age the veins are so small and narrow that they "prevent the passage of sperm."[13] In any case, emanating from the whole body, or coming for the most part from the head, semen is regarded as the result of a process that separates, isolates, and concentrates "the most potent part" of the bodily fluid: *to ischyrotaton.* This force is manifested in the rich and foamy nature of semen, and in the violence with which it is expelled; it is also evidenced by the weakness that is always felt after coition, however small the amount excreted.[14]

Actually, the origin of semen remained a topic of debate in the medical and philosophical literature. But no matter what explanations were submitted, they had to account for what enabled semen to transmit life, to give rise to another living creature. And where did the seminal substance get its potency if not from the source of life that was found in the individual from whom it came? The life that it imparted had to have been borrowed and separated from the living being where it originated. In every emission of sperm there was something that issued, and was withdrawn, from the most precious elements of the individual. The creator in the *Timaeus* thus rooted this seed in what constituted, for humans, the nexus of the body and the soul, of death and immortality. This nexus was the marrow (which, in its round cranial part, housed the seat of the immortal soul): "For it was in this that the bonds of life by which the soul is bound to the body were fastened, and implanted the roots of the mortal kind."[15] From this source flowed, via the two dorsal veins, the moisture which the body needed and which remained enclosed within it; this was also the source of the semen that was emitted through the sex organ to conceive another individual. Living beings and their offspring had one and the same life principle.

Aristotle's analysis is very different from those of both Plato and Hippocrates. Different as to localizations, different as to mechanisms. And yet here, too, one finds the same principle of precious loss. In the *Generation of Animals,* the sperm is explained as the residue *(perittōma)* of nutriment: the end product, concentrated in very small quantities and useful in the same way as is the raw material for growth that the organism draws from food. For Aristotle, in fact, the final processing of what alimentation brings into the body furnishes a material, one portion of which is conveyed to all parts of the body, causing them to grow, imperceptibly, every day—while the other portion awaits the expulsion that will enable it, once inside the womb of a woman, to give rise to the formation of an embryo.[16] The development and reproduction of the individual thus depend on the same elements and have their source in the same substance. The growth elements and the seminal fluid are doublets resulting from an alimentary processing that maintains the life of one individual and makes possible the birth of another. Given these conditions, it is understandable that the discharge of this semen constitutes an important event for the body: it withdraws a substance that is precious, being the end result of a lengthy distillation by the organism and concentrating elements which, in accordance with nature, might have gone "to all parts of the body," and hence might have made it grow if they had not been removed from the body. It is also understandable why this discharge— which is entirely possible at an age when a human being needs only to renew his organism without having to develop it—does not take place in early youth when all the resources of nourishment are used for development; at that age, "all the nutriment is used up too soon," says Aristotle; it is understandable, too, that in old age, the production of sperm slows down: "The organism does not concoct enough."[17] The entire life of the individual—from youth, when one needs to grow, to old age, when one has so much trouble sustaining oneself—is marked by this relation of complementarity between the power to procreate and the capacity to develop or continue existing.

Whether the semen is drawn from the whole organism, or

originates where the body and the soul are joined to one another, or is formed at the end of a lengthy internal processing of food, the sexual act that expels it constitutes a costly expenditure for the human being. Pleasure may well accompany it, as nature intended, so that men would think of providing themselves with descendants; it nonetheless constitutes a hard jolt for the being itself, involving as it does the relinquishing of a whole portion of that which contains a "being itself." This is how Aristotle explains the "obvious" dejection that follows intercourse[18]; it is also how the author of the *Problems* explains the dislike felt by young men for the first woman with whom they chanced to have sexual relations.[19] Although the volume is small—proportionately larger, however, in men than in other animals—living creatures deprive themselves of a whole portion of the elements that are essential to their own existence.[20] One sees how in certain instances, as in the case of dorsal consumption described by Hippocrates, the misuse of sexual pleasure might lead to death.

3. Death and Immortality.   It was not just the fear of excessive expenditure that caused medical and philosophical reflection to associate sexual activity with death. This reflection also linked them together in the very principle of reproduction, by holding that the purpose of reproduction was to compensate for the passing away of living beings and to provide the species as a whole with the eternity that could not be given to each individual. If animals united in sexual intercourse, and if this relation gave them descendants, it was in order that the species might—as the *Laws* puts it—endlessly accompany the march of time. This was its way of cheating death: leaving "the children of children" behind it while remaining the same, it "partakes of immortality by means of coming-into-being."[21] For Aristotle and Plato alike, the sexual act was at the point of junction of an individual life that was bound to perish—and from which, moreover, it drew off a portion of its most precious resources—and an immortality that assumed the con-

crete form of a survival of the species. Between these two lives,
the sexual relation constituted, as Plato says, an "artifice"
(mēchanē) that was designed to join them together so that the
first might, in its own way, participate in the second; this
mēchanē provided the individual with an "offspring" of himself *(apoblastēma)*.

In Plato this link, contrived and natural at the same time,
is sustained by the longing for self-perpetuation and immortality, which characterizes every perishable creature.[22] In the
Symposium, Diotima points out that such a longing exists in
animals which, seized by the urge to procreate, "fall prey to
a violent love-sickness," and they are "ready to die if need be
in order to secure the survival of their progeny."[23] It also exists
in the human animal who, once his life is over, does not want
to lie in a grave uncelebrated and "nameless."[24] This is why,
according to the *Laws,* he should marry and provide himself
with descendants in the best possible circumstances. But it is
this same desire that makes some individuals who love boys
eager, not to sow their seed in the body, but to engender in the
soul and to give birth to that which is, of itself, beautiful.[25] In
Aristotle, in certain early texts like the treatise *On the Soul,*
sexual activity's connection with death and immortality is still
expressed in the somewhat "Platonizing" form of a desire for
participation in the eternal;[26] in later texts such as the treatise
On Generation and Corruption, or *Generation of Animals,* it
is conceived in the form of a differentiation and distribution
of beings in the natural order, according to a set of ontological
principles concerning being, nonbeing, and the better. Proposing to explain in terms of final causes why there is procreation
of animals and separate existence of the sexes, the second book
of the *Generation of Animals* invokes a few basic principles
governing the relationships of the myriads of beings to being
per se. First, some things are eternal and divine, while others
can be or not be; second, the beautiful and divine is always the
better and what is not eternal can participate in the better and
the worse; third, it is better to be than not to be, to live than

not to live, to be animate than inanimate. And, observing that beings who are subject to becoming can be eternal only within the limits of their capability, he concludes that this is why there is generation of animals, and that the latter, excluded from eternity as individuals, can be eternal as a species: "numerically," an animal "cannot be eternal, for the substance of things that are is particular; and if it were such, it would be eternal—but it is possible for it as a species."[27]

Hence sexual activity was located within the broad parameters of life and death, of time, becoming, and eternity. It became necessary because the individual was fated to die, and in order that he might in a sense escape death. To be sure, these philosophical speculations were not immediately present in reflection regarding the use of pleasures and their regimen. But notice the solemnity with which Plato refers to these themes in the "persuasive" legislation—laws that must be of first importance since they were to be "the first laid down in every city"—that he proposes concerning marriage: "A man is to marry after he reaches the age of thirty and before he reaches thirty-five, bearing in mind that there is a sense in which the human species has by a certain nature a share in immortality, and that it is the nature of everyone to desire immortality in every way. For the desire to become famous and not to lie nameless after one has died is a desire for such a thing. Thus the species of human beings has something in its nature that is bound together with all of time, which it accompanies and will always accompany to the end. In this way the species is immortal; by leaving behind the children of children and remaining one and the same for always, it partakes of immortality by means of coming-into-being."[28] The interlocutors of the *Laws* know that these lengthy considerations are not part of the customary practice of legislators. But the Athenian remarks that things are the same in this sphere as in medicine; the latter, when it speaks to reasonable and free men, cannot be content to lay down precepts; it must explain, give reasons, and persuade so that the patient might regulate his way of living. To give such explanations about the individual and the species, time and eternity, life and death, is to ensure that citizens will accept, "in a frame of mind more favorably disposed and therefore more apt to learn something," the prescriptions that are meant to regulate their sexual activity and their marriage, the reasonable regimen of their moderate life.[29]

Greek medicine and philosophy concerned themselves with the *aphrodisia* and the use that ought to be made of them if one wished to care properly for one's body. This problematization did not lead to a drawing of distinctions among those acts, their possible forms and varieties, in order to decide which ones were admissible and which were harmful or "abnormal." By considering them in the aggregate, as the manifestation of a generic activity, it sought to determine the principles that would enable individuals to engage in them at the appropriate intensity and to distribute them in the right way, according to circumstances. Yet the clearly restrictive tendencies of such an economy attest to an anxiety about this sexual activity. An anxiety that related to the possible consequences of abuses; an anxiety that also related—especially so—to the act itself, which was always perceived in terms of a male, ejaculatory, "paroxystic" schema that appeared to adequately define all sexual activity. We see, then, that the importance that was accorded to the sexual act and to the forms of its rarefaction was owing not only to its negative effects on the body, but to what it was in itself and by nature: a violence that confounded the will, an expenditure that wasted the body's resources, a procreation that was linked to the future death of the individual. The sexual act did not occasion anxiety because it was associated with evil but because it disturbed and threatened the individual's relationship with himself and his integrity as an ethical subject in the making; if it was not properly measured and distributed, it carried the threat of a breaking forth of involuntary forces, a lessening of energy, and death without honorable descendants.

We may note that these three great themes of preoccupation are not peculiar to ancient culture: indications of this anxiety, which identify the sexual act with the "virile" form of semen and associate it with violence, exhaustion, and death, could doubtless be found frequently elsewhere. For example, the documents assembled by Van Gulik, pertaining to ancient Chinese culture, seem to show the presence of this same thematic complex: fear of the irrepressible and costly act, dread of its harmful consequences for the body and health, representation of the man-woman relationship in the form of a contest, preoccupation with obtaining descendants of good quality by means of a well-regulated sexual activity.[30] But the ancient Chinese "bedroom" treatises responded to that anxiety in a manner completely different from what one finds in classical Greece. The dread one felt when faced with the violence of the act and the fear of losing one's semen were answered by methods of willful retention; the encounter with the other sex was perceived as a way to come into contact with the vital principle the latter held in her possession and, by absorbing it, to internalize it for one's own benefit. So that a well-managed sexual activity not only precluded any danger, it could also result in a strengthening of one's existence and it could be a means of restoring one's youthfulness. Elaboration and exercise in this case concerned the act itself, its unfolding, the play of forces that sustained it, and of course the pleasure with which it was associated; the nullification or indefinite postponement of its completion enabled one both to carry it to its highest degree in the realm of pleasure and to turn it to one's greatest advantage in life. In this "erotic art," which sought, with pronounced ethical concerns, to intensify insofar as possible the positive effects of a controlled, deliberate, multifarious, and prolonged sexual activity, time—a time that terminated the act, aged the body, and brought death—was exorcised.

It would also be easy to find in the Christian doctrine of the flesh closely related themes of anxiety: the involuntary violence of the act, its kinship with evil, and its place in the play of life and death. But in the irrepressible force of desire and the sexual act, Saint Augustine was to see one of the main stigmata of the Fall (that involuntary movement reproduced in the human body man's rebellion against God); the Christian pastoral ministry was to set the rules of economy, on a precise calendar and according to a detailed morphology of acts; and the doctrine of marriage was to give the procreative finality the dual role of ensuring the survival or even the proliferation of God's people, and of making it possible for individuals to avoid pledging their souls to eternal death through indulgence in that activity. In short, this was a juridico-moral codification of acts, moments, and intentions that legitimated an activity that was of itself a bearer of negative values; and it inscribed it in the dual order of the ecclesiastical institution and the matrimonial institution. The time of rites and the time of legitimate procreation could absolve it of blame.

Among the Greeks, these same anxiety themes (violence, expenditure, and death) took shape within a reflection that did not aim at a codification of acts, nor at the creation of an erotic art; rather, its objective was to develop a technique of existence. This technique did not require that the acts be divested of their primordial naturalness; nor did it attempt to augment their pleasurable effects; it sought to distribute them in the closest conformity with what nature demanded. The material it sought to elaborate was not, as in an erotic art, the unfolding of the act; nor was it the conditions of the act's institutional legitimation, as it would be in Christianity; it was much more the relationship between oneself and that activity "considered in the aggregate," the ability to control, limit, and apportion it in the right manner. This *technē* created the possibility of forming oneself as a subject in control of his conduct; that is, the possibility of making oneself like the doctor treating sickness, the pilot steering between the rocks, or the statesman governing the city*—a skillful and prudent guide of himself, one who had a sense of the right time and the right measure. We can thus understand why the necessity of a regimen for the *aphrodisia* was underscored so insistently, while so few details were given regarding the troubles that an abuse could bring about, and very few particulars concerning what one should or shouldn't do. Because it was the most violent of all the pleasures, because it was more costly than most physical activities, and because it participated in the game of life and death, it constituted a privileged domain for the ethical formation of the subject: a subject who ought to be distinguished by his ability to subdue the tumultuous forces that were loosed within him, to stay in control of his store of energy, and to make his life into an *oeuvre* that would endure beyond his own ephemeral existence. The physical regimen of pleasures and the economy it required were part of a whole art of the self.

*These three "arts of governing" were often likened to one another, as arts that demanded a knowledge and prudence attuned to circumstances; they were also comparable because they were knowledges that were associated with an ability to command. They were frequently referred to where it was a question of an individual's search for the principles or the authority that would help him to "conduct himself."

PART THREE

Economics

1

The Wisdom of Marriage

How, in what form, and why were sexual relations between husband and wife "problematical" in Greek thought? What reason was there to be worried about them? And above all, what reason was there to question the husband's behavior, to reflect on the moderation it necessitated, and—in a society so strongly marked by the rule of "free men"—to make it a theme of moral preoccupation? It looks as if there were none, or in any case very little. At the end of the legal argument *Against Neaera,* attributed to Demosthenes, the author delivers a sort of aphorism that has remained famous: "Mistresses we keep for the sake of pleasure, concubines for the daily care of our persons, but wives to bear us legitimate children and to be faithful guardians of our households."[1]

With a formula like this one, which seems to speak of a strict distribution of roles, we could not be further from the arts of conjugal pleasure such as one finds, according to Van Gulik, in ancient China. There, prescriptions concerning the woman's obedience, her respect, and her devotion were closely linked with advice on the correct erotic behavior to manifest in order to increase the partners' pleasure, or at least that of the man, and with opinions on the right conditions for obtaining the best possible progeny.[2] This was because, in that polygamous society, the wife found herself in a competitive situation where her status was tied directly to her ability to give pleasure; questions concerning sexual behavior and the forms of its possible improvement formed part of the society's reflection about existence; the skillful practice of pleasures and the equilibrium of married life belonged to the same set of concerns.

The *Against Neaera* formula is also far removed from what one finds in the Christian doctrine and its pastoral application, but for entirely different reasons. In that strictly monogamous situation, the man was to be prohibited from going in pursuit of any other form of pleasure beyond the pleasure he was allowed to take with his lawful wife; and even that pleasure was to pose a number of problems, seeing that the stated goal of sexual relations was not in sensual delight but in procreation. Around this central cluster of themes, a whole inquiry was to develop regarding the status of pleasures within the conjugal relationship. In this case, the problematization did not grow out of a polygamous structure but out of a monogamous obligation; and it did not seek to tie the quality of the relationship to the intensity of pleasure and the variety of partners, but on the contrary it sought to dissociate, insofar as possible, the constancy of a single conjugal relationship from the pursuit of pleasure.*

The formula expressed in *Against Neaera* appears to have been based on an altogether different system. On the one hand, this system operated on the principle of a single lawful wife; but on the other hand, it very clearly located the domain of pleasures outside the marital relationship. In it, marriage would encounter the sexual relation only in its reproductive function, while the sexual relation would raise the question of pleasure only outside of marriage. And consequently one does not see why sexual relations would be a problem in married

*We have to be careful not to schematize, not to reduce the Christian doctrine or marital relations to the procreative function, excluding pleasure. In actual fact, the doctrine was to be complex and open to discussion, and it was to have numerous variants. But the thing to bear in mind in our context is that the question of pleasure in the conjugal relationship and the question of the place it ought to be given, of the precautions that one had to take against it, as well as of the concessions that one had to grant it (taking account of the weakness and lustfulness of the other), constituted an active focus of reflection.

life, unless it was a matter of the husband's obtaining legitimate and promising descendants. Thus, it is quite logical that one finds in Greek thought technical and medical inquiries concerning sterility and its causes,[3] considerations from the viewpoint of dietetics and hygiene on how to have healthy children (and boys rather than girls),[4] political and social reflections on the best possible matching of marriage partners,[5] and finally, juridical debates on the conditions in which descendants could be considered legitimate and have the benefit of citizenship (this was what was at issue in *Against Neaera*).

Moreover, one fails to see why the problematization of sexual relations between spouses would take other forms or become attached to other questions, given the status of married couples in Athens and the obligations to which both husband and wife were held. The definition of what was allowed, forbidden, and prescribed for spouses by the institution of marriage in matters of sexual practice was simple enough, and clearly symmetrical enough so that additional moral regulation did not appear necessary. As far as women were concerned, in fact, they were bound by their juridical and social status as wives; all their sexual activity had to be within the conjugal relationship and their husband had to be their exclusive partner. They were under his power; it was to him that they had to give their children, who would be citizens and heirs. In case of adultery, the punishment meted out was private, but it was also public (a woman guilty of adultery no longer had the right to appear in public religious ceremonies): as Demosthenes says, the law "has declared that our women may be inspired with a fear sufficient to make them live soberly [*sōphronein*], and avoid all vice [*mēden hamartanein*] and, as their duty is, to keep to their household tasks"; the law warns them that "if a woman is guilty of any such sin, she will be outcast from her husband's home and from the sanctuaries of the city."[6] The familial and civic status of a married woman made her subject to the rules of a conduct that was character-

ized by a strictly conjugal sexual practice. It was not that
virtue was of no use to women, far from it; but their *sōphrosynē*
had the role of ensuring that they would manage, by an exercise of will and reason, to respect the rules that were laid down
for them.

For his part, the husband was bound by a certain number
of obligations toward his wife (one of Solon's laws[7] required
the husband to have sexual relations with his wife at least
three times a month if she was an "heiress").* But having
sexual relations only with his lawful wife did not by any means
form part of his obligations. It is true that every man, whoever
he might be, married or not, had to respect a married woman
(or a girl under parental control); but this was because she was
under someone else's authority; it was not his own status that
prevented him, but that of the girl or woman who was the
object of his attack. His offense was essentially against the man
who held authority over the woman; this was why, if he was
an Athenian, he would be punished less severely if he committed rape, overcome by the voracity of his desire, than if he
deliberately and artfully seduced a woman; as Lysias says in
On the Murder of Eratosthenes, seducers "corrupt their victims' souls, thus making the wives of others more closely
attached to themselves than to their husbands, and get the
whole house into their hands, and cause uncertainty as to
whose the children really are."[9] The rapist violated only the
woman's body, while the seducer violated the husband's authority. All things considered, the married man was prohibited only from contracting another marriage; no sexual
relation was forbidden him as a consequence of the marriage
obligation he had entered into; he could have an intimate
affair, he could frequent prostitutes, he could be the lover of
a boy—to say nothing of the men or women slaves he had in

*One also finds evidence of an obligation in regard to conjugal duties in Pythagorean
teaching, as reported by Diogenes Laertius: "Hieronymus, however, says that, when
he had descended into Hades . . . he saw under torture those who had neglected to
fulfill their conjugal duties [*tous mē thelontes syneinai tais heautōn gunaixi*]."[8]

his household at his disposal. A man's marriage did not restrict him sexually.

Juridically, this meant that adultery was not a breach of the marriage contract if it was committed by one of the two partners. It constituted an infraction only in cases where a married woman had relations with a man who was not her husband; it was the marital status of the woman, never that of the man, that made it possible to define a relation as adultery. And from a moral standpoint, it is clear that there did not exist for the Greeks that category of "mutual fidelity" which would later introduce into married life a sort of "sexual right" having moral weight, juridical effects, and religious significance. The principle of a double monopoly, making exclusive partners of the two spouses, was not required in the marital relation. For while the wife belonged to the husband, the husband belonged only to himself. Reciprocal sexual fidelity, as a duty, a commitment, and a feeling shared equally, did not constitute the necessary guarantee nor the highest expression of married life. All this favors the conclusion that sexual pleasures posed their problems, and while married life posed problems of its own, there were few meeting points between the two problematizations. At any rate, marriage ought not to have raised any questions as far as the ethics of pleasure was concerned, for the reasons we have just considered: in the case of one of the partners—the wife—the restrictions were defined by status, law, and custom, and they were guaranteed by punishments or sanctions; in the case of the other—the husband—marital status did not impose precise rules on him, except to designate the woman from whom he must expect to obtain his legitimate heirs.

We cannot stop at that, however. It is true that, at least during that era, marriage—and within marriage, sexual relations between partners—did not constitute a very intense focus of questioning; it is true that less thought seems to have been given to sexual conduct in the relation that one might have with one's wife than in the relation that one might have with one's own body, or, as we shall see, in the relationship with boys. But it would be incorrect to think that things were so simple that the behavior of women—as wives—was too imperiously set to need any reflection, or that the behavior of men—as husbands—was so free that there was no need to question oneself concerning it. First, we have many statements about feelings of jealousy; wives commonly reproached their husbands for the pleasures they would go elsewhere to enjoy, and the fickle wife of Euphiletus took exception to his intimacies with a mere slave girl.[10] More generally, public opinion expected a man who was about to be married to exhibit a certain change in his sexual behavior; it was understood that during youthful bachelorhood (it often happened that men would not marry before they reached thirty) one would readily tolerate an intensity and variety of pleasures that it was good to curtail after marriage, even though the latter did not explicitly impose any precise limitation. But apart from these common behaviors and attitudes, there also existed a conceptual thematics of marital austerity. The moralists—some of them, at any rate—gave it to be understood in clear terms that a married man could not rightly feel free to indulge in pleasures as if he were not married. One was to hear Nicocles, in the speech Isocrates attributes to him, declare not only that he ruled his subjects justly, but that since his marriage he had had sexual relations only with his own wife. And Aristotle was to assert in the *Politics* that intercourse "of the husband with another woman, or the wife with another man" must be considered "a dishonorable action." An isolated and unimportant phenomenon? Already the birth of a new ethics? But as few in number as these texts are, and especially considering how far removed they are from real social practice and from the actual behavior of individuals, it is still pertinent to ask ourselves: why did moral reflection concern itself with the sexual behavior of married men? What was the nature of this concern, what was its origin, and what were its forms?

We will do well in this connection to avoid two interpretations, neither one of which seems entirely adequate.

One of them would consist in thinking that intercourse between husband and wife had no other function for the Greeks in the classical period than the calculation which allied two families, two strategies, and two fortunes, and which had the sole objective of producing descendants. The *Against Neaera* aphorism, which seems to sharply differentiate the roles that ought to be played in a man's life by the courtesan, the concubine, and the wife, has sometimes been read as a tripartition that implies exclusive functions: sexual pleasure on one side, everyday life on the other, and for the wife nothing more than the maintenance of the line of descent. But one has to consider the context in which this harsh-sounding maxim was formulated. It was part of a litigant's attempt to invalidate the apparently legitimate marriage of one of his enemies, as well as the claim to citizenship of the children born of that marriage. And the arguments given had to do with the wife's birth, her past as a prostitute, and her current status, which could only be that of a concubine. The object therefore was not to show that pleasure was to be sought elsewhere than with the legal wife, but that legitimate descendants could not be obtained except with the wife herself. This is why, as Lacey comments, it would be a mistake to interpret this text as offering a definition of three distinct roles; it is more in the nature of a cumulative enumeration, to be read as follows: pleasure is the only thing a courtesan can give; as for the concubine, she is capable of providing the satisfactions of everyday life besides; but only the wife can exercise a certain function that is owing to her special status: she can bear legitimate children and ensure the continuity of the family institution.[11] It needs to be understood that in Athens marriage was not the only kind of union that was accepted; it actually formed a particular and privileged union, which alone could lead to matrimonial cohabitation and legitimate offspring. Further, there exists a good deal of evidence testifying to the value that was attached to the wife's beauty, to the importance of the sexual relations that one might have with her, and to the existence of mutual love (as in the play of Eros and Anteros that unites Niceratus and his wife in Xenophon's *Symposium*).[12] The radical separation between marriage and the play of pleasures and passions is doubtless not an adequate formula for characterizing marital life in antiquity.

By being too intent on detaching Greek marriage from affective and personal implications that did in fact assume much greater importance in later times, and by insisting on distinguishing it from subsequent forms of conjugality, one is led, by an opposite impulse, to draw too close a parallel between the austere ethics of the philosophers and Christian morality. Often in these texts where good behavior is conceived, evaluated, and regulated in the form of "sexual fidelity," people are tempted to perceive the first draft of a still nonexistent moral code: the code that was to symmetrically impose the same obligation on the two spouses to engage in sexual relations only within the marital union, and the same duty to give these relations procreation as the privileged if not exclusive aim. There is a tendency to regard the passages that Xenophon or Isocrates devote to the husband's duties as "exceptional in view of the morals of the time."[13] They are exceptional inasmuch as they are rare. But even so, is that a reason to see in them the anticipation of a future ethics or the sign heralding a new sensibility? That these texts have shown a retrospective similarity to later formulations is a fact. Does it suffice to sever this moral reflection and this demand for austerity from contemporaneous behaviors and attitudes? Is it a reason for seeing in them the isolated forerunner of an ethics to come?

If one is willing to examine these texts, not for the bit of code they formulate, but for the manner in which the sexual behavior of men is problematized, one soon realizes that this problematization did not have to do with the marriage tie itself and with the direct, symmetrical, and reciprocal obligation that might derive from it. To be sure, it was insofar as he was married that a man needed to restrict his pleasures, or at least his partners; but being married in this case meant, above all, being the head of a family, having authority, exercising a power whose locus of application was in the "home," and fulfilling household obligations that affected his reputation as a citizen. This is why reflection on marriage and the good behavior of husbands was regularly combined with reflection concerning the *oikos* (house and household).

Thus, it becomes clear that the principle that obligated a man to have no partner outside the couple he formed was different in nature from that which tied a woman to an analogous obligation. In the case of the woman, it was insofar as she was under the authority of her husband that this obligation was imposed on her. In the man's case, it was because he exercised authority and because he was expected to exhibit self-mastery in the use of this authority, that he needed to limit his sexual options. For the wife, having sexual relations only with her husband was a consequence of the fact that she was under his control. For the husband, having sexual relations only with his wife was the most elegant way of exercising his control. This was not nearly so much the prefiguration of a symmetry that was to appear in the subsequent ethics, as it was the stylization of an actual dissymmetry. The restriction, which was analogous in what it allowed or forbade the two spouses, did not cover the same manner of "conducting oneself." This is exemplified very well in a text devoted to the way in which a man was to conduct the affairs of his household and conduct himself as the master of the household.

2

Ischomachus'
Household

Xenophon's *Oeconomicus* contains the most fully developed treatise on married life that classical Greece has left us. The text is presented as a set of precepts concerning the way to manage one's estate. In conjunction with some specific advice on administering the domain, supervising the workers, undertaking different kinds of cultivation, applying the right techniques at the right time, and selling or buying as one should and when one should, Xenophon develops a number of general ideas: considerations on the need, in these matters, to rely on rational practices, which he sometimes designates by the term "knowledge" *(epistēmē)* and sometimes by the term signifying art or technique *(technē);* considerations on the goal to have in view (to preserve and develop the estate); and lastly, considerations on the means of achieving this objective—that is, on the art of ruling. It is this theme that recurs most often through the whole length of the text.

The mileu in which this analysis is placed is socially and politically quite distinct. It is the small society of landholders who must maintain and increase the family wealth and bequeath it to those who bear their name. Xenophon explicitly contrasts this world with that of craftsmen, whose life is not beneficial either to their own health (because of their way of living), or to their friends, or to the city (seeing that they do not have the leisure to attend to its affairs).[1] The activity of landowners, on the other hand, is practiced in the market-

152

place, in the *agora*, where they can fulfill their duties as friends and as citizens, as well as in the *oikos*. But the *oikos* comprises more than just the house proper; it also includes the fields and possessions, wherever they may be located (even outside the boundaries of the city): "whatever someone possesses is part of his household"; it defines a whole sphere of activities.² And this activity is connected to a lifestyle and an ethical order. The landowner's existence, if he takes proper care of his estate, is good for him first of all; in any case it is an endurance exercise, physical training that is good for the body, for its health and vigor; it also encourages piety by making it possible to offer rich sacrifices to the gods; it favors friendship relations by providing the occasion to show generosity, to satisfy fully one's hospitality obligations, and to manifest one's beneficence toward other citizens. Further, this activity is useful to the entire city in that it adds to its wealth and especially because it supplies it with good defenders: the landowner, being used to strenuous work, is a strong soldier and the wealth he possesses motivates him to courageously defend the homeland.³

All these personal and civic advantages of the landowner's life center on what is given to be the principal merit of the "economic" art: it teaches the practice of commanding and is indissociable from the latter. To manage the *oikos* is to command, and being in charge of the household is not different from the power that is to be exercised in the city. Socrates says to Nicomachides in the *Memorabilia:* "Don't look down on businessmen. For the management of private concerns differs only in point of number from that of public affairs. In other respects they are much alike . . . those who take charge of public affairs employ just the same men when they attend to their own; and those who understand how to employ them are successful directors of public and private concerns."⁴ The dialogue on "economics" is structured as a grand analysis of the art of commanding. The beginning of the text evokes Cyrus the Younger, who personally supervised the cultivation of his land, worked in his garden as a daily practice, and who had in this way acquired so much skill at leading men that when he was obliged to go to war, none of his soldiers ever deserted his army; rather than abandon him, they preferred to die fighting near his corpse.[5] In symmetrical fashion, the end of the text evokes the replica of that model ruler, such as one might find personified in those "great-minded" leaders whose armies always followed them without faltering, or in the estate master whose kingly ways sufficed to stir the workers to greater efforts as soon as they saw him, without his having to lose his temper, threaten, or punish. The domestic art was of the same nature as the political art or the military art, at least insofar as all three involved ruling others.[6]

It is in this framework of an art of "economy" that Xenophon introduces the problem of the relations between husband and wife. Now, the wife, as mistress of the house, is a key figure in the management of the *oikos* and she is essential for its good government. Socrates asks Critobulus: "Is there anyone to whom you entrust more serious matters than to your wife?"; and a little later, he adds: "I hold that a woman who is a good partner in the household is a proper counterweight to the man in attaining the good"; and in this sphere, "when things turn out well, the households increase, but when done badly, the households diminish."[7] But, in spite of the wife's importance, nothing has really prepared her to play the required role, given her extreme youth, first of all, and the very brief education she has received ("Did you marry her when she was a very young girl and had seen and heard as little as possible?"), and also the near-total absence of relations with her husband, with whom she rarely converses ("is there anyone with whom you discuss fewer things than with your wife?").[8] This is precisely where the need exists for the husband to establish relations with his wife that are for the purpose of training and guidance at the same time. In a society in which girls were given at a very young age—often around fifteen—to men who were often twice as old as they, the marital relationship, for which the *oikos* served as a support and context, took the form of a pedagogy and a government of behavior. This was the husband's responsibility. When the wife's conduct, instead of bringing profit to the husband, caused him only detriment, who should get the blame? The husband. "When sheep fare badly, we usually fault the shepherd, and when a horse behaves badly, we usually speak badly of the horseman; as for the woman, if she has been taught the good things by the man and still acts badly, the woman could perhaps justly be held at fault; on the other hand, if he doesn't teach the fine and good things but makes use of her as though she is quite ignorant of them, wouldn't the man justly be held at fault?"[9]

We see, then, that relations between spouses are not questioned in themselves; they are not first seen as the simple relationship of a couple comprised of a man and a woman who might, in addition, have to attend to a house and family. Xenophon deals at length with the marital relation, but in an indirect, contextual, and technical fashion: he deals with it in the context of the *oikos,* as one aspect of the husband's governmental responsibility and with a view to determining how the husband will be able to make his wife into the co-worker, the partner, the *synergos* he needs for the reasonable practice of economy.

Ischomachus is asked to show that this technique can be taught; he has nothing more, and nothing less, in the way of teaching credentials than the fact of being a "gentleman"; he once found himself in the same situation as Critobulus is in; he married a woman who was quite young—she was fifteen, and her education had scarcely taught her more than how to make a cloak and how to give out the wool to the spinner maids;[10] but he had trained her so well and had made her such a valuable partner that he could put the house in her care while he went about his work, whether this was in the fields or in the *agora*—that is, in those places where male activity ought to be exercised in a privileged way. Thus, Ischomachus will set forth the principles of "economy," the art of managing the *oikos,* for the benefit of Socrates and Critobulus. Before giving advice on administering an agricultural domain, he will quite naturally begin by speaking of the household proper, whose administration must be well thought out if one wishes to have the time to take care of the animals and the fields, and if one does not want all the effort expended there to be wasted on account of domestic disorder.

1. Ischomachus recalls the first principle of marriage by citing the discourse he remembers having addressed to his young wife shortly after marriage, when she had become "accustomed" to her husband and "domesticated to the extent that we could have discussions": "Tell me, woman, have you thought yet why it was that I took you and your parents gave you to me?" Ischomachus answers the question himself: "I considered for myself, and your parents for you, whom we might take as the best partner for the household and children."[11] The marriage bond is thus represented in its original dissymmetry—the man decides for himself whereas it is the family that decides for the young woman—and in its dual finality: the house and the children. We may note, further, that the question of descendants is left aside for the moment and that before being trained for motherhood, the young woman must become a good mistress of the house.[12] And Ischomachus shows that this role is that of partner; the respective contribution of each does not have to be taken into consideration,* but only the way each one acts with a view to the common goal, which is "to keep their substance in the best condition but also to add as much as possible to it by fine and just means."[14] One should note this emphasis on the necessary equalization of initial differences between the husband and the wife, and on the partnership that must be established between them; and yet it is clear that this community, this *koinōnia,* is not established in the dual relation between two individuals,

---

*Ischomachus stresses this cancelling of differences between spouses, differences that may be substantial in terms of what each partner contributes.[13]

but is mediated by a common purpose, which is the household: its maintenance and also the dynamics of its increase. This will serve as a starting point for analyzing the forms of that "community" and the specific nature of the roles that the two marriage partners should play.

2. In order to define the respective functions of the two spouses in the household, Xenophon starts from the notion of the "shelter" *(stegos):* it seems that when the gods created the human couple, they were thinking of offspring and of the perpetuation of the race, of the support one needs in old age, and of the necessity "not to live in the open air, like beasts" —humans "obviously need shelter." At first it looks as if descendants provide the family with its temporal dimension and shelter gives it its spatial organization. But things are a little more complex than that. The "shelter" does delimit an outside and an inside, the first being the man's domain and the second constituting the privileged place of the woman; but it is also the place where they bring in, store, and preserve that which has been acquired; to shelter is to provide for future distribution at the right times. Outside, therefore, the man sows, cultivates, plows, and tends the flocks; he brings back the things he has produced, earned, or acquired through exchange. Indoors, the woman for her part receives, preserves, and allocates according to need. Generally speaking, it is the husband's activity that brings provisions into the house, but it is the wife's management that regulates their expenditure.[15] The two roles are exactly complementary and the absence of one would make the other useless: "My guarding and distribution of the indoor things would look somewhat ridiculous," says the wife, "if it weren't your concern to bring in something from outside." To which the husband replies that if there were no one to keep secure the things that are brought into the house, he would look as ridiculous as "those who are said to draw water with a leaking jar."[16] Thus, two places, two forms of activity, and two ways of organizing time: on one side (that

of the man), production, the rhythm of the seasons, waiting for the harvest, respecting and foreseeing the opportune time; on the other side (that of the woman), preservation and expenditure, ordering and distributing what is needed, orderly storage above all: Ischomachus dwells at length on all the advice he remembers giving his wife on how to store things in the space of the house so that she might find what she has put away, thus making her home a place of order and memory.

In order that they might work together in the exercise of these different functions, the gods endowed each of the two sexes with particular qualities. Physical traits, first of all: to men, who must work in the open air "plowing, sowing, planting, herding," they gave the capacity to endure cold, heat, and journeys on foot; women, who work indoors, were given bodies that are less resistant. Character traits as well: women have a natural fear, but one that has positive effects—it induces them to be mindful of the provisions, to worry about losing them, to be in dread of using them up. The man, on the other hand, is brave, for he is obliged to defend himself outdoors against everything that might cause him injury. In short, "the god directly prepared the woman's nature for indoor works and the man for works of the open air."[17] But he also equipped them with common qualities: since in their respective roles men and women have to "give and take," since in their activity as household managers they have to gather in and mete out, they both received memory and diligence (mnēmē and epimeleia).[18]

Hence each of the two marriage partners has a nature, a form of activity, and a place, which are defined in relation to the necessities of the oikos. That they remain steadfast partners is a good thing in the eyes of the "law," the nomos—i.e., the regular custom that conforms exactly to nature's intentions, assigns each person his role, and defines what is good and fine to do and not to do. This "law" declares good (kala) "what the god has brought forth each to be capable of": hence "it is a finer thing [kallion] for the woman to stay indoors than to spend her time in the open" and not good for the man "to stay indoors instead of concerning himself with outdoor things." To alter this division, going from one activity to the other, is to be in contempt of this *nomos;* it is at the same time to go against nature and to abandon one's place: "When someone acts in a way contrary to what the god has brought forth, perhaps in causing some disorder [*ataktōn*] he is noticed by the gods and pays the penalty for neglecting his own works or for doing the woman's works."[19] The natural oppositeness of man and woman and the specificity of their aptitudes are indissociably tied to the good order of the household; they are designed for this order, and inversely, order demands them as obligations.

3.   This text, so detailed when it is a matter of determining the division of household tasks, is quite discrete on the question of sexual relations, both in terms of their place in the marital relationship and in regard to the prohibitions that might result from marriage as such. It is not that the importance of having descendants is neglected; the fact is noted several times in the course of Ischomachus' speech: he remarks that it is one of the main objectives of marriage;* he also points out that nature has endowed the woman with a special affection that makes her better suited to take care of children; and he remarks how fortunate it is when one grows old to find the support that one needs in one's children.[21] But nothing is said in this text about either procreation itself or the precautions to take in order to have the finest possible offspring: it is not yet time to take up this kind of question with the young bride.

And yet several passages do refer to sexual conduct, to the necessary moderation and to the physical attachment between husband and wife. We first have to recall the very beginning of the text, where the two interlocutors start to talk about

---

*He specifies that the deity brings the man and woman together with a view to children, and the law makes them partners with a view to the household.[20]

economy as a knowledge that enables one to manage a household. Socrates evokes those people who have the talents and
resources but refuse to put them to work because they obey
invisible masters or mistresses within themselves: indolence,
softness of soul, insouciance, but also—mistresses more inflex-
ible than the others—gluttony, drunkenness, lust, and foolish,
expensive ambitions. Those who yield to this sort of despotism
of the appetites will only bring ruin to their bodies, their souls,
and their households.[22] But Critobulus prides himself on having already defeated these enemies; his moral training has
supplied him with a sufficient amount of *enkrateia:* "On exam-
ining myself I seem to find I am fairly self-controlled in such
matters, so that if you advise me about what I might do to
increase my household, it seems to me I wouldn't be prevented
from doing it, at least by those things you call mistresses."[23]
This is what entitles Critobulus to say that he is now ready to
play the role of master of a household and to learn the difficult
tasks that are involved. It has to be understood that marriage,
the functions of a head of a family, and the government of an
oikos presuppose that one has acquired the ability to govern
oneself.

Further on, in Ischomachus' listing of different qualities
with which nature has supplied each of the two sexes in order
for them to play their domestic roles, he mentions self-control
(*enkrateia*). He does not describe it as a trait belonging specifically to the man or the woman, but as a virtue common to both
sexes, like memory and diligence; individual differences may
modulate the distribution of this quality; and what shows its
high value in married life is that it is awarded to the better of
the marriage partners: be it the husband or the wife, the better
one has the larger share of this virtue.[24]

Now, in the case of Ischomachus, we see how his self-
restraint is manifested for its own sake and how it guides that
of his wife. As a matter of fact, there is an incident spoken of
in the dialogue that relates rather explicitly to certain aspects
of the sexual life of the couple: I am thinking of the one having

to do with makeup and face paint.²⁵ This is an important theme in ancient morality, for adornment posed the problem of the relationships between truth and the pleasures, and by bringing the play of artifice into the latter, it confused the principles of their natural regulation. The question of coquetry in Ischomachus' wife has nothing to do with her faithfulness, which is taken for granted throughout the text; nor does it concern her lack of thrift: it is a matter of knowing how the wife can display herself and be recognized by her husband as an object of pleasure and a sexual partner in the marital relation. It is this question that Ischomachus addresses, in the form of a lesson, one day when, thinking to please him (by seeming to have "a fairer complexion" than she really has, "rosier" cheeks, and a "taller and more slender" figure), his wife appears before him perched on high sandals and all made up with ceruse and alkanet dye. Ischomachus will respond to this reprehensible behavior by giving a two-part lesson.

The first part is negative; it consists in criticizing makeup as deception. This deception may fool strangers, but there is no way it can delude a man with whom one lives and who therefore has the possibility of seeing his wife when she rises from her bed, when she is sweating or in tears, and when she leaves her bath. But most important, Ischomachus criticizes this trickery for violating a basic principle of marriage. Xenophon does not appeal directly to the long-lived and often encountered aphorism that said marriage was a community *(koinōnia)* of property, of life, and of bodies; but it is clear that the theme of a threefold community is at work throughout the text: a community of property concerning which the author declares that each partner ought to forget the share he or she has contributed; a community of life that makes the prosperity of the estate one of its objectives; and a community of bodies that is explicitly emphasized *(ton sōmatōn koinōnēsantes)*. Now, the community of property rules out deception; and the man would behave badly toward his wife if he made her think he possessed more than was really the case; in the same way, they must not try to deceive one another about their bodies; for his part, he would not apply vermilion to his face; in the same way, she must not embellish herself with ceruse. The just community of bodies demands this consideration. The attraction that should come into play between husband and wife is the kind that expresses itself naturally—as in every animal species—between male and female: "Just as the gods have made horses most pleasant to horses, oxen to oxen, and sheep to sheep, so human beings [*anthrōpoi*] suppose the undisguised body of a human being is most pleasant."[26] It is natural attraction that should serve as the basis for sexual relations between spouses and for the community of bodies they constitute. Ischomachus' *enkrateia* rejects all the artifices that people use in order to increase desires and pleasures.

But a question arises: how can the wife remain an object of desire for her husband? How can she be sure of not being supplanted someday by someone younger and prettier? The young wife of Ischomachus asks him directly: what can she do not just to seem beautiful but to be beautiful and remain so?[27] And once again, by a logic that may appear strange to us, the household and the government of the household will be the crucial factor. According to Ischomachus, at any rate, the wife's real beauty is sufficiently guaranteed by her household occupations, provided that she goes about them in the right way. He explains that by performing her appointed tasks, she will not sit about, huddled up like a slave, or remain idle like a coquette. She will stand, she will observe, she will supervise, she will go from room to room checking the work that is in progress; standing and walking will give her body that certain demeanor, that carriage which in the eyes of the Greeks characterized the physique of the free individual (Ischomachus will later show that a man becomes vigorous as a soldier and free citizen through his active participation in the responsibilities of a taskmaster).[28] In the same way, it is good for the mistress of the house to mix flour and knead dough, and to shake out and fold the bedcovers.[29] In this way the body's handsomeness will be shaped and maintained; the condition of mastery has its physical version, which is beauty. Further, the wife's clothes have a freshness and elegance that set her apart from her servants. In any case, she will always enjoy an advantage over the latter from the fact that she seeks willingly to please instead of being obliged to submit under compulsion like a slave girl. Here Xenophon seems to be referring to the same principle he evokes elsewhere: the pleasure that one takes by force is much less agreeable than that which is freely offered.[30] It is the latter pleasure that the wife can give her husband. Thus, by virtue of the forms of a physical beauty that is indissociable from her privileged status and by virtue of her unconstrained willingness to gratify *(charizesthai),* the mistress of the household will always be preeminent over the other women of the household.

In this text devoted to the "masculine" art of governing a household—wife, servants, estate—there is no allusion to the sexual faithfulness of the wife or to the fact that her husband should be her only sexual partner: this is taken for granted as a necessary principle. As for the self-restrained attitude of the husband, it is never defined as the monopoly over all his sexual activity which he would concede to his wife. What is at stake in this reflective practice of marital life, what appears as essential to the orderliness of the household, to the peace that must reign within it, and to the woman's expectations, is that she be able, as the lawful wife, to keep the preeminent place that marriage has assigned to her: not to see another woman given preference over her, not to suffer a loss of status and dignity, not to be replaced at her husband's side by another—this was what mattered to her above all else. For the threat to marriage did not come from the pleasure which the husband happened to enjoy here or there, but from the rivalries that might form between the wife and the other women over one's position in the household and over the order of precedence to be observed. The "faithful" husband *(pistos)* was not the one who linked the state of marriage to the renunciation of all sexual pleasure enjoyed with someone else; it was the husband who steadfastly maintained the privileges to which the wife was entitled by marriage. Moreover, this is how the "betrayed" women who appear in Euripides' tragedies understand the matter. Medea complains bitterly of Jason's "unfaithfulness": he has forsaken her for a royal bride and he will beget descendants who will reduce his children by Medea to a state of humiliation and servitude.[31] What makes Creusa lament the imagined "betrayal" of Xuthus is the thought of living "a childless life, in a house forsaken and solitary"; it is that—at least this is what she is made to believe—"into her house," which was the house of Erechtheus, will come "a motherless nobody, some slave's brat."[32]

This preeminence of the wife, which the husband must protect, was implied by the act of marriage. But it was not acquired once and for all; it was not guaranteed by any moral pledge on the part of the husband; even in addition to the possibility of repudiation and divorce, there was always the threat of a *de facto* loss of prestige. Now, what Xenophon's *Oeconomicus* and Ischomachus' discourse show is that while the husband's wisdom—his *enkrateia* but also his knowledge as head of a family—was always ready to acknowledge the wife's privileges, the wife, if she was to preserve them, must in return exercise her function in the house and accomplish the tasks that were associated with it in the best possible way. Ischomachus does not promise his wife at the outset either "sexual fidelity" in the way we understand it, or even that she will never have to fear any other preference on his part; but just as he assures her that her activity as mistress of the house, her bearing and her way of dressing, will give her a greater charm than that of the servants, he also assures her that she can keep the place of honor in the house until old age. And he suggests a kind of contest between the two of them to see who behaves best and who is the most diligent in caring for the household; if she manages to win, she will then have nothing more to fear from any sort of rival, even a young one.

"But the most pleasant thing of all: if you look to be better than I and make me your servant, you will have no need to fear that with advancing age you will be honored any less in the household, and you may trust that as you grow older, the better a partner you prove to be for me, and for the children a better guardian of the household, by so much more will you be honored in the household."[33]

In this ethics of married life, the "fidelity" that is recommended to the husband is therefore something quite different from the sexual exclusivity that marriage imposes on the wife. It has to do with maintaining the wife's status and privileges, and her preeminence over other women. And while it does imply a certain reciprocity of behavior between the man and the woman, this is in the sense that the man's faithfulness would correspond not so much to the good sexual conduct of the wife, which is always presupposed, but to the way in which she conducts the household and conducts herself in the household. A reciprocity, then, but a fundamental dissymmetry since the two interdependent behaviors are not based on the same exigencies and do not obey the same principles. The husband's self-restraint pertains to an art of governing—governing in general, governing oneself, and governing a wife who must be kept under control and respected at the same time, since in relation to her husband she is the obedient mistress of the household.

3

Three Policies of
Moderation

Other texts, dating from the fourth century and the beginning of the fifth, also develop the theme that the state of
marriage calls for at least some form of sexual moderation.
Three of these texts are especially noteworthy: the passage in
the *Laws* where Plato discusses the rules and obligations of
marriage; Isocrates' exposition concerning the way Nicocles
manages his life as a married man; and a treatise on economics
attributed to Aristotle and definitely a product of his school.
These texts are very different from one another in their subject
matter: the first offers a system of authoritarian regulation of
behaviors in the context of an ideal city; the second characterizes the personal lifestyle of an autocrat who is respectful of
himself and others; the third seeks to define the principles that
any man will find useful for directing his household. In any
case, unlike Xenophon's *Oeconomicus,* none of them refers to
the appropriate way of life of a landowner nor consequently
to the tasks associated with the management of an estate, tasks
that he must assume in complementarity with his wife. In spite
of the differences that separate them, these texts all seem to
emphasize—more clearly than that of Xenophon—a demand
resembling something that could be called the principle of
"double sexual monopoly"; that is, they seem to want to local-
ize a whole class of sexual activity, both for the man and for
the woman, in the marital relation alone. In the same way as
his spouse, the man is presented as being obligated, or at least

disposed, not to seek his pleasure with anyone else but her. A demand for a certain symmetry, therefore; and a tendency to define marriage not just as the privileged place, but perhaps as the only place for morally acceptable sexual relations. However, a reading of these three texts shows that it would clearly be a mistake to project onto them retrospectively a principle of "reciprocal sexual fidelity" like the one that served as a juridico-moral pillar for later forms of matrimonial practice. The fact is that in all these texts, the obligation the husband is under, or the recommendation that is made to him, to be moderate to the extent of having no other sexual partner but his own wife is not the result of a personal commitment he might make with respect to her; it is the result of a political regulation that is imposed by fiat in the case of the Platonic laws, or—in the case of Isocrates or Aristotle—by the husband himself through a sort of deliberate self-limitation of his power.

1. Thus, when it is stipulated in the *Laws* that one should marry at the proper age (for men, between the ages of twenty-five and thirty-five), beget children in the best possible conditions, and not have relations—whether one is a man or a woman—with anyone other than one's marriage partner, all these injunctions take the form, not of a voluntary ethics, but of a coercive regimentation; it is true that the author remarks several times on the difficulty of legislating in this area and on the desirability for some measures to take the form of an ordinance only in the case of disorders and where the greatest number is no longer capable of moderation.[1] In any case, the principles of this moral code are always directly referred to the needs of the state, and never to the internal demands of the household, the family, or married life: one should bear in mind that the good marriage is the one that benefits the city and it is for the sake of the latter that the children ought to be "the noblest and best possible."[2] Unions that—with respect to proportions beneficial to the state—should not be instances of the

rich marrying the rich;[3] meticulous inspections that would
verify that young couples are carefully preparing themselves
for the procreative task;[4] the injunction, backed up by penal-
ties, to inseminate only one's lawful wife without having any
other sexual relations during the period in which one is capable of procreation[5]—all this is tied to the particular structures
of an ideal city and is rather foreign to a style of moderation
based on the voluntary pursuit of moderation.*

It should be noted, however, that Plato puts only a limited
amount of trust in the law when it is a question of regulating
sexual conduct. He does not believe it will achieve adequate
results if one does not use measures other than its prescriptions and threats for controlling such violent desires.[7] More
effective means of persuasion are needed for this, and Plato
lists four. (1) *Public opinion:* Plato refers to what happens in
the case of incest; how is it, he asks, that men have come to
the point where they don't even feel any desire for their brothers and sisters, their sons and daughters, however beautiful
they may be? The explanation is that they have heard it said
constantly that these acts are "hateful to the gods" and that
no one has ever had the occasion to hear different pronounce-
ments on the subject; what is needed, therefore, in regard to
all blameworthy sexual acts, is for "the unanimous public
voice" to be similarly "sanctified." (2) *Glory:* Plato cites the
example of athletes who, in their desire to win a victory in the
games, place themselves under a strict regimen, not going near
a woman, or a boy either, the whole time of their training:
surely victory over those internal enemies, the pleasures, is
finer than the victory one may win over rivals.[9] (3) *The honor
of the human being:* Here Plato gives an example that will be
used often subsequently; he speaks of those animals which live
in bands, each in the midst of others, but "which live celibate,

---

*Note that once past the age limit for having children, "the man or woman
who behaves moderately [sōphronōn kai sōphronousa] in all such respects should be
accorded an entirely good reputation; he who behaves in the opposite fashion should
be honored in the opposite way—or rather dishonored."[6]

pure, and chaste"; when the age for procreation is reached, they separate from the group and pair into couples that will last. Now, it will be noticed that this animal conjugality is not cited as a natural principle that would be universal, but rather as a challenge that men ought to take up: how could calling attention to such a practice fail to prompt reasonable men to prove themselves "superior to the beasts."[10] (4) *Shame:* By reducing the frequency of sexual activity, shame will "weaken the sway of this mistress"; without there being the need to prohibit the acts, it will be held "noble to engage in them if one escapes notice," and people will have to learn that to commit them openly is "shameful" by "the custom laid down in habit and unwritten law."[11]

Hence Plato's legislation does set a requirement that is symmetrical for the man and the woman, each on their own account. It is because they have a certain role to play for the common purpose—that of father and mother of future citizens —that they are bound exactly in the same way by the same laws, which impose the same restrictions on both. But it is important to see that this symmetry in no way implies that husband and wife are held to "sexual fidelity" by a personal bond that would be intrinsic to the matrimonial relation and constitute a mutual commitment. The symmetry is not based on a direct and reciprocal relation between the two, but on an element that dominates both of them: principles and laws to which they are both subjected in the same way. It is true that their compliance must be voluntary, the result of an internal persuasion; but the latter does not involve an attachment they should have for one another; it involves the reverence one should feel for the law, or the concern one should have for oneself, one's reputation, one's honor. The relation of the individual to himself and to his city in the form of respect or shame, honor or glory—not the relation to the other person —is what imposes this obedience.

And we may note that in Plato's proposal for the law concerning "the choices of love," he envisages two possible formulations. According to one, every individual would be forbidden to touch any woman of good birth who is not his lawful wife, to procreate outside of marriage, and to "go against nature and sow sterile seed in males." The other formulation repeats the prohibition against male love relations, making it absolute this time; as for extramarital sexual relations, he contemplates punishment only in cases where the wrongdoing would not go unnoticed by "all men and women."* Clearly, then, the double obligation to limit sexual activities relates to the stability of the city, to its public morality, to the conditions of good procreation, and not to the reciprocal obligations that attach to a dual relation between husbands and wives.

2.   In the text by Isocrates, which has the form of an address by Nicocles to his fellow citizens, an explicit connection is established between the views on moderation and marriage it sets forth and the exercise of political power. This speech is a companion piece to the one Isocrates addressed to Nicocles shortly after the latter came to power: the orator gave the young man advice on personal conduct and government, advice that ought to serve him well for the rest of his life. Nicocles' speech is supposed to be an address by the monarch in which he explains to his subjects how they ought to behave toward him. Now, the whole first part of the text is devoted to justifying his power: the merits of a monarchical regime, the rights of the ruling family, the personal qualities of the ruler; and it is only once these justifications have been given that the obedience and attachment the citizens owe their ruler will be defined. By reason of his special virtues, the monarch is entitled to demand his subjects' submission. Nicocles will therefore dwell at some length on the qualities he sees himself as having: first, the justice—*dikaiosynē*—he has manifested in

---

*Note that, at least in the first formulation of the law, Plato seems to say that only women who are "free" and of "good birth" are forbidden to a married man. At any rate this is how Diès translates the passage. Robin interprets the text as meaning that this law applies only to free *men* of good birth.[12]

financial affairs, in matters of penal jurisdiction, and in the good relations he has established or reestablished with the foreign powers;[13] next, his *sōphrosynē,* his moderation, which he speaks of as if it were nothing but the control of sexual pleasures. And he explains the forms and reasons of this moderation in direct connection with the sovereign authority he exercises in his country.

The last consideration he invokes concerns his lineage and the necessity of a bastardless race that can claim the distinction of a noble birth and the continuity of a genealogy that can be traced all the way back to the gods: "Nor was I of the same mind as most kings in regard to the begetting of children. I did not think I should have some children by a woman of humbler station and others by one of higher degree, nor that I should leave after me bastard progeny, as well as progeny of legitimate birth; but that all my children should be able to trace their lineage back through the same father and the same mother to Evagoras, my father, among mortals, to the Aeacides among the demigods, and to Zeus among the gods, and that not one of the children sprung from my loins should be cheated of this noble origin."[14]

Another reason for Nicocles to be moderate has to do with the continuity and homogeneity between the government of a state and that of a household. This continuity is defined in two ways: by the principle that one should respect all associations *(koinōniai)* that one has formed with others; thus Nicocles does not want to be like those men who respect their other commitments but behave badly toward a wife, despite the lifelong association *(koinōnia pantos tou biou)* they have formed with her: since one does not feel obliged to suffer any hurt from one's wife, one must not make her suffer any because of the pleasures that one enjoys; the king who wishes to be just must be so with his own wife.[15] But there is also the continuity and a kind of isomorphism between the good order that should reign in the monarch's house and the order that should prevail in his government: "If kings are to rule well, they must try to preserve harmony, not only in the states over which they hold dominion, but also in their own households and in their places of abode; for all these things are the works of temperance and justice."[16]

The link between moderation and power that Nicocles refers to throughout the text is conceived primarily as an essential relationship between dominion over others and dominion over oneself, following the general principle that was stated in the discourse addressed to Nicocles: "Govern yourself no less than your subjects, and consider that you are in the highest sense a king when you are a slave to no pleasure, but rule over your desires more firmly than over your people."[17] As for this self-mastery as a moral precondition for leading others, Nicocles starts out by proving that he has it: unlike so many tyrants, he has not used his power to possess himself of other men's wives and children by force; he has been mindful of how attached men are to their spouses and their progeny and of how often political crises and revolutions originated in abuses of this nature;[18]* he has therefore taken the greatest care to avoid such reproaches: no one can charge him with having had physical relations "with any person other than his wife" from the time he took the supreme office.[20] Nicocles has more positive reasons for being moderate, however. First, he wants to be an example to his fellow citizens; doubtless this does not mean that he expects the inhabitants of his country to practice the same sexual faithfulness as he; it is unlikely that he intends to make a general rule of it; the strictness of his morals should be understood as a general invitation to be virtuous and as a model standing against the laxity that is always harmful to the state.[21] This principle of a rough analogy between the morals of the prince and those of the people was alluded to in the address to Nicocles: "Let your own self-control [sōphrosynē] stand as an example to the rest, realizing that the manners [ēthos] of the whole state are copied from its rulers. Let it be

---

*We may note that Isocrates does remark on the people's forbearance for leaders who take their pleasure everywhere but still govern justly.[19]

a sign to you that you rule wisely if you see all your subjects growing more prosperous and more temperate [*euporōterous kai sōphronesterous gignomenous*] because of your oversight [*epimeleia*]."[22] But Nicocles would not be content merely to make the majority behave like him; at the same time, and without there being a contradiction, he wants to be distinguished from others, from the elite and even from those who are the most virtuous. What we are dealing with, therefore, is the moral formula of example (to be a model for everyone by being better than the best) combined with the political formula of competition for personal power in an aristocracy and the principle of a stable basis for wise and moderate tyranny (to be, in the eyes of the people, better endowed with virtue than the most virtuous): "I saw that while the majority of people are masters of themselves in other matters, even the best are slaves to the passions whose objects are boys and women; and therefore I wanted to show that I could be strong in those things in which I should be superior, not merely to people in general, but even to those who pride themselves on their virtue."[23]

But it is essential to understand that this virtue that functions as an example and a sign of superiority does not owe its political value simply to the fact that it is an honorable behavior in everyone's eyes. In reality, as far as the subjects are concerned, it reveals the form of relationship that the prince maintains with himself. This is an important political point because it is this relationship with the self that modulates and regulates the use the prince makes of the power he exercises over others. It is therefore important in itself, for the visible excellence it displays, and because of the rational frame that braces it. This is why Nicocles points out that his *sōphrosynē* has passed a test before everyone's witness; there are clearly circumstances and ages in which it is not difficult to show that one can be just and forgo money and pleasure; but when one assumes power in the midst of one's youth, to give proof of moderation then constitutes a kind of qualifying test.[24] Moreover, he makes it clear that his virtue is not just a matter of nature but a result of reasoning *(logismos)* as well: consequently, his good behavior will not be due to chance or circumstance; it will be deliberate and constant.

Thus, the prince's moderation, tested in the most hazardous of situations, and ensured by the continuous exercise of reason, serves as the basis of a sort of compact between the ruler and the ruled: the latter can obey him, seeing that he is master of himself. One can demand the subjects' obedience, since it is warranted by the prince's virtue. The prince is indeed capable of moderating the power he exercises over others by means of the mastery he establishes over himself. This is in fact how the passage ends where Nicocles, having finished talking about himself, draws on what he has said in order to exhort his subjects to obey him: "The reason I have spoken at some length about myself . . . is that I might leave you no excuse for not doing willingly and zealously whatever I counsel and command."[25] The prince's relationship with himself and the manner in which he forms himself as an ethical subject are an important component of the political structure; his austerity is part of it, contributing to its solidity. The prince, too, must practice an ascesis and exercise himself: "Therefore, no athlete is so called upon to train his body as is a king to train his soul; for not all the public festivals in the world offer a price comparable to those for which you who are kings strive every day of your lives."[26]*

3.   As for the *Economics* attributed to Aristotle, we are aware of the difficulties with respect to the date of its composition. The text that forms Books I and II is rather generally recognized as being from the "right period"—either edited from notes by an immediate disciple of Aristotle or the work of one of the very first generations of Peripatetics. In any case, we can leave aside the third part for the moment, or at least

---

*The theme of the prince's private virtue as a political problem would merit a whole study of its own.

the Latin text, which has been regarded as a "version" or an "adaptation" of the "lost" third book of the *Economics*. Much shorter and infinitely less rich than the text by Xenophon, Book I is likewise presented as a reflection on the art *(technē)* of economics. It aims to explain how to "own" a household and how to "make use of" it *(ktēsasthai, chrēsasthai).* [27] The text purports to be an art of governing, and not so much things as people. This is in keeping with a principle stated elsewhere by Aristotle; namely, that in economics one is more concerned with persons than with inanimate property. [28] And the treatise *Economics* actually does devote the bulk of its instructions (without giving much space to the techniques of cultivation, as Xenophon does) to the tasks of leadership, oversight, and control. It is a master's manual, for a master who must "concern himself" *(epimelein)* first and foremost with his wife. [29]

This text promotes more or less the same values as the treatise by Xenophon: praise of agriculture, which is capable of forming "virile" individuals, unlike the handicrafts and trades; affirmation of its primordial and fundamental character as determined by nature, and of its integral value for the city. [30] But many of its elements also carry the Aristotelian stamp; in particular, the emphasis on both the natural basis of the marital relation and the specificity of its form in human society.

The partnership *(koinōnia)* of man and woman is presented by the author as being something that exists "by nature" and as being exemplified among the animals: "their common life has necessarily arisen." [31] This is a constant argument in Aristotle—whether in the *Politics,* where this necessity is linked directly to procreation, or in the *Nicomachean Ethics,* which presents man as being a naturally "syndastic" creature destined to live in pairs. [32] But the author of the *Economics* remarks that this *koinōnia* has peculiar features not found in the other animal species: other animals practice forms of association that go well beyond mere procreative coupling, so it is not that; [33] it is that in humans, the finality of the tie that unites man and woman concerns not just "being" but "well-being" *(einai, eu einai)*—an important distinction in Aristotle. In humans, in any case, the existence of the couple allows for mutual help and support throughout existence; as for their offspring, they do not merely ensure the survival of the species; they are a means of "securing advantage" for the parents, for "the care which parents bestow on their helpless children when they are themselves vigorous is repaid to them in old age when they are helpless by their children, who are then in full vigor."[34] And it was with this life enhancement in mind that nature arranged man and woman in the way that she did; it was with a view to their common life that "she organized both sexes." The first is strong, the second is held back by fear; one finds his health in movement, the other is inclined to live a sedentary life; one brings provisions back to the house, the other watches over what is there; one nurtures the children, the other educates them. In a manner of speaking, nature has programmed the household economy and the parts that both spouses must take within it. Here, starting from Aristotelian principles, the author links up with the general outline of a traditional description, which had already been illustrated by Xenophon.

It is immediately after this analysis of natural complementarities that the author of the *Economics* addresses the question of sexual behavior. And this comes in a brief, elliptical passage that is worth quoting in its entirety: "First, then, he must do her no wrong, for thus a man is less likely himself to be wronged. This is indicated by the general law, as the Pythagoreans say, that one least of all should injure a wife as being 'a suppliant and taken from her hearth.' Now wrong inflicted by a husband is the formation of connections outside his own house [*thyraze synousiai*]."[35] It is hardly surprising that nothing is said about the wife's conduct, since in her case the rules are well known and since we are dealing here with a manual for masters: it is their way of acting that is in question. We may also note that there is nothing said—here or in Xenophon—about what the husband's sexual behavior should be with respect to his wife, nothing about fulfilling the marital obligation, or about the rules of modesty. But the main concern is elsewhere.

We may note first of all that the text situates the question of sexual relations squarely within the general framework of relations of justice between husband and wife. Now, what do these relations involve? What forms must they have? In spite of the text's declaration a little earlier regarding the need to determine what kind of "association" *(homilia)* should unite man and woman, nothing is said in the *Economics* concerning its general form or its principle. In other texts, however, and particularly in the *Nicomachean Ethics* and the *Politics,* Aristotle does reply to this question when he analyzes the political nature of the marriage tie; that is, the type of authority that is exercised within marriage. In his view, the relationship between man and wife is plainly nonegalitarian, since it is the man's role to govern the wife (the reverse situation, which can be due to several causes, is "contrary to nature").[36] However, this inequality must be carefully distinguished from three other inequalities: that which separates the master from the slave (the wife is a free being), that which separates a father from his children (and which makes for a kingly type of authority), and lastly, that which in a city separates the citizens who rule from those who are ruled. While the husband's authority is in fact weaker, less total than in the first two relations, it does not have the provisional character one finds in the "political" relation in the strict sense of the term; that is, in relations between citizens in a state. This is because under a free constitution the citizens take turns ruling and being ruled, whereas in the household the man must always maintain superiority.[37] An inequality of free beings, therefore, but one that is permanent and based on a natural difference. It is in this sense that the political form of the association of husband and wife will be aristocracy: a government in which it is always the best who rules, but where everyone receives his share of authority, his role, and his functions according to his merit and his worth. As the *Nicomachean Ethics* expresses it: "The association of man and wife seems to be aristocratic; for the man rules in accordance with his fitness [*kat'axian*], and in those matters in which man should rule"; which implies, as in every aristocratic government, that he will delegate to his wife the part she is suited to play (if he tried to do everything by himself, the husband would transform his authority into an "oligarchy").[38] The relationship with the wife is thus posited as a question of justice which is linked directly to the "political" nature of the marriage bond. Between father and son, says the *Magna Moralia,* the relationship cannot be one of justice, at least so long as the son has still not gained his independence, for he is only "a part of his father"; nor can it be a question of justice between master and servants unless by this is meant a justice "of the economic or household kind." The same does not hold with the wife: doubtless the latter is and will always be inferior to the man, and the justice that should govern relations between spouses cannot be the same as the justice that obtains between citizens; and yet, because of their resemblance, man and wife should be in a relationship that "approaches near to political justice."[39] Now, in the *Economics* passage where it is a question of the sexual behavior that the husband ought to exhibit, the author seems to be referring to a very different kind of justice; recalling a Pythagorean observation, he declares that the wife is like "a supplicant and taken from her hearth." However, a closer look at this passage indicates that this reference to the suppliant—and more generally, to the fact that the wife was born in another household and that in her husband's house she is not "at home"—is not meant to define the type of relations that should ordinarily obtain between a man and his wife. These relations, in their positive form and their conformity with the nonegalitarian justice that should govern them, had been spoken of indirectly in the preceding passage. We may suppose that by evoking the figure of the suppliant the author is saying that the marriage itself does not authorize the wife to demand sexual faithfulness of her husband, but that there is something in the married woman's situation that calls for restraint and limitation on the part of the husband. The thing to note is precisely her position of weakness, which makes her subject to the benevolence of her husband, like a suppliant who has been taken from her household of birth.

As for the nature of these unjust acts, it is not at all easy to specify in terms of the *Economics.* The text speaks of *thyraze synousiai* ("outside connections"). The word *synousiai* can signify a particular sexual union; it can also mean a "commerce", an "intimate relationship." If we had to give the word its narrowest meaning here, it would denote any sexual act committed "outside the house," which would constitute an injustice with regard to the wife. Such a standard appears rather improbable in a text that holds rather closely to the current thinking about ethics. If, on the other hand, we give the word *synousia* the more general meaning of "relationship," we can easily see why there would be injustice in the exercise of an authority that is supposed to mete out to each according to his value, his merit, and his status: an extramarital liaison, a concubinage, and perhaps illegitimate children would be serious instances of derogation from the respect that is owing to the wife. In any case, as far as the husband's sexual relations are concerned, anything that threatens the privileged position of the wife in the aristocratic government of the household also compromises the necessary and essential justice of that government. Understood in this way, the formulation found in the *Economics* is not far removed in its concrete significance from what Xenophon implied by having Ischomachus promise his wife never to violate her privileges and status so long as she behaved well.* It should be noted, moreover, that the themes evoked in the lines that immediately follow are

---

*It should be remarked, however, that Ischomachus was evoking situations of rivalry that could be produced by relations with the maidservants of the household, whereas here it is exterior liaisons that appear threatening.

quite close to those of Xenophon: the husband's responsibility in the moral training of his spouse and the criticism of adornment *(kosmēsis)* as mendacity and trickery that must not be allowed to come between spouses. But whereas Xenophon makes the husband's moderation an appropriate style for a vigilant and wise master of a household, the Aristotelian text seems to place it within the multifarious interaction of the different forms of justice that should govern relations of humans in society.

It is no doubt difficult to identify exactly which sexual practices the author of the *Economics* would allow or forbid the husband who wished to conduct himself properly. Even so, it does seem that the husband's moderation—whatever its precise form—does not derive from the personal bond between the spouses and that it is not imposed on him in the same way that strict faithfulness can be required of the wife. It is in the context of an unequal distribution of powers and functions that the husband has to privilege his wife; and it is through a voluntary attitude—based on interest and wisdom —that he will be able, as one who knows how to manage an aristocratic authority, to judge what is owing to each individual. The husband's moderation in this case is still an ethics of power that one exercises, but this ethics is conceived as one of the forms of justice. This is a nonegalitarian and formal way of defining the association between husband and wife and the place that their respective virtues ought to have in that association. Let us not forget that this way of thinking about marital relations did not in the least exclude the kind of intensity that was acknowledged in relations of friendship. The *Nicomachean Ethics* brings together all these elements—justice, inequality, virtue, the aristocratic form of government; and it is through them that Aristotle defines the special nature of the husband's friendship for his wife; this *philia* between spouses "is the same as that which is found in an aristocracy; for it is in accordance with excellence—the better gets more of what is good, and each gets what befits him; and so, too, with the justice in these relations."[40] And further on, Aristotle adds: "How man and wife and in general friend and friend ought mutually to behave seems to be the same question as how it is just for them to behave."[41]*

One thus finds, in Greek thought of the classical period, elements of a marriage ethics that seems to demand on the part of both spouses a similar renunciation of all extramarital sexual activity. Now, the rule prescribing an exclusively conjugal sexual practice, which in theory was imposed on the wife by her status and by the laws of the city and the family alike —it seems that some people may have believed that this rule was applicable to men as well; at any rate, this is the lesson that seems to emerge from Xenophon's *Oeconomicus* and from the Aristotelian *Economics,* or from certain texts by Plato and Isocrates. These few texts appear quite isolated in the midst of a society in which neither the laws nor the customs contained any such requirements. True. But it does not appear possible to see in this the first outlines of an ethics of reciprocal conjugal fidelity, or the beginnings of a codification of married life to which Christianity was to give a universal form, an imperative value, and the support of a whole institutional system.

There are several reasons for this. Except in the Platonic city, where the same laws apply to everyone in the same way, the moderation that is demanded of the husband does not have the same ethical basis or the same forms as that which is imposed on the wife; in the latter case, these derive directly

*It should be noted that in the ideal city described by Aristotle in the *Politics*, relations between husband and wife are defined in a way that is rather similar to what one finds in Plato. The obligation to procreate will be lifted when the parents risk being too old: "from that time forward we must regard them as indulging in intercourse for reasons of health, or for some similar cause." As for adulterous relations of the husband with another woman or the wife with another man, they will rightly be regarded as a disgraceful action *(mē kalon)* "in whatever shape or form, during all the period of their being married and being called husband and wife." For reasons easy to understand, this offense will have legal consequences—*atimia*—if it is committed "during the period of bringing children into the world."[42]

from a *de jure* situation, and from a statutory dependence that places her under the authority of her husband; in the case of the husband, they depend on a choice, on a willingness to give his life a certain form. A matter of style, as it were: the man is called upon to temper his conduct in terms of the mastery he intends to bring to bear on himself, and in terms of the moderation with which he aims to exercise his mastery over others. Whence the fact that this austerity is presented—in Isocrates, for instance—as a refinement whose exemplary value does not take the form of a universal principle; whence, too, the fact that the renunciation of every relation outside the conjugal relation is not explicitly prescribed by Xenophon or perhaps even by the Aristotelian author, and it does not take the form of a permanent commitment in Isocrates but that of an achievement instead.

Furthermore, whether the prescription is symmetrical (as in Plato) or not, the moderation that is demanded of the husband is not based on the special nature and peculiar form of the conjugal relationship. No doubt it is because he is married that his sexual activity must undergo some restrictions and accept a certain delimitation. But it is the status of a married man, not the relation to the wife, that requires this: married—in Plato's city—according to the forms that the state will decide, and in order to provide it with the citizens it needs; married and thus having to manage a household that should prosper in an orderly fashion and be maintained in a condition that will be, in everyone's eyes, the image and proof of a good government (Xenophon and Isocrates); married and obligated to apply the rules of justice in the forms of inequality appropriate to marriage and to the wife's nature (Aristotle). There is nothing in all this that would rule out personal feelings of attachment, affection, and concern. But it should be clearly understood that it is never vis-à-vis the wife that this *sōphrosynē* is necessary, in the association that joins them together as individuals. The husband is self-obligated in this respect, since the fact of being married commits him to a particular interplay of duties and demands in which his reputation, his relation to others, his prestige in the city, and his willingness to lead a fine and good existence are at stake.

One understands, therefore, how the man's moderation and the wife's virtue could be presented as two simultaneous requirements, each deriving, in its own way and its own forms, from the state of marriage; and yet it is as if the question of sexual practice as an element—a crucial element—of the conjugal relationship were hardly raised. Later, sexual relations between spouses, the form they should take, the acts that were permitted, the rules of decency they should observe—but also the intensity of the bonds they manifested and drew closer—were to be an important subject of reflection. The entire sexual life between husbands and wives was to give rise, in the Christian pastoral ministry, to a codification that was often quite detailed; but already before this, Plutarch had broached questions concerning not only the form of sexual relations between spouses but their affective significance as well; he had underscored the importance of reciprocal pleasures for the mutual attachment of husband and wife. This new ethics would be characterized, not simply by the fact that man and wife would be restricted to one sexual partner, the spouse, but also by the fact that their sexual activity would be problematized as an essential, decisive, and especially delicate component of their personal conjugal relation. Nothing of the sort is visible in the moral reflection of the fourth century B.C. This is not to suggest that sexual pleasures had little importance in the married life of the Greeks of that period, or that they did not contribute to a couple's mutual understanding: that is another question in any case. But in order to understand the working out of sexual conduct as a moral problem, it is necessary to emphasize that, in classical Greek thought, the sexual behavior of the two spouses was not questioned from the standpoint of their personal relationship. What occurred between them assumed importance from the moment it became a question of having children. Apart from that, their mutual sex life was not an object of reflection and prescription: the point of problematization was in the moderation that each of the two partners needed to show for reasons and in forms corresponding to their sex and their status. Moderation was not a matter shared between them and requiring concern on the part of the one for the other. In this we are far from the Christian teaching where each spouse would have to ensure the other's chastity, being careful not to cause him or her to commit the sin of the flesh—either through indecent entreaties or through harsh refusals. For the Greek moralists of the classical epoch, moderation was prescribed to both partners in matrimony; but it depended on two distinct modes of relation to self, corresponding to the two individuals. The wife's virtue constituted the correlative and the proof of a submissive behavior; the man's austerity was part of an ethics of self-delimiting domination.

PART FOUR

Erotics

1

A Problematic Relation

The use of pleasures in the relationship with boys was a theme of anxiety for Greek thought—which is paradoxical in a society that is believed to have "tolerated" what we call "homosexuality." But perhaps it would be just as well if we avoided those two terms here.

As matter of fact, the notion of homosexuality is plainly inadequate as a means of referring to an experience, forms of valuation, and a system of categorization so different from ours. The Greeks did not see love for one's own sex and love for the other sex as opposites, as two exclusive choices, two radically different types of behavior. The dividing lines did not follow that kind of boundary. What distinguished a moderate, self-possessed man from one given to pleasures was, from the viewpoint of ethics, much more important than what differentiated, among themselves, the categories of pleasures that invited the greatest devotion. To have loose morals was to be incapable of resisting either women or boys, without it being any more serious than that. When he portrays the tyrannical man—that is, one "in whose soul dwells the tyrant Eros who directs everything"[1]—Plato shows him from two equivalent angles, so that what we see in both instances is contempt for the most fundamental obligations and subjection to the rule of pleasure: "Do you think he would sacrifice his long beloved and irreplaceable mother for a recently acquired mistress whom he can do without, or, for the sake of a young boy recently become dear to him, sacrifice his aged and irreplaceable father, his oldest friend, beat him, and make his parents slaves of those others if he brought them under the same roof?"[2] When Alcibiades was censured for his debauchery, it was not for the former kind in contradistinction to the latter, it was, as Bion the Borysthenite put it, "that in his adolescence he drew away the husbands from their wives, and as a young man the wives from their husbands."[3]

Conversely, if one wanted to show that a man was self-controlled, it was said of him—as Plato said concerning Iccus of Tarentum[4]—that he was able to abstain from relations with boys and women alike; and, according to Xenophon, the advantage that Cyrus saw in relying on eunuchs for court service was that they were incapable of offending the honor of either women or boys.[5] So it seemed to people that of these two inclinations one was not more likely than the other, and the two could easily coexist in the same individual.

Were the Greeks bisexual, then? Yes, if we mean by this that a Greek could, simultaneously or in turn, be enamored of a boy or a girl; that a married man could have *paidika;* that it was common for a male to change to a preference for women after "boy-loving" inclinations in his youth. But if we wish to turn our attention to the way in which they conceived of this dual practice, we need to take note of the fact that they did not recognize two kinds of "desire," two different or competing "drives," each claiming a share of men's hearts or appetites. We can talk about their "bisexuality," thinking of the free choice they allowed themselves between the two sexes, but for them this option was not referred to a dual, ambivalent, and "bisexual" structure of desire. To their way of thinking, what made it possible to desire a man or a woman was simply the appetite that nature had implanted in man's heart for "beautiful" human beings, whatever their sex might be.[6]

True, one finds in Pausanias' speech a theory of two loves,[7] the second of which—Urania, the heavenly love—is directed exclusively to boys. But the distinction that is made is not between a heterosexual love and a homosexual love; Pausanias draws the dividing line between "the love which the baser sort of men feel"—its object is both women and boys, it only looks to the act itself *(to diaprattesthai)*—and the more ancient, nobler, and more reasonable love that is drawn to what has the most vigor and intelligence, which obviously can only mean the male sex. Xenophon's *Symposium* shows very well that the choice between girls and boys in no way relates to the distinction between two tendencies or to the opposition between two forms of desire. The dinner is given by Callias in honor of the very young Autolycus whom he is enamored of; the boy's beauty is so striking that he draws looks from all the guests as "the sudden glow of a light at night draws all eyes to itself"; "there was not one . . . who did not feel his soul strangely stirred by the boy."[8] Now, among the participants, several were engaged or married, like Niceratus—who felt a love for his wife that she reciprocated, in the play of Eros and Anteros—or Critobulus, who was nonetheless still of an age to have suitors and male lovers;[9] further, Critobulus tells of his love for Cleinias, a boy he has met at school and, in a comic joust with Socrates, he matches his own beauty against that of the latter; the contest prize is to be a kiss from a boy and one from a girl: the boy and girl belong to a Syracusan who has taught them a dance whose graceful charm and acrobatic movements are the delight of everyone present. He has also taught them to mime the loves of Dionysus and Ariadne; and the guests, who have just heard Socrates say what true love for boys should be, all feel extremely "excited" *(aneptoromenoi)* on seeing this "Dionysus truly handsome" and this "Ariadne truly fair" exchanging real kisses; one can tell from the lovers' vows pronounced by the young acrobats that they "are now permitted to satisfy their long cherished desires."[10] So many different incitements to love put everyone in the mood for pleasure: at the end of the *Symposium,* some ride off on their horses to reunite with their wives, while Callias and Socrates leave to rejoin the handsome Autolycus. At this banquet where they felt a common enchantment with the beauty of a girl or the charm of boys, men of various ages kindled the appetite for pleasure or serious love—love that some would look for in women, others in young men.

To be sure, the preference for boys or girls was easily recognized as a character trait: men could be distinguished by the pleasure they were most fond of;[11] a matter of taste that could lend itself to humorous treatment, not a matter of topology involving the individual's very nature, the truth of his desire, or the natural legitimacy of his predilection. People did not have the notion of two distinct appetites allotted to different individuals or at odds with each other in the same soul; rather, they saw two ways of enjoying one's pleasure, one of which was more suited to certain individuals or certain periods of existence. The enjoyment of boys and of women did not constitute two classificatory categories between which individuals could be distributed; a man who preferred *paidika* did not think of himself as being "different" from those who pursued women.

As for the notions of "tolerance" or "intolerance," they too would be completely inadequate to account for the complexity of the phenomena we are considering. To love boys was a "free" practice in the sense that it was not only permitted by the laws (except in particular circumstances), it was accepted by opinion. Moreover, it found solid support in different (military or educational) institutions. It had religious guarantees in rites and festivals where the protection of the divine powers was invoked on its behalf.[12] And finally, it was a cultural practice that enjoyed the prestige of a whole literature that sang of it and a body of reflection that vouched for its excellence. Mixed in with all this, however, there were some quite different attitudes: a contempt for young men who were too "easy," or too self-interested; a disqualification of effeminate men, who were so often mocked by Aristophanes and the comic authors;* a disallowance of certain shameful behaviors,

*For example, Cleisthenes in the *Acharnians* or Agathon in the *Thesmophoriazusae.*

such as that of the catamites, which Callicles could not bear to talk about despite his boldness and plainness of speech, and which he saw as the proof that not every pleasure could be good and honorable.* Indeed, it seems that this practice—though it was common and accepted—was surrounded by a diversity of judgments, that it was subjected to an interplay of positive and negative appraisals so complex as to make the ethics that governed it difficult to decipher. And there was a clear awareness of this complexity at the time; at least, that is what emerges from the passage in Pausanias' speech where he shows how hard it is to know if people in Athens are in favor of or hostile to that form of love. On one hand, it was accepted so well—better still: it was valued so highly—that certain kinds of behavior on the part of male lovers were honored which were judged to be folly or dishonesty on the part of anyone else: the prayers, the entreaties, the stubborn wooings, all their false vows. But on the other hand, one noted the care fathers took to protect their sons from love affairs, how they demanded that tutors prevent them from occurring, and one heard boys' comrades teasing each other for accepting such relationships.[14]

Simple linear schemas do not enable us to understand the singular kind of attention that people of the fourth century gave to the love of boys. We need to take up the question afresh, using terms other than those of "tolerance" toward "homosexuality." And instead of trying to determine the extent to which the latter was free in ancient Greece (as if we were dealing with an unvarying experience uniformly subtending mechanisms of repression that change in the course of time), it would be more worthwhile to ask how and in what form the pleasure enjoyed between men was problematic. How did people think of it in relation to themselves? What

---

*"Socrates: The life of the catamites *(ho ton kinaidōn bios)* isn't that strange and shameful and wretched? Or will you dare to say that these people are happy if they have what they need without restriction? —Callicles: Aren't you ashamed to lead the discussion to such things, Socrates?"[14]

specific questions did it raise and what debate was it brought into? In short, given that it was a widespread practice, and the laws in no way condemned it, and its attraction was commonly recognized, why was it the object of a special—and especially intense—moral preoccupation? So much so that it was invested with values, imperatives, demands, rules, advice, and exhortations that were as numerous as they were emphatic and singular.

To put things in a very schematic way: we tend nowadays to think that practices aimed at pleasure, when they are carried out between two partners of the same sex, are governed by a desire whose structure is particular; but we agree—if we are "tolerant"—that this is not a reason to refer them to a moral standard, to say nothing of a legislation, different from the one that is shared by all. We focus our questioning on the singularity of a desire that is not directed toward the other sex; and at the same time, we affirm that this type of relation should not be assigned a lesser value, nor given a special status. Now, it seems that the Greeks thought very differently about these things: they believed that the same desire attached to anything that was desirable—boy or girl—subject to the condition that the appetite was nobler that inclined toward what was more beautiful and more honorable; but they also thought that this desire called for a particular mode of behavior when it made a place for itself in a relationship between two male individuals. The Greeks could not imagine that a man might need a different nature—an "other" nature—in order to love a man; but they were inclined to think that the pleasures one enjoyed in such a relationship ought to be given an ethical form different from the one that was required when it came to loving a woman. In this sort of relation, the pleasures did not reveal an alien nature in the person who experienced them; but their use demanded a special stylistics.

And it is a fact that male loves were the object, in Greek culture, of a whole agitated production of ideas, observations, and discussions concerning the forms they should take or the value one might attribute to them. It would be less than adequate if we saw in this discursive activity only the immediate and spontaneous representation of a free practice that chanced to express itself naturally in this fashion, as if all that was needed for a behavior to become a domain of inquiry or a focus of theoretical and moral concerns was that it not be prohibited. But we would be just as remiss if we assumed that these texts were only an attempt to clothe the love one could direct to boys in an honorable justification: such an undertaking would presuppose condemnations or disqualifications, which in fact were declared much later. Rather, we must try and learn how and why this practice gave rise to an extraordinarily complex problematization.

Very little remains of what Greek philosophers wrote on the subject of love and on the subject of *that* love in particular. The idea that one can justifiably form concerning these reflections and their general thematics is bound to be rather uncertain considering that such a limited number of texts have been preserved; moreover, nearly all these belong to the Socratic-Platonic tradition, while we do not have, for example, the works that Diogenes Laertius mentions, by Antisthenes, Diogenes the Cynic, Aristotle, Theophrastus, Zeno, Chrysippus, and Crantor. Nevertheless, the speeches that are more or less ironically reported by Plato can give us some notion of what was at issue in these reflections and debates on love.

1. The first thing to note is that the philosophical and moral reflections concerning love did not cover the whole field of sexual relations. Attention was focused for the most part on a "privileged" relationship—a problem area, an object of special concern: this was a relationship that implied an age difference and, connected with it, a certain difference of status. The relationship that concerned people, that they discussed and reflected upon, was not the one that joined together two mature adult males or two schoolboys of the same age; it was the relationship that developed between two men (and nothing prevented them from both being young and rather near in age to one another) who were considered as belonging to two distinct age groups and one of whom was still quite young, had not finished his education, and had not attained his definitive status.* It is the existence of this disparity that marked the relationship that philosophers and moralists concerned themselves with. This special attention should not lead us to draw hasty conclusions either about the sexual behaviors of the Greeks or about the details of their tastes (even though there is evidence from many areas of their culture that very young men were both represented and recognized as highly desirable erotic objects). We must not imagine in any case that only this type of relation was practiced; one finds many references to male love relationships that did not conform to this schema and did not include this "age differential." We would be just as mistaken to suppose that, though practiced, these other forms of relations were frowned upon and regarded as unseemly. Relations between young boys were deemed completely natural and in keeping with their condition.† On the other hand, people could mention as a special case—without censure—an abiding love relationship between two men who were well past adolescence.‡ Doubtless for reasons having to do, as we shall see, with the polar opposition of activity and passivity, an opposition regarded as necessary, relations between two grown men were more apt to be an object of criticism and irony. Passivity was always disliked, and for an adult to be suspected of it was especially serious. But whether these

*Although the texts often refer to this difference of age and status, it should be noted that the real age that is given for the partners tends to "float."[15] Further, we see characters who play the role of lover in relation to some, and that of beloved in relation to others: e.g., Critobulus in Xenophon's *Symposium,* where he tells of his love for Cleinias, whom he has met at school and who is a very young man like himself.[16]

†In the *Charmides,* Plato describes the arrival of a youth whom everyone fastened their eyes upon, adults *and* boys, "down to the very smallest."[17]

‡There was the long cited example of Euripides who still loved Agathon when the latter was already a man in his prime. F. Buffière notes in this connection an anecdote told by Aelian.[18]

relations met with easy acceptance or tended to be suspect, the important thing for the moment is to see that they were not an object of moral solicitude or of a very great theoretical interest. Without being ignored or nonexistent, they did not belong to the domain of active and intense problematization. The attention and concern was concentrated on relations in which one can tell that much was at stake: relations that could be established between an older male who had finished his education—and who was expected to play the socially, morally, and sexually active role—and a younger one, who had not yet achieved his definitive status and who was in need of assistance, advice, and support. This disparity was at the heart of the relationship; in fact, it was what made it valuable and conceivable. Because of it, the relationship was considered in a positive light, made a subject of reflection; and where it was not apparent, people sought to discover it. Thus, one liked to talk about the relationship of Achilles and Patroclus, trying to determine what differentiated them from one another and which of the two had precedence over the other (since Homer's text was ambiguous on this point).* A male relationship gave rise to a theoretical and moral interest when it was based on a rather pronounced difference on either side of the threshold separating adolescence from manhood.

2.   It does not appear that the privilege accorded to this particular type of relation can be attributed solely to the pedagogical concerns of moralists and philosophers. We are in the habit of seeing a close connection between the Greek love of boys and Greek educational practice and philosophical instruction. The story of Socrates invites this, as does the way in which the love of boys was constantly portrayed in antiquity. In reality, a very large context contributed to the valorization and elaboration of the relationship between men and adolescents. The philosophical reflection that took it as a

*Homer gave one the advantage of birth, the other that of age; one was stronger, the other more intelligent.[19]

theme actually had its roots in practices that were widespread, accepted, and relatively complex. Unlike other sexual relations, it seems—or in any case, more than they—the relations that united man and boy across a certain age and status threshold separating them were the object of a sort of ritualization, which by imposing certain rules on them gave them form, value, and interest. Even before they were taken up by philosophical reflection, these relations were already the pretext for a whole social game.

"Courtship" practices had formed around them. Doubtless these practices did not have the complexity found in other arts of loving such as those that would be developed in the Middle Ages. But by the same token, they were something quite different from the formalities that one observed in order to qualify for the hand of a young lady. They defined a whole set of conventional and appropriate behaviors, making this relation a culturally and morally overloaded domain. These practices— the reality of which has been amply documented by K. J. Dover[20]—defined the mutual behavior and the respective strategies that both partners should observe in order to give their relations a "beautiful" form; that is, one that was aesthetically and morally valuable. They determined the role of the *erastes* and that of the *eromenos.* The first was in a position of initiative—he was the suitor—and this gave him rights and obligations; he was expected to show his ardor, and to restrain it; he had gifts to make, services to render; he had functions to exercise with regard to the *eromenos;* and all this entitled him to expect a just reward. The other partner, the one who was loved and courted, had to be careful not to yield too easily; he also had to keep from accepting too many tokens of love, and from granting his favors heedlessly and out of self-interest, without testing the worth of his partner; he must also show gratitude for what the lover had done for him. Now, this courtship practice alone shows very well that the sexual relation between man and boy did not "go without saying": it had to be accompanied by conventions, rules of conduct, ways of

going about it, by a whole game of delays and obstacles designed to put off the moment of closure, and to integrate it into
a series of subsidiary activities and relations. In other words,
while this type of relation was fully accepted, it was not a
matter of "indifference." One would be missing the essential
thing if one regarded all these precautions that were taken and
the interest that was shown merely as the proof that this love
was freely engaged in; it would be to ignore the distinction that
was made between this sexual behavior and all the others whose
recommended modalities were of little concern. All these
preoccupations make it clear that pleasure relations between
men and adolescent boys already constituted a delicate factor
in society, an area so sensitive that one could not fail to be
concerned about the conduct of the participants on both sides.

3. But we may note at once a considerable difference in
comparison with that other focus of interest and inquiry, matrimonial life: in the case of relations between men and boys,
we are dealing with a game that was "open," at least up to a
certain point.

Open "spatially." In economics and the art of the household, we saw a binary spatial structure where the spaces of the
two marriage partners were carefully distinguished (the exterior for the husband, the interior for the wife; the men's quar-
ters on one side, the women's on the other). With boys, the
game unfolded in a very different space: a common space, at
least from the time when they had reached a certain age—the
space of the street and the gathering places, with some
strategically important points (such as the gymnasium); but a
space in which everyone moved about freely,* so that one had
to pursue a boy, chase after him, watch for him in those places
where he might pass and catch hold of him where he happened
to be; it was a theme of ironic complaint on the part of lovers,
that they were obliged to haunt the gymnasium, go hunting

*In the schools, this freedom was supervised and limited.[21]

with the *eromenos,* and pant alongside him in exercises, which
they were no longer in any condition to do.

But, more important, the game was also open in that one
could not exercise any statutory authority over the boy, as
long as he was not slaveborn—he was free in his choices, in
what he accepted or rejected, in his preferences or his decisions. In order to get from him something that he always had
the right to refuse, one had to be able to persuade him; anyone
who wished to remain his favorite had, in his eyes, to outshine
such rivals as might present themselves, and for this it was
necessary to highlight one's achievements, one's qualities, or
one's presents; but the decision was the boy's alone to make:
in this game that one had initiated, one was never sure of
winning. And yet this was the very thing that made it interesting. Nothing illustrates this better than the charming complaint of Hiero the tyrant, as reported by Xenophon.[22] Being
a tyrant, he explains, does not make things pleasant either in
regard to a wife or in regard to a boy. For a tyrant cannot help
but take a wife from an inferior family, thus losing all the
advantages of marrying into a family "of greater wealth and
influence." As for the boy—and Hiero is enamored of Daïlo-
chus—the fact of having despotic power at one's disposal
raises other obstacles; the favors that Hiero would like so
much to obtain, he would like the boy to give them out of
friendship and of his own accord; but "to take them from him
by force," he would sooner desire "to do himself an injury."
To take something from one's enemy against his will is the
greatest of pleasures; but when it comes to the favors of boys,
the sweetest are those that are freely granted. For example,
what a pleasure it is to "exchange looks, how pleasant his
questions and answers; how very pleasant and ravishing
are the struggles and bickerings. But to take advantage of a
favorite against his will seems to me more like brigan-
dage than love."

In the case of marriage, the problematization of sexual
pleasures and of the practices associated with them was car-

ried out on the basis of the statutory relation that empowered
the husband to govern the wife, other individuals, the estate,
and the household; the essential question concerned the moderation that needed to be shown in exercising power. In the
case of the relationship with boys, the ethics of pleasures
would have to bring into play—across age differences—subtle
strategies that would make allowance for the other's freedom,
his ability to refuse, and his required consent.

4. In this problematization of relationships with adolescent boys, the question of timing was important, but it was
raised in a singular fashion; what mattered was not, as in
dietetics, the opportune moment for the act, nor, as in economics, the continual maintenance of a relational structure;
rather, it was the difficult question of precarious time and
fugitive passage. It was expressed in different ways—as a problem of "limit" first of all: what was the age limit after which
a boy ought to be considered too old to be an honorable
partner in a love relation? At what age was it no longer good
for him to accept this role, nor for his lover to want to assign
it to him? This involved the familiar casuistry of the signs of
manhood. These were supposed to mark a threshold, one that
was all the more intangible in theory as it must have very often
been crossed in practice and as it offered the possibility of
finding fault with those who had done so. As we know, the first
beard was believed to be that fateful mark, and it was said that
the razor that shaved it must sever the ties of love.[23] In any
case, one should note that people criticized not only boys who
were willing to play a role that no longer corresponded to their
virility, but also the men who frequented overaged boys.[24] The
Stoics were criticized for keeping their lovers too long—up to
the age of twenty-eight—but the argument they gave, which
was more or less an extension of that given by Pausanias in
the *Symposium* (he held that in order to make sure that men
became attached only to youths of merit, the law should prohibit relations with boys who were too young),[25] shows that

this limit was less a universal rule than a subject of debate that permitted a variety of solutions.

This attention to the period of adolescence and its boundaries no doubt helped to increase people's sensitivity to the juvenile body, to its special beauty, and to the different signs of its development; the adolescent physique became the object of a kind of cultural valorization that was quite pronounced. That the male body might be beautiful, well beyond its first bloom, was something that the Greeks were not blind to nor inclined to forget; classical figure sculpture paid more attention to the adult body; and it is recalled in Xenophon's *Symposium* that in choosing garland-bearers for Athena, they were careful to select the most beautiful old men.[26] But in the sphere of sexual ethics, it was the juvenile body with its peculiar charm that was regularly suggested as the "right object" of pleasure. And it would be a mistake to think that its traits were valued because of what they shared with feminine beauty. They were appreciated in themselves or in their juxtaposition with the signs and guarantees of a developing virility. Strength, endurance, and spirit also formed part of this beauty; hence it was good in fact if exercises, gymnastics, competitions, and hunting expeditions reinforced these qualities, guaranteeing that this gracefulness would not degenerate into softness and effeminization.[27] The feminine ambiguity that would be perceived later (and already in the course of antiquity, even) as a component—more exactly, as the secret cause—of the adolescent's beauty, was, in the classical period, more something from which the boy needed to protect himself and be protected. Among the Greeks there was a whole moral aesthetics of the boy's body; it told of his personal merit and of that of the love one felt for him. Virility as a physical mark should be absent from it; but it should be present as a precocious form and as a promise of future behavior: already to conduct oneself as the man one has not yet become.

But this sensibility was also connected with feelings of anxiety in the face of those rapid changes and the nearness of their completion; by a sense of the fleeting character of that beauty and of its legitimate desirability; and by fear, the double fear so often expressed in the lover, of seeing his beloved lose his charm, and in the beloved, of seeing his lover turn away from him. And the question that was then posed concerned the possible conversion—an ethically necessary and socially useful one—of the bond of love (doomed to disappear) into a relation of friendship, of *philia.* The latter differed from the love relation, out of which it would ideally and sometimes actually be formed: it was lasting, having no other limit than life itself; and it obliterated the dissymmetries that were implied in the erotic relation between man and adolescent. It was one of the frequent themes in moral reflection on this type of relation, that these relations needed to rid themselves of their precariousness: a precariousness that was due to the inconstancy of the partners, and that was a consequence of the boy's growing older and thereby losing his charm; but it was also a precept, since it was not good to love a boy who was past a certain age, just as it was not good for him to allow himself to be loved. This precariousness could be avoided only if, in the fervor of love, *philia*—friendship—already began to develop: *philia,* i.e., an affinity of character and mode of life, a sharing of thoughts and existence, mutual benevolence.[28] The beginning of this cultivation of indestructible friendship in the love relation is what Xenophon is describing when he portrays two lovers who look into each other's faces, converse, confide in one another, rejoice together or feel a common distress over successes and failures, and look after each other: "It is by conducting themselves thus that men continue to love their mutual affection and enjoy it down to old age."*

5. On a very general level, this inquiry concerning relationships with boys took the form of a reflection on love. This

---

*This whole passage of Socrates' speech is a good illustration of the anxiety that was felt in view of the precariousness of male love relationships, and of the role that the permanence of friendship was supposed to play in the scheme of things.[29]

fact should not lead us to conclude that for the Greeks Eros had no place except in this type of relation, and that it could not play a part in relations with a woman: Eros could unite human beings no matter what their sex happened to be; in Xenophon, one can see that Niceratus and his wife are joined together by the ties of Eros and Anteros.[30] Eros was not necessarily "homosexual," nor was it exclusive of marriage; and the marriage tie did not differ from the relation with boys by being incompatible with love's intensity and reciprocity. The difference was elsewhere. Matrimonial morality, and more precisely the sexual ethics of the married man, did not depend on the existence of an erotic relation in order to constitute itself and define its rules (although it was quite possible for this kind of bond to exist between marriage partners). On the other hand, when it was a matter of determining what use they might make of their pleasures within the relationship, then the reference to Eros became necessary; the problematization of their relationship belonged to an "erotics." This was because, in the case of two spouses, marital status, management of the *oikos,* and maintenance of the lineage could create standards of behavior, define the rules of that behavior, and determine the forms of the requisite moderation. But in the case of a man or boy who were in a position of reciprocal independence and between whom there was no institutional constraint, but rather an open game (with preferences, choices, freedom of movement, uncertain outcome), the principle of regulation of behaviors was to be sought in the relation itself, in the nature of the attraction that drew them toward one another, and in the mutual attachment that connected them. Hence the problematization would be carried out in the form of a reflection on the relation itself: an inquiry that was both theoretical about love and prescriptive about the way one lived.

But in actual fact, this art of loving was intended for two classes of individuals. To be sure, the wife and her behavior were not completely absent from reflection on economics; but she was placed under her husband's exclusive authority and while it was right that she be respected in her privileges, this was insofar as she proved worthy of respect, the important thing being that the head of a family remain master of himself. The boy, on the other hand, could be expected to maintain the reserve that was appropriate at that age; with his possible refusals (dreaded but honorable) and his eventual acceptances (desired but likely to be suspect), he constituted an independent center vis-à-vis the lover. And this erotics would have to be deployed from one fixed point of this elliptical configuration to the other. In economics and dietetics, the voluntary moderation of the man was based mainly on his relation to himself; in erotics, the game was more complicated; it implied self-mastery on the part of the lover; it also implied an ability on the part of the beloved to establish a relation of dominion over himself; and lastly, it implied a relationship between their two moderations, expressed in their deliberate choice of one another. One can even note a certain tendency to privilege the boy's point of view. The questions that were raised had to do with his conduct in particular, and it was to him that one offered observations, advice, and precepts: as if it were important above all to constitute an erotics of the loved object, or at least, of the loved object insofar as he had to form himself as a subject of ethical behavior; this is in fact what becomes apparent in a text like the eulogy of Epicrates, attributed to Demosthenes.

2

A Boy's Honor

In comparison with the two great *Symposiums,* Plato's and Xenophon's, and with the *Phaedrus,* Demosthenes' *Erotic Essay* appears rather mediocre. A formulaic speech, it is both the encomium of a young man and an exhortation addressed to him. This was in fact the traditional function of encomiums, and the function that Xenophon alludes to in the *Symposium:* "in the very act of flattering Callias, you are educating him to conform to the ideal."[1] Praise and lesson at the same time, therefore. But despite the banality of the themes and their treatment—a kind of insipid Platonism—it is possible to discover a few traits that were characteristic of other discourses on love and of the way in which the question of "pleasures" was posed within them.

1. One preoccupation animates the entire text. It finds expression in a vocabulary that refers constantly to honor and shame. Throughout the speech it is a question of *aischynē,* that shame which is both the dishonor with which one can be branded and the feeling that causes one to turn away from it; it is a question of that which is ugly and shameful *(aischron),* in contrast to that which is fine, or both fine and honorable. Much is said, too, about that which results in blame and contempt *(oneidos, epitimē),* as opposed to that which brings honor and leads to a good reputation *(endoxos, entimos).* In any case, Epicrates' admirer states his objective from the very start of the *Erotic Essay:* may this praise bring honor to his beloved, and not shame, as sometimes happens when eulogies are delivered by indiscreet suitors.[2] And he returns again and again to this concern: it is important that the young man remember that because of his birth and standing, the least negligence where honor is at stake may well cover him with shame; he must always keep in mind the example of those who, by being vigilant, have managed to preserve their honor in the course of their relationship;[3] he must take care not to "dishonor his natural qualities" and not to disappoint the hopes of those who are proud of him.[4]*

The behavior of young men thus appears to have been a domain that was especially sensitive to the division between what was shameful and what was proper, between what reflected credit and what brought dishonor. It was this question that preoccupied those who chose to reflect on young men, on the love that was manifested for them and the conduct they needed to exhibit. Pausanias, in Plato's *Symposium,* calls attention to the diversity of morals and customs having to do with boys. He points out what is considered "disgraceful" or "good" in Elis, in Sparta, in Thebes, in Ionia or in areas under Persian rule, and lastly, in Athens.[6] And Phaedrus recalls the principle that should be one's guide in the love of young men as well as in life in general: "shame at what is disgraceful and ambition for what is noble; without these feelings neither a state nor an individual can accomplish anything great or fine."[7] But it should be remarked that this question was not confined to a few exacting moralists. A young man's behavior, his honor and his disgrace were also the object of much social curiosity; people payed attention to this, spoke about it, remembered it. For example, in order to attack Timarchus, Aeschines had no qualms about rehashing the gossip that may have gone round many years previously, when his adversary was still a very young man.[8] Moreover, the *Erotic Essay* shows

---

*Aristotle's *Rhetoric* shows the importance of the categories of *kalon* and *aischron* in speeches of praise.[5]

very well in passing just what sort of distrustful solicitude a
boy could quite naturally be subjected to by his entourage;
people watched him, spied on him, remarked on his demeanor
and his relations; vicious tongues were active around him;
spiteful people were ready to blame him if he showed arro-
gance or conceit, but they were also quick to criticize him if
he was too gracious.[9] Naturally, one cannot help but think
about what the situation of girls in other societies must have
been when—the age for marriage being much earlier for
women—their premarital conduct became an important
moral and social concern, of itself and for their families.

2.   But in regard to the Greek boy, the importance of his
honor did not concern—as it would later in the case of the
European girl—his future marriage; rather, it related to his
status, his eventual place in the city. Of course, there is abun-
dant evidence that boys of dubious reputation could exercise
the highest political functions; but there is also evidence that
this very thing could be held against them—without counting
the substantial judicial consequences that certain kinds of misconduct might produce: the Timarchus affair makes this clear.
The author of the *Erotic Essay* points it out to the young
Epicrates; part of his future, including the rank he will be able
to occupy in the city, depends this very day on the manner,
honorable or not, in which he conducts himself: considering
that the city cannot call upon just anyone, it will have to take
account of established reputations;[10] and the man who scoffs
at good advice will be punished all his life for his blindness.
Two things are necessary, therefore: to mind one's own conduct when one is still very young, but also to look after the
honor of younger men, when one has grown older.
This transitional age, when the young man was so desirable
and his honor so fragile, thus constituted a trial period: a time
when his worth was tested, in the sense that it had to be
formed, exercised, and measured all at the same time. A few
lines at the end of the text point up the testlike characteristics

that the boy's behavior assumed in this period of his life. In exhorting Epicrates, the author of the encomium reminds him that he will be put to the test *(agōn),* and that the debate will be a *dokimasia:* [11] this was the word that designated the examination upon whose completion young men were enrolled among the *ephebi* or citizens were admitted to certain magistracies. The young man's conduct owed its importance and the attention that everyone needed to give it, to the fact that everyone saw it as a qualifying test. The text says this plainly, moreover: "I think . . . that the city will appoint you to be in charge of some department of her business, and in proportion as your natural gifts are more conspicuous it will judge you worthy of greater responsibilities and will the sooner desire to make trial of your abilities."[12]

3.   What exactly was being tested? And with respect to what type of behavior was Epicrates supposed to draw the line between that which was honorable and that which was disgraceful? The test pertained to the familiar points of Greek education: the demeanor of the body (carefully avoid *rhathymia,* the sluggishness which was always a defamatory sign); one's gaze (in which *aidōs,* dignity, could be read), one's way of talking (don't take the easy option of silence, but be able to mix serious talk with casual talk); and the quality of one's acquaintances.

But it was especially in the sphere of amorous conduct that the distinction between what was honorable and what was shameful operated. On this point, we may note first of all that the author—and this is what makes the text both a eulogy of love and praise of a young man—criticizes the opinion that would tie a boy's honor to the systematic rejection of suitors: doubtless certain lovers defile the relation itself *(lymainesthai tōi pragmati),* [13] but one should not put them in the same class as those admirers who show moderation. The text does not draw the boundary line of honor between those who spurn their suitors and those who accept them. For a Greek youth, to be pursued by would-be lovers was obviously not a dishonor: it was, rather, the visible mark of his qualities; the number of admirers could be an object of legitimate pride, and sometimes an object of vainglory. But to accept the love relation, to enter the game (even if one did not play exactly the game the lover proposed) was not considered to be a disgrace either. The man who praises Epicrates explains to him that being beautiful and being loved constitute a double stroke of fortune *(eutychia);* [14] it only remains for him to make the right use *(orthōs chrēsthai)* of it. It is this point that the text emphasizes and makes a "point of honor," so to speak: these things *(ta pragmata)* are not, in themselves and absolutely, good or bad; they vary according to who practices them *(para tous chrōmenous).* [15] It is "use" that determines their moral value, according to a principle that one sees often formulated elsewhere; in any case, we find quite similar expressions in the *Symposium:* "The truth of the matter I believe to be this. There is, as I stated at first, no absolute right and wrong in love, but everything depends upon the circumstances; to yield to a bad man in a bad way is wrong, but to yield to a worthy man in a right way is right." [16]

Now, as for knowing precisely how the distribution of honor is to be carried out in the love relation, one must admit that the text is extremely elliptical. While it does offer specifics regarding what Epicrates should do or has done in order to exercise his body and develop his courage, or to acquire the philosophical knowledge that he will need, nothing is said concerning what is acceptable or objectionable in physical relations. One thing is clear: not everything should be refused (the young man "grants his favors"), but not everything should be consented to: "No one finds himself disappointed of favors from you which it is just and fair to ask, but no one is permitted even to hope for such liberties as lead to shame. So great is the latitude your discreetness permits to those who have the best intentions; so great is the discouragement it presents to those who would fling off restraint." [17] The modera-

tion—the *sōphrosynē*—that is one of the major qualities required of boys clearly implies a discrimination in physical
contacts. But it is not possible to infer from this text the acts
and gestures that honor would compel one to refuse. It should
be noted that in the *Phaedrus* the lack of precision is almost
as great, even though the theme is developed more fully.
Throughout the first two speeches on the advisability of yielding to a lover or a nonlover, and in the great fable of the soul
as a team with its restive steed and its obedient steed, Plato's
text shows that the question of what constitutes "honorable"
practice is crucial: and yet the acts are never designated except
by expressions like "to gratify" or "to grant one's favors"
(charizesthai), "to do the thing" *(diaprattesthai),* "to derive
the greatest possible pleasure from the beloved," "to obtain
what one wants" *(pleithesthai),* "to enjoy" *(apolauesthai).* A
reticence inherent in this type of discourse? Without doubt,
the Greeks would have found it improper that someone would
call by name, in a set speech, things that were only vaguely
alluded to even in polemics and law court addresses. One
imagines, too, that it was hardly necessary to insist on distinctions that were common knowledge: everyone must have
known what it was honorable or shameful for a boy to consent
to. But we may also recall an observation that was made in our
discussion of dietetics and economics, where it became apparent that moral reflection was less concerned with specifying
the codes to be respected and the list of acts that were permitted and prohibited than it was concerned with characterizing
the type of attitude, of relationship with oneself that was
required.

4. Actually, while the text does not indicate the practical
forms that are to be respected and the physical boundaries that
are not to be crossed, it does at least designate the general
principle that determines the way to conduct oneself in these
matters. The entire eulogy of Epicrates refers to an agonistic
context in which the worth and brilliance of the young man

must affirm itself through his superiority over others. Let us quickly review these motifs that were so frequent in set speeches. The individual being eulogized is greater than the praise that one offers him, and the words risk being less beautiful than the one to whom they are addressed; or the boy surpasses all others in physical and moral qualities; not only his gifts but his conversation places him above all others; among all the exercises in which one can excel, he has chosen the most noble, the most rewarding; his soul is prepared for "the rivalries of ambition," and not content to distinguish himself by one quality, he combines "all the qualities of which a man might justly feel proud."[18]

However, the merit of Epicrates is not just in this abundance of qualities that enable him to outstrip all his rivals and bring glory to his parents;[19] it also consists in the fact that with respect to all those who approach him he always maintains his eminent worth; he does not allow himself to be dominated by any of them; they all want to draw him into their intimacy—the word *synētheia* has both the general meaning of living together and the specific meaning of sexual relations—but he surpasses them in such a way, he gains such an ascendancy over them that they derive all their pleasure from the friendship they feel for him.[20] By not yielding, not submitting, remaining the strongest, triumphing over suitors and lovers through one's resistance, one's firmness, one's moderation *(sōphrosynē)*—the young man proves his excellence in the sphere of love relations.

Given this general indication, must we imagine a precise code based on the analogy—so familiar to the Greeks—between positions in the social field (with the difference between "the first ones" and the others, the great who rule and those who obey, the masters and the servants) and the form of sexual relations (with dominant and subordinate positions, active and passive roles, penetration carried out by the man and undergone by his partner)? To say that one must not yield, not let others get the best of one, not accept a subordinate position where one would get the worst of it, is doubtless to exclude or advise against sexual practices that would be humiliating for the boy, putting him in a position of inferiority.[21]

But it is likely that the principle of honor and maintenance of "superiority" refers—beyond a few precise prescriptions—to a kind of general style: it was not good (especially in the eyes of public opinion) for a boy to behave "passively," to let himself be manipulated and dominated, to yield without resistance, to become an obliging partner in the sensual pleasures of the other, to indulge his whims, and to offer his body to whomever it pleased and however it pleased them, out of weakness, lust, or self-interest. This was what dishonored boys who accepted the first comer, who showed off unscrupulously, who passed from hand to hand, who granted everything to the highest bidder. This was what Epicrates did not and would not do, mindful as he was of the opinion people had of him, of the rank he would have to hold, and of the useful relations he might enter into.

5. I would like just to mention again briefly the role that the author of the *Erotic Essay* has philosophy play in this safeguarding of honor and these contests of superiority by which the boy is invited to test himself in a manner that befits his age. This philosophy, whose content is not specified apart from a reference to the Socratic theme of *epimeleia heautou*, "care of the self,"[22] and to the necessity, also Socratic, of combining knowledge and exercise *(epistēmē, meletē)*—this philosophy is not presented as a guide for leading a different life, nor for abstaining from all the pleasures. It is invoked by Demosthenes as an indispensable complement of the other tests: "Reflect that . . . of all things the most irrational is to be ambitious for wealth, bodily strength, and such things, and for their sake to submit to many tests . . . but not to aim at the improvement of the mind, which has supervision over all other powers."[23] What philosophy can show, in fact, is how to become "stronger than oneself" and when one has become so,

it also enables one to prevail over others. It is by nature a leadership principle since it alone is capable of directing thought: "Of the powers residing in human beings we shall find that thought leads all the rest and that philosophy alone is capable of directing it rightly and training it."[24] It is clear that philosophy is an asset that is necessary for the young man's wise conduct; not, however, in order to guide him toward another form of life, but to enable him to exercise self-mastery and to triumph over others in the difficult game of ordeals to be undergone and honor to be safeguarded.

The entire *Erotic Essay* revolves, as we see, around the problem of this twofold superiority over oneself and over others in that difficult phase when the boy's youth and beauty attract one man after the other, each trying to "get the best" of him. In dietetics, it was mainly a question of mastery over oneself and over the violence of a perilous act; in economics, it was a question of the control that one had to exercise over oneself in the practice of the authority that one exercised over one's wife. Here, where erotics takes the boy's point of view, the problem is to see how the boy is going to be able to achieve self-mastery in not yielding to others. The point at issue is not the sense of measure that one brings to one's own power, but the best way to measure one's strength against the power of others while ensuring one's own mastery over self. In this regard, a brief narration that appears in the middle of the speech acquires a symbolic value. It is a commonplace account of a chariot race, but a direct relation is established between the little sports drama that is reported and the public test that the young man undergoes in his behavior with his suitors. We see Epicrates driving his team (a likely reference to the *Phaedrus*); he is on the verge of defeat, his chariot is about to be smashed to pieces by an opposing team; the crowd, despite the taste it ordinarily has for accidents, cheers for the hero, while he, "stronger even than the vigor of his team, manages to win the victory over the most favored of his rivals."[25]

This prosaic address to Epicrates is certainly not one of the highest forms of Greek reflection on love. But in its very banality it does bring out some important aspects of "the Greek problem of boys." The young man—between the end of childhood and the age when he attained manly status—constituted a delicate and difficult factor for Greek ethics and Greek thought. His youth with its particular beauty (to which every man was believed to be naturally sensitive) and the status that would be his (and for which, with the help and protection of his entourage, he must prepare himself) formed a "strategic" point around which a complex game was required; his honor—which depended in part on the use he made of his body and which would also partly determine his future role and reputation—was an important stake in the game. For him, there was a test in all this, one that demanded diligence and training; there was also, for others, an occasion for care and concern. At the very end of his eulogy of Epicrates, the author declares that the life of the boy, his *bios,* must be a "common" work; and, as if it were a matter of a work of art to be finished, he urges all who know Epicrates to give this future figure "the greatest possible brilliance."

Later, in European culture, girls or married women, with their behavior, their beauty, and their feelings, were to become themes of special concern; a new art of courting them, a literature that was basically romantic in form, an exacting morality that was attentive to the integrity of their bodies and the solidity of their matrimonial commitment—all this would draw curiosity and desires around them. No matter what inferior position may have been reserved for them in the family or in society, there would be an accentuation, a valorization, of the "problem" of women. Their nature, their conduct, the feelings they inspired or experienced, the permitted or forbidden relationship that one might have with them were to become themes of reflection, knowledge, analysis, and prescription. It seems clear, on the other hand, that in classical Greece the problematization was more active in regard to boys, maintaining an intense moral concern around their fragile beauty, their corporal honor, their ethical judgment and the training it required. What is historically singular is not that the Greeks found pleasure in boys, nor even that they accepted this pleasure as legitimate; it is that this acceptance of pleasure was not simple, and that it gave rise to a whole cultural elaboration. In broad terms, what is important to grasp here is not why the Greeks had a fondness for boys but why they had a "pederasty"; that is, why they elaborated a courtship practice, a moral reflection, and—as we shall see— a philosophical asceticism, around that fondness.

3

The Object of Pleasure

In order to understand how the use of the *aphrodisia* was problematized in reflection on the love of boys, we have to recall a principle, which is doubtless not peculiar to Greek culture, but which assumed considerable importance within it and exercised a decisive authority in its moral valuations. I am referring to the principle of isomorphism between sexual relations and social relations. What this means is that sexual relations—always conceived in terms of the model act of penetration, assuming a polarity that opposed activity and passivity—were seen as being of the same type as the relationship between a superior and a subordinate, an individual who dominates and one who is dominated, one who commands and one who complies, one who vanquishes and one who is vanquished. Pleasure practices were conceptualized using the same categories as those in the field of social rivalries and hierarchies: an analogous agonistic structure, analogous oppositions and differentiations, analogous values attributed to the respective roles of the partners. And this suggests that in sexual behavior there was one role that was intrinsically honorable and valorized without question: the one that consisted in being active, in dominating, in penetrating, in asserting one's superiority.

This principle had several consequences relating to the status of those who were supposed to be the passive partners in this activity. Slaves were at the master's disposition, of course:

215

their condition made them sexual objects and this was taken for granted—so much so that people could be astonished that the same law would forbid the rape of slaves and that of children. In order to explain this anomaly, Aeschines submits that the aim was to show, by prohibiting violence even in the case of slaves, what a serious thing it was when directed at children of good birth. As for the woman's passivity, it did denote an inferiority of nature and condition; but there was no reason to criticize it as a behavior, precisely because it was in conformity with what nature intended and with what the law prescribed. On the other hand, everything in the way of sexual behavior that might cause a free man—to say nothing of someone who, by birth, fortune, and prestige, held or should hold one of the first ranks among men—to bear the marks of inferiority, submission to domination, and acceptance of servitude, could only be considered as shameful: a shame that was even greater if he offered himself as the obliging object of another's pleasure.

Now, in a game regulated according to such principles, the position of the (freeborn) boy was difficult. To be sure, he was still in an "inferior" position in the sense that he was a long way from benefiting from the rights and powers that would be his when he attained the full enjoyment of his status. And yet his place was not assimilable to that of a slave, nor to that of a woman. This was true even in the context of the household and the family. A passage from Aristotle's *Politics* makes this clear. Discussing the relations of authority and forms of government that are appropriate for the family, Aristotle defines the positions of the slave, the wife, and the (male) child in relation to the head of the family. Governing slaves, Aristotle says, is not like governing free beings; to govern a wife is to exercise a "political" authority in which relations are permanently unequal; in contrast, the governing of children can be called "royal" because it is based "on affection and seniority."[1] Indeed, the deliberative faculty is lacking in the slave; it is present in the woman, but she doesn't exercise the decision-making function in her house; in the boy, the deficiency relates only to his incomplete development. And while the moral education of women is important, seeing that they constitute half the free population, that of male children is more so, for it concerns future citizens who will participate in the government of the city.[2] We can see, therefore, that the specific nature of the boy's position, the particular form of his dependence, and the manner in which he is to be treated, even in the space where the considerable power of the patriarch is exercised, were marked by the status that would be his in future years.

The same held true up to a point in the game of sexual relations. Among the various legitimate "objects," the boy occupied a special position. He was definitely not a forbidden object; in Athens, certain laws protected free children (from adults, who at least for a time did not have the right to go into the schools; from slaves, who incurred the death penalty if they tried corrupting them; and from their fathers or tutors, who were punished if they prostituted them);[3] but nothing prevented or prohibited an adolescent from being the openly recognized sexual partner of a man. Yet there was a sort of intrinsic difficulty in this role: something that simultaneously made it hard to define clearly and specify exactly what the role implied in the sexual relation, and nonetheless drew attention to this point and made people attach much importance and value to what should or should not occur in that regard. All this constituted something of a blind spot and a point of overvaluation. The role of the boy was a focus of a good deal of uncertainty, combined with an intense interest.

Aeschines, in *Against Timarchus,* makes use of a law that is very interesting in itself because it concerns the effects of civic and political disqualification that a man's sexual misconduct—"prostitution" in the precise sense—could entail in that it would prohibit him from subsequently "becoming one of the nine archons or discharging the office of priest or acting as an advocate for the state." An individual who had prostituted

himself was debarred from holding any magistracy in the city
or abroad, be it elective or conferred by lot. He could not serve
as a herald or ambassador, nor become a prosecutor of ambas-
sadors or a paid slanderer.* Further, he could not address the
council or the assembly, even though he were "the most elo-
quent orator in Athens."⁴ Hence this law made male prostitution an instance of *atimia*—of public disgrace—that excluded
a citizen from certain responsibilities.† But the way in which
Aeschines conducts his prosecution, and tries through a
strictly juridical discussion to compromise his adversary,
points up the relation of incompatibility—ethical as much as
legal—that was recognized as existing between certain sexual
roles assumed by boys and certain social roles assumed by
adults.

Aeschines' legal argumentation, which is based on Timarchus' "bad conduct" as alleged via rumors, gossip, and testi-
mony, consists in going back and finding certain factors that
constitute prostitution (number of partners, indiscriminate-
ness, payment for services) whereas others are lacking (he
hadn't been registered as a prostitute and he hadn't stayed in
a house). When he was young and good-looking, he passed
through many hands, and not always honorable ones since he
is known to have lived with a man of servile status and in the
house of a notorious lecher who surrounded himself with
singers and zither players; he received gifts, he was kept, he
took part in the excesses of his protectors; he is known to have
been with Cedonides, Autocleides, Thersandrus, Misgolas,
Anticles, Pittalacus, and Hegesandrus. Thus it is not possible
to say simply that he has had many relationships *(hetairēkōs)*,
but that he has "prostituted" himself *(peporneumenos):* "For

---

Translator's note. Foucault says here: "accusateur ou denonciateur salarié." The
relevant phrase from Aeschines' speech, as translated by K. J. Dover in *Greek
Homosexuality*, reads: "or take money for threatening false accusations." Dover
notes that this disqualification is fictitious, a rhetorical maneuver by Aeschines.
Obviously, slander was not something that Athenian law explicitly condoned.

†K. J. Dover points out that what was punishable was not prostitution itself; rather,
it was the fact of violating the disqualifications that resulted from having been a
prostitute.⁵

the man who practices this thing with one person, and practices it for pay, seems to me to be liable to precisely this charge."[6]

But the accusation also operates on a moral level that makes it possible not only to establish the crime, but to compromise the adversary politically and in general. Perhaps Timarchus was not formally a professional prostitute, but he is definitely not one of those respectable men who make no secret of their taste for male loves and who maintain honorable relations with free boys, relations that are valuable to the young partner: Aeschines acknowledges that he is partial to this kind of love. He describes Timarchus as a man who in the course of his youth placed himself and showed himself to everyone, in the inferior and humiliating position of a pleasure object for others; he wanted this role, he sought it, took pleasure in it, and profited from it. And this is what Aeschines would have his audience see as morally and politically incompatible with civic responsibilities and the exercise of political power. A man who has been marked by this role which he was pleased to assume in his youth would not now be able to play, without provoking indignation, the role of a man who is over others in the city, who provides them with friends, counsels them in their decisions, leads them and represents them. What was hard for Athenians to accept—and this is the feeling that Aeschines tries to play upon in the speech against Timarchus —was not that they might be governed by someone who loved boys, or who as a youth was loved by a man; but that they might come under the authority of a leader who once identified with the role of pleasure object for others.

It is this feeling, moreover, that Aristophanes had appealed to so often in his comedies; the point of mockery and the thing that was meant to be scandalous were that these orators, these leaders who were followed and loved, these citizens who sought to seduce the people in order to rule over them, such as Cleon or Agyrrhius, were also individuals who had consented and still consented to play the role of passive, obliging objects. And Aristophanes spoke ironically of an Athenian democracy where one's chances of being heard in the assembly were greater the more one had a taste for pleasures of this sort.[7] In the same way and the same spirit, Diogenes made fun of Demosthenes and the morals he had while pretending to be the leader *(dēmagōgos)* of the Athenian people.[8] When one played the role of subordinate partner in the game of pleasure relations, one could not be truly dominant in the game of civic and political activity.

The extent to which these criticisms and satires may have been justified in reality matters little. There is at least one thing that they show clearly by their mere existence: namely, the difficulty caused, in this society that accepted sexual relations between men, by the juxtaposition of an ethos of male superiority and a conception of all sexual intercourse in terms of the schema of penetration and male domination. The consequence of this was that on the one hand the "active" and dominant role was always assigned positive values, but on the other hand it was necessary to attribute to one of the partners in the sexual act the passive, dominated, and inferior position. And while this was no problem when it involved a woman or a slave, the case was altered when it involved a man. It is doubtless the existence of this difficulty that explains both the silence in which this relationship between adults was actually enveloped, and the noisy disqualification of those who broke this silence by declaring their acceptance of, or rather, their preference for this "subordinate" role. It was also in view of this difficulty that all the attention was concentrated on the relationship between men and boys, since in this case one of the two partners, owing to his youth and to the fact that he had not yet attained manly status, could be—for a period that everyone knew to be brief—an admissible object of pleasure. But while the boy, because of his peculiar charm, could be a prey that men might pursue without causing a scandal or a problem, one had to keep in mind that the day would come when he would have to be a man, to exercise powers and responsibilities, so that obviously he could then no longer be an object of pleasure—but then, to what extent could he *have been* such an object?

Hence the problem that we may call the "antinomy of the boy" in the Greek ethics of *aphrodisia*. On the one hand, young men were recognized as objects of pleasure—and even as the only honorable and legitimate objects among the possible male partners of men: no one would ever reproach a man for loving a boy, for desiring and enjoying him, provided that the laws and proprieties were respected. But on the other hand, the boy, whose youth must be a training for manhood, could not and must not identify with that role. He could not of his own accord, in his own eyes, and for his own sake, be that object of pleasure, even though the man was quite naturally fond of appointing him as an object of pleasure. In short, to delight in and be a subject of pleasure with a boy did not cause a problem for the Greeks; but to be an object of pleasure and to acknowledge oneself as such constituted a major difficulty for the boy. The relationship that he was expected to establish with himself in order to become a free man, master of himself and capable of prevailing over others, was at variance with a form of relationship in which he would be an object of pleasure for another. This noncoincidence was ethically necessary.

Such a difference explains certain characteristic features of the Greeks' reflection on the love of boys.

In the first place, there was an oscillation—enigmatic for us—concerning the natural or "unnatural" character of that type of love. On one side, it was held for granted that the attraction to boys was natural in just the same way as all movement that carried one in the direction of the beautiful was natural. And yet it is not unusual to find the assertion that relations between men, or more generally, between two individuals of the same sex, is *para physin*, beside nature. Of course one can infer that these two views indicate two different attitudes, one favorable and the other hostile to that kind of love. But the very possibility of these two opinions was probably owing to the fact that while people deemed it quite natural that one might find pleasure with a boy, it was much harder to accept as natural that which made a boy an object of pleasure. So that one could take exception to the very act that was carried out between two male individuals on the grounds that it was *para physin*—because it *feminized* one of the partners, whereas the desire that one could have for beauty was nevertheless regarded as natural. The Cynics were not against the love of boys, even though they heaped sarcasm on all those boys whose passivity caused them to accept being estranged from their own nature, thus becoming "worse than they were."[9] As for Plato, there is no reason to suppose that, having been a believer in male love as a youth, he later "got wise" to the extent that he condemned it as being a relationship "contrary to nature." It should be noted, rather, that at the beginning of the *Laws*, when he draws a contrast between relations with women as an element of nature and relations between men (or between women) as an effect of incontinence *(akrasia)*, he is referring to the act of copulation itself (provided for by nature for procreation) and he is thinking of institutions that are likely to promote or on the other hand pervert citizens' morals.[10] Similarly, in the passage from Book VIII where he foresees the need—and the difficulty—of a law concerning sexual relations, the arguments he puts forward have to do with the harmfulness of "using" men and boys "like females" in sexual intercourse *(mixis aphrodisiōn)*: in the one seduced, how might a "courageous, manly disposition [*to tēs andreias ethos*] be formed? And in the seducer, what would nurture "the offspring of the idea of a moderate man"? "Everyone blames the softness of the one who gives in to the pleasures and is incapable of mastering them," and "reproves the resemblance in image of the one who undertakes the imitation of the female."[11]*

*In the *Phaedrus*, the physical form of the relation where a man behaves like a "four-footed beast" is said to be "unnatural."[12]

The problem of considering the boy as an object of pleasure was also manifested by a noticeable reticence on several points. There was a reluctance to evoke directly and in so many words the role of the boy in sexual intercourse: sometimes quite general expressions are employed, such as "to do the thing" *(diaprattesthai to pragma);*[13] other times the "thing" is designated by the very impossibility of naming it;[14] or again—and this is what says most about the problem posed by the relation—people resorted to metaphorical terms that were "agnostic" or political: "to yield," to "submit" *(hypē-retein),* "to render a service" *(therapeuein, hypourgein).*[15]

But there was also a reluctance to concede that the boy might experience pleasure. This "denial" should be interpreted both as the affirmation that such a pleasure could not exist and as the prescription that it ought not to be experienced. Having to explain why love so often turns into hatred when it is mediated by physical relations, Socrates, in Xenophon's *Symposium,* speaks of the unpleasant feelings that may arise in a youth because of his relationship *(homilein)* with an aging man. But he immediately adds as a general principle: "A youth does not share in the pleasure of the intercourse as a woman does, but looks on, sober, at another in love's intoxication."[16] Between the man and the boy, there is not—there cannot and should not be—a community of pleasure. The author of the *Problems* admits the possibility only for a few individuals and only in the case of an anatomical irregularity. And no one was more severely criticized than boys who showed by their willingness to yield, by their many relationships, or by their dress, their makeup, their adornments or their perfumes, that they might enjoy playing that role.

Which does not mean, however, that when the boy happened to give in, he had to do it coldly somehow. On the contrary, he was supposed to yield only if he had feelings of admiration, gratitude, or affection for his lover, which made him want to please the latter. The verb *charizesthai* was commonly employed in order to indicate the fact that the boy "complied" and "granted his favors."[17] The word does suggest that there was something other than a simple "surrender" by the beloved to the lover; the youth "granted his favors" through a movement that yielded to a desire and a demand on the part of the other, but was not of the same nature. It was a response; it was not the sharing of a sensation. The boy was not supposed to experience a physical pleasure; he was not even supposed quite to take pleasure in the man's pleasure; he was supposed to feel pleased about giving pleasure to the other, provided he yielded when he should—that is, not too hastily, nor too reluctantly either.

Sexual relations thus demanded particular behaviors on the part of both partners. A consequence of the fact that the boy could not identify with the part he had to play; he was supposed to refuse, resist, flee, escape.[18] He was also supposed to make his consent, if he finally gave it, subject to conditions relating to the man to whom he yielded (his merit, his status, his virtue) and to the benefit he could expect to gain from him (a benefit that was rather shameful if it was only a question of money, but honorable if it involved training for manhood, social connections for the future, or a lasting friendship). And in fact it was benefits of this kind that the lover was supposed to be able to provide, in addition to the customary gifts, which depended more on status considerations (and whose importance and value varied with the condition of the partners). So that the sexual act, in the relation between a man and a boy, needed to be taken up in a game of refusals, evasions, and escapes that tended to postpone it as long as possible, but also in a process of exchanges that determined the right time and the right conditions for it to take place.

Thus, the boy was expected to give—out of kindness and hence not for his own pleasure—something that his partner sought with a view to the pleasure he would enjoy; but the partner could not rightfully ask for it without a matching offer of presents, services, promises, and commitments that were altogether different in nature from the "gift" that was made to him. Which explains that tendency which was so visibly marked in Greek reflection on the love of boys: how was this relation to be integrated into a larger whole and enabled to transform itself into another type of relationship, a stable relationship where physical relations would no longer be important and where the two partners would be able to share the same feelings and the same possessions? The love of boys could not be morally honorable unless it comprised (as a result of the reasonable gifts and services of the lover and the reserved compliance of the beloved) the elements that would form the basis of a transformation of this love into a definitive and socially valuable tie, that of *philia*.

One would be quite mistaken to think that since the Greeks did not prohibit this kind of relationship, they did not worry about its implications. It "interested" them more than any other sexual relation, and there is every indication that they were anxious about it. But we can say that in a thinking such as ours, the relationship between two individuals of the same sex is questioned primarily from the viewpoint of the subject of desire: how can it be that in a man a desire forms whose object is another man? And we know very well that it is in a certain structuring of this desire (in its ambivalence, or in what it lacks) that the rudiments of an answer will be sought. The preoccupation of the Greeks, on the other hand, did not concern the desire that might incline an individual to this kind of relationship, nor did it concern the subject of this desire; their anxiety was focused on the object of pleasure, or more precisely, on that object insofar as he would have to become in turn the master in the pleasure that was enjoyed with others and in the power that was exercised over oneself.

It was here, at this point of problematization (how to make the object of pleasure into a subject who was in control of his pleasures), that philosophical erotics, or in any case Socratic-Platonic reflection on love, was to take its point of departure.

PART FIVE

True Love

Erotics, as a purposeful art of love (the love of boys in particular), will be our topic in this section as well. But this time it will be treated as a developmental context for the fourth of the great austerity themes that have run through the ethics of pleasure over the entire course of its history in the Western world. After the relation to the body and to health, after the relation to wives and to the institution of marriage, and after the relation to boys, to their freedom and their virility—three motifs in the problematization of sexual activity—I would like now to consider the relation to truth. For it is one of the most remarkable aspects of Greek reflection on the love of boys that not only does it show how—for reasons we have seen—this love constituted a sensitive point that demanded an elaboration of behavior and a rather delicate stylization of the use of the *aphrodisia,* but it was around this issue that the question of the relations between the use of pleasures and access to truth was developed, in the form of an inquiry into the nature of true love.

In the Christian and modern cultures these same questions —of truth, of love, and of pleasure—were to be framed, rather, in terms of the constituent elements of the man-woman relationship: the themes of virginity, of spiritual matrimony, of the soul-wife soon marked the shift from a basically masculine scene—occupied by the *erastes* and the *eromenos*—to one dominated by the figures of femininity and of the relationship between the two sexes.* Much later, *Faust* would be an example of the way in which the question of pleasure and that of access to knowledge would be linked to the theme of love for

*Which does not mean that the figures of male love disappeared entirely.[1]

woman, for her virginity, her purity, her fall, and her redemptive power. With the Greeks, on the other hand, reflection on the reciprocal ties between access to truth and sexual austerity seems to have been developed primarily in connection with the love of boys. Of course we have to make allowance for the fact that little has survived of the things that may have been said and recommended, in the Pythagorean circles of the period, concerning the relations between purity and knowledge. We also have to allow for the fact that we do not have the treatises on love that were written by Antisthenes, Diogenes the Cynic, Aristotle, or Theophrastus. It would be unwise, therefore, to generalize the particular features of the Socratic-Platonic doctrine, as if the latter provided a compendium of all the forms the philosophy of Eros may have taken in classical Greece. All the same, it did remain a pole of reflection for a very long time, as texts such as Plutarch's dialogue, Lucian's *Affairs of the Heart*, or the speeches of Maximus of Tyre show very well.

As it appears in the *Symposium* or the *Phaedrus* in any case, and considering the references it makes to other ways of discoursing on love, we can see the distance that separates this doctrine from the ordinary erotics that posed questions concerning the reciprocal good behavior of the young man and his suitor, and concerning the way in which behavior could accord with honor. We can also see how, while being deeply rooted in the habitual themes of the ethics of pleasure, it broached questions that would later have a very great importance for the transformation of this ethics into a morality of renunciation and for the constitution of a hermeneutics of desire.

An entire large section of the *Symposium* and of the *Phaedrus* is devoted to the "reproduction"—imitation or pastiche —of what was customarily said in speeches on love. The "reference speeches" of Phaedrus, Pausanias, Eryximachus, and Agathon in the *Symposium;* that of Lysias in the *Phaedrus;* and the first counter-speech by Socrates are of this type. They illuminate the background of the Platonic doctrine, the raw material that Plato elaborates and transforms when he replaces the problematics of "courtship" and honor with that of truth and ascesis. In these reference speeches, one element is essential: through the praise of love, of its power and its divinity, the question of consent comes up again and again: should the young man yield? To whom? In what conditions and with what guarantees? And can the individual who loves him justifiably hope to see him yield easily? A question characteristic of an erotics conceived as an art of give and take between the one who courts and the one who is courted.

It is this question that appears in the form of an absolutely general and amusingly tautological principle in the first speech of the *Symposium* at Agathon's house: "shame [*aischynē*] at what is disgraceful [*aischrois*] and ambition for what is noble";[2] but Pausanias immediately takes up the principle in a more serious way, differentiating between two loves, the one "whose only aim is the satisfaction of its desires," and the other which desires above all to test the soul.[3] We may also note that in the *Phaedrus* the first two speeches—both of which will be dismissed, the first becoming the object of an ironic recapitulation, and the second, that of a reparative palinode—pose, each in its own way, the question of "to whom should one yield?"; and that they answer the question by saying that one must yield to the person who loves. And all these first speeches appeal to a common thematics: that of transitory loves that disintegrate when the beloved comes of age, leaving him stranded;[4] that of dishonorable relations that place the boy under the domination of the lover,[5] compromise him in the eyes of everyone, and alienate him from his family or from honorable relations from which he could benefit;[6] that of the feelings of disgust and contempt the lover might have for the boy due to the satisfactions the latter grants him, or the feelings of hatred the young man might experience for the aging man who imposes disagreeable relations on him;[7] that of the feminine role the boy is led to assume, and the effects of physical and moral deterioration that this kind of relation invites;[8] that of the often burdensome compensations, benefits, and services that the lover must impose on himself, obligations that he tries to escape by abandoning his erstwhile companion to shame and solitude.[9] All of that constituted the elementary problematics of the pleasures and their use in the love of boys. It was these difficulties that the customs, courtship practices, and regulated games of love attempted to overcome.

One might think that Aristophanes' speech in the *Symposium* constituted an exception: in telling of the bisection of primeval human beings due to the wrath of the gods, their separation into two halves (males and females, or both halves being of the same sex, depending on whether the original individual was androgynous or entirely male or female), it seems to go far beyond the problems of the art of courtship. It raises the question of the nature of love; and it could pass for an amusing approach—ironically placed in the mouth of Aristophanes, the old adversary of Socrates—to the theses of Plato himself. Doesn't it speak of lovers who are searching for their lost half, just as Plato's souls remember and long for what used to be their homeland? However, restricting ourselves to the parts of the speech that concern male love, it is clear that Aristophanes also tends to answer the question of consent. And the thing that makes his speech and his irony unusual and a bit scandalous is that his answer is completely affirmative. Moreover, his mythical tale upsets the generally accepted principle of dissymmetry of age, feelings, and behavior between the lover and the beloved. He posits a symmetry and equality between the two, since he has them originate in the division of a single being; the same pleasure and the same desire attract the *erastes* and the *eromenos* to one another. A boy will naturally love men if he is half a male being: he will "take pleasure" in "lying beside males" and in "being entwined with them" *(sympeplegmenoi).*[10] And far from revealing a feminine nature, this shows that he is the mere "tally" of a being that is entirely male. And Plato amuses himself by having Aristophanes reverse the reproach that the latter, in his comedies, had so often aimed at the politicians of Athens: "in after years they are the only men who show any real manliness in public life."[11] In their youth they gave themselves to men because they were looking for their male half; for the same reason, once they are adults they will pursue boys. "Loving boys" and "cherishing lovers" (to be *paiderastēs* and *philerastēs*)[12] are the two sides of the same being. Hence, to the traditional question of consent, Aristophanes gives an answer that is direct, simple, and entirely affirmative, and he thereby abolishes the game of dissymmetries that structured the complex relations between man and boy: the whole question of love and right conduct thus becomes nothing more than the problem of finding one's lost half.

Now, Socratic-Platonic erotics is radically different: not only because of the solution it proposes, but also and especially because it tends to frame the question in very different terms. Knowing the nature of true love will no longer be a matter of answering the question: who must one love and under what conditions can love be honorable both for the beloved and for the lover? Or at least, all these questions will be subordinated to another, primary and fundamental question: what is love in its very being?[13]

In order to measure the Platonic elaboration and the distance that separates it from the prevailing erotics, it may be useful to recall the way in which Xenophon replies to this same question. He stresses the traditional elements: the opposition between the love that seeks only the pleasure of the lover and that which also manifests a concern for the beloved himself; the necessity of transforming ephemeral love into a mutual, egalitarian, and lasting friendship. In the *Symposium* and the *Memorabilia,* Xenophon presents a Socrates who draws a strict dividing line between love of the soul and love of the body, disqualifies the love of the body in his own person, makes love of the soul the true love and seeks in friendship *(philia)* the principle that gives value to every relation *(synousia).* [14] It follows that to join love of the soul to love of the body is not sufficient; one must rid every attachment of its physical dimensions (when one loves "the body and the soul at the same time," it is the first that will dominate, and the fading of youth causes friendship itself to wither away);[15] one should follow the example of Socrates and shun all contact, forgo the kisses that are likely to hinder the soul, and even take care that one's body doesn't touch another's, and doesn't feel its "bite."[16] In positive terms, every relationship must be based on the constituent elements of friendship: benefits and services rendered, efforts for the improvement of the boy one loves, mutual affection, a permanent bond established once and for all.[17] Does this mean that for Xenophon (or for the Socrates that Xenophon portrays) there should not be any *eros* between two men, but only a relationship of *philia?* This is in fact the ideal that Xenophon claims to recognize in the Sparta of Lycurgus.[18] According to him, Spartan men who were attracted to the bodies of boys were declared "vile," whereas people praised and encouraged "honest" adults who loved nothing but the soul of youths and aspired only to become friends with them; so that in Sparta "lovers were no less restrained in their love for children than were fathers with respect to their sons, or brothers with respect to their brothers." But in the *Symposium,* Xenophon gives a less schematic image of this division. He outlines a conception of *eros* and its pleasures that would have friendship itself as the goal. Friendship, insofar as it implies a life in common, reciprocal attention, kindness to one another, and shared feelings, is not made a substitute for love or something that would take over from it in due time. Xenophon makes it the very thing lovers should be enamored of: *erōntes tēs philias,* he says, employing a characteristic expression that makes it possible to save *eros,* to maintain its force, but without giving it a concrete content apart from the behavior that results from the mutual and lasting affection of friendship.[19]

Platonic erotics is constructed very differently, even if the starting point of reflection is in the familiar question of the place to assign the *aphrodisia* in the love relation. For in fact Plato takes up these traditional questions only in order to show how, in the hasty replies that are given to them, the basic problem is overlooked.

The first two speeches of the *Phaedrus*, the naive speech of Lysias and the facetious speech of Socrates, argue that a boy should not yield to the one who loves him. Such talk, Socrates remarks, cannot tell the truth: "False is the tale [*ouk esti etymos logos*] which says that because the lover is mad and the non-lover sane the non-lover should be given the preference when one might have a lover."[20] In contrary fashion, and out of a concern to praise love instead of offending it, the beginning speeches of the *Symposium* assert that it is fine to yield provided one does so in the right way, to a noble lover,[21] that there is nothing indecent or shameful in it, and that under the law of love "where there is mutual consent there is what the law proclaims to be right."[22] These speeches are more respectful of love, but that does not make them any more *etymoi* than those of Lysias and his ironic fault-finder in the *Phaedrus*.

Counterposed to them, the words of Diotima, reported in the *Symposium*, and the great fable of the *Phaedrus*, narrated by Socrates himself, stand as discourses *etymoi*: true discourses, and related by their origin to the truth that they tell. What makes them such? How are they different from the panegyrics or disqualifications that preceded them? The difference is not in the fact that Diotima or Socrates are more rigorous or more austere than the other interlocutors; they do not oppose these other speeches because the latter are too accommodating, making too much allowance for the body and the pleasures in a love that should be directed only to souls. They set themselves apart because they do not pose the problem in the same way; they carry out a certain number of basic transformations and displacements with regard to the game of questions that were traditional in discussions about love.

1. From the question of amorous behavior to an inquiry into the nature of love.   In the debate as it is formulated in the other speeches, love and the intense and forceful movement that takes hold of the lover are presupposed; this love "being granted,"[23] the main point of preoccupation is in knowing how the two partners ought to conduct themselves; how, in what form, to what extent, with the help of what means of persuasion or by giving what assurances of friendship, should the lover seek to attain "that to which he aspires"; and how, in what conditions, after what resistances and tests, should the beloved yield? A question of conduct, grounded in a preexisting love. Now, the subject of Diotima and Socrates' inquiry is the very being of this love, its nature and its origin, that which makes it strong, and that which moves it so stubbornly or so madly toward its object: "What is the essential nature of Love, what are his characteristics, and then what are his works?"[24] An ontological inquiry and no longer a question of deontology. All the other interlocutors orient their speeches toward praise or criticism, toward the division between good and bad love, toward the delimitation of what one should and should not do; in the customary thematics with its search for appropriateness and its elaboration of an art of courtship, the primary object of reflection is conduct or the game of reciprocal conducts. Plato puts this question aside, at least provisionally, and, going beyond the division of good and bad, he raises the question of what it means to love.*

Now, to state the question in this way implies, first of all, a displacement of the very object of discourse. Diotima reproaches Socrates—and in fact all the authors of the preceding encomiums—for having looked to the "beloved" object *(ton erōmenon)* for the principle of what needed to be said about love; they thus let themselves be blinded by the charm, beauty, and perfection of the beloved boy, and they mistakenly attributed his merits to love itself; the latter will manifest its

---

*After Phaedrus' speeches, Socrates points out that there has to be in the mind of the speaker "knowledge of the truth about the subject of the speech."[25]

characteristic truth only if that truth is sought in its nature and not in its object. So it is necessary to leave off thinking about the beloved and redirect one's inquiry to the one who loves *(to erōn)*, questioning him in his own condition.[26] The same thing will be done in the *Phaedrus* when, replying to the first two counter-panegyrics, Socrates makes his long detour via the theory of souls. But as a result of this displacement, the discourse on love will have to face the risk of being nothing more than an "encomium" (in the composite form of praise addressed both to love and to the beloved); it will have to speak—as in the *Symposium*—of the "intermediate" nature of love, the deficiency that characterizes it (since it does not possess the beautiful things that it desires), the parentage of poverty and contrivance, of ignorance and knowledge from which it is born; it will also have to speak, as in the *Symposium,* of the way in which forgetfulness and remembrance of the supracelestial vision are mixed in love, and of the long road of suffering that will lead it finally to its goal.

2. From the question of the boy's honor to that of love of truth. To say, as Diotima does, that it is better to turn one's thoughts from the beloved object to the loving principle does not mean that the question of the object is no longer posed: on the contrary, the whole development that follows that basic formulation is devoted to determining what is loved when there is love. But as soon as one undertakes to speak of love in a discourse that aims to define its nature instead of praising that which one loves, the question of the object will be posed in different terms.

In the traditional debate, the starting point for inquiry was on the side of the love object itself: given what the person whom one loved was, and what he was supposed to be—the beauty not only of his body but of his soul, the education that he needed, the free, noble, manly, and courageous character he must acquire—what form of love was honorable, for him and for the lover? It was respect for the beloved, for his real nature, that ought to give its own form and its sober style to whatever one might ask of him. In the Platonic inquiry, on the other hand, it is reflection on the nature of love itself that ought to lead to a true determination of its object. Beyond the different beautiful objects that the amorous individual may become attached to, Diotima shows Socrates that love seeks to beget spiritual children, and to contemplate "absolute beauty" in its true nature, in its unalloyed purity, and in the "oneness of its form." And in the *Phaedrus,* it is Socrates himself who shows how the soul, if it has a strong enough memory of what it has seen beyond the heavens, if it is energetically driven, and if it does not allow impure appetites to rob it of its momentum, will attach itself to the beloved object only insofar as the latter reflects and imitates beauty itself.

One does find in Plato the theme that love should be directed to the soul of boys rather than to their bodies. But he was not the first or the only one to say this. It was a theme that ran through the traditional discussions on love, with consequences that varied in their rigor. Attributing the theme to Socrates, Xenophon gives it a radical form. What is peculiar to Plato is not the dichotomy, but the way in which he establishes the inferiority of love for bodies. He bases this notion not on the dignity of the boy who is loved, but on that which, in the lover himself, determines the nature and form of his love (his desire for immortality, his yearning for the beautiful in its purity, the recollection of what he has seen beyond the heavens). Moreover (and both the *Symposium* and the *Phaedrus* are quite explicit on this point), he does not trace a clear, definitive, and uncrossable dividing line between the bad love of the body and the glorious love of the soul; however devalued and inferior the relation to the body compared with that motion toward beauty, and however dangerous it can sometimes be since it cannot deflect and stop that motion, it is not excluded out of hand or condemned for all time. From one beautiful body to other beautiful bodies, according to the famous formula of the *Symposium,* and on to the beauty that is found in "occupations," "rules of conduct," "the sciences," the motion is continuous, until one gazes at last upon "the vast ocean of beauty."[27] And the same holds for the *Phaedrus*. While it praises the courage and perfection of souls who have not yielded, it does not promise punishment for those who, leading a life devoted to honor rather than to philosophy, let themselves be taken by surprise, so that, carried away by their passion, they chance to "commit the thing." No doubt, at the moment when their souls leave their bodies, their lives here below having run their course, they will find themselves without wings (unlike what happens to those who have remained "masters of themselves"). So they will not be compelled to voyage in the underworld; the two lovers will accompany one another on the voyage beneath the heavens, until they in turn receive wings, "because of their love."[28] For Plato, it is not exclusion of the body that characterizes true love in a fundamental way; it is rather that, beyond the appearances of the object, love is a relation to truth.

3. *From the question of the dissymmetry of partners to that of the convergence of love.* According to accepted conventions, it was understood that the *Eros* came from the lover; as for the beloved, he could not be an active subject of love on the same basis as the *erastes*. Doubtless a corresponding attachment, an *Anteros,* was expected of him. But the nature of this response was problematic: it could not be exactly symmetrical to that which gave rise to it; more than the lover's desire and pleasure, it was his benevolence, his good turns, his tender care, and his example that the boy was supposed to reciprocate, and it was necessary to await the time when the transports of love would cease and age would calm the passions and so remove the dangers before the two friends could become bound to one another by a relationship of exact reciprocity.

But if Eros was a relation to truth, the two lovers could only be rejoined provided that the beloved too had been moved in the direction of truth by the force of the same Eros. In Platonic erotics, the beloved cannot settle into the position of object in relation to the other's love, simply waiting to receive, by the terms of the exchange to which he is entitled (since he is loved), the counsel he needs and the knowledge to which he aspires. It is right that he should actually become a subject in this love relation. In fact, this is the reason for the reversal, toward the end of the third speech of the *Phaedrus,* that changes the focus of the discussion from the lover to the one who is loved. Socrates has described the journey, the fervor, and the suffering of the one who loves, and the hard struggle he has had to conduct in order to gain control of his team. Now he turns his attention to the loved one: the young boy's companions have perhaps made him think that it is not good to yield to a lover; nevertheless he begins to accept the company of his lover; the latter's presence excites him to distraction; he in his turn feels uplifted by the rising wave of desire, wings and plumage start to grow in his soul.[29] Of course, he still does not know the true nature of that which he longs for, and he finds no words with which to name it; but he "throws his arms" around his lover and "gives him kisses."[30] This moment is important: unlike what occurs in the art of courtship, the "dialectic of love" in this case calls for two movements exactly alike on the part of the two lovers; the love is the same for both of them, since it is the motion that carries them toward truth.

4. *From the virtue of the loved boy to the master's love and wisdom.* In the art of courtship, it fell to the lover to do the wooing; and even though he was expected to keep control of himself, it was clear that the compelling force of his love risked overcoming him in spite of himself. The solid point of resistance was the boy's honor, his dignity, the reasonable obstinacy with which he might refuse. But from the moment when Eros appeals to truth, it is the one who is the more advanced on the road of love, the one who is more truly

enamored of truth, who will best be able to guide the other and help him to keep from degrading himself in all the base pleasures. The one who is better versed in love will also be the master of truth; and it will be his role to teach the loved one how to triumph over his desires and become "stronger than himself." In the love relation, and as a consequence of that relation to truth which now structures it, a new figure makes its appearance: that of the master, coming to take the place of the lover; moreover, this personage, through the complete mastery that he exercises over himself, will turn the game upside down, reverse the roles, establish the principle of a renunciation of the *aphrodisia,* and become, for all young men who are eager for truth, an object of love.

This is doubtless the meaning that should be given to the description, in the last pages of the *Symposium,* of the relations that Socrates maintains not only with Alcibiades, but also with Charmides, the son of Glaucon; with Euthydemus, the son of Diocles; and with many others in addition.[31] The distribution of roles is completely reversed: it is the young boys—those who are beautiful, with many suitors—who are enamored of Socrates; they dog his footsteps, they try to seduce him, they would like very much to grant him their favors —that is, for him to communicate the treasure of his wisdom. They are in the position of *erastes,* and he, the old man with the ugly body, is in the position of *eromenos.* But what they are not aware of, and what Alcibiades discovers in the course of the famous "test," is that Socrates is loved by them only to the extent that he is able to resist their seduction; which does not mean that he feels no love or desire for them, but that he is moved by the force of true love, and that he knows how truly to love the truth that must be loved. Diotima had said this before: it was he who was wisest of all on the subject of love. Henceforth the master's wisdom (and no longer the boy's honor) would mark both the object of true love and the principle that kept one from "yielding."

The Socrates that appears in this passage is invested with

powers that are characteristic of the traditional figure of the *theios anēr:* physical endurance, the ability to make oneself indifferent to sensations, and the power to absent oneself from the body and to concentrate all the soul's energy on oneself.[32] But it should be understood that these powers are operative here in the quite particular game of Eros; they ensure the domination that Socrates is able to exercise over himself in the game; and hence they qualify him as the highest object of love to which young men might appeal, but at the same time, as the only one who can guide their love all the way to truth. Into the lover's game where different dominations confronted one another (that of the lover seeking to get control of the beloved, that of the beloved seeking to escape, and seeking, by means of his resistance, to enslave the lover), Socrates introduces another type of domination: that which is exercised by the master of truth and for which he is qualified by the dominion he exercises over himself.

Platonic erotics can thus be considered from three viewpoints. First, it is a way of responding to an inherent difficulty, for Greek culture, in relationships between men and boys: namely, the question of what status to give the latter as objects of pleasure. From this angle, Plato's answer seems only more complex and more elaborate than those that might have been put forward in the various "debates" on love, or—by "Socrates"—in the texts of Xenophon. Actually, Plato resolves the difficulty of the object of pleasure by bringing the question of the loved individual back to the nature of love itself; by structuring the love relation as a relation to truth; by doubling it and placing it in the one who is loved as well as in the one who is in love; and by reversing the role of the loved young man, making him a lover of the master of truth. In this sense, one can say that it meets the challenge that was issued by Aristophanes' fable: it gives the latter a true content. It shows how it is indeed the same love which, in the same movement, can make a man both *paiderastēs* and *philerastēs.* The dissymmetries, the disparities, the resistances, and the evasions that organized the always difficult relations between the *erastes* and the *eromenos*—the active subject and the pursued object—in the practice of love no longer have any justification; or rather, they can develop according to a completely different movement, by taking a completely different form, and by imposing a quite different game: that of a process in which the master of truth teaches the boy the meaning of wisdom.

But it becomes apparent that Platonic erotics—and this is the other side of it—thereby introduces the question of truth into the love relation as a fundamental question. And this is in an altogether different form from that of the *logos* to which it is necessary to submit one's appetites in the use of pleasures. The lover's task, the accomplishment of which will in fact enable him to reach his goal, is to recognize the true nature of the love that has seized him. And here the answer to the challenge of Aristophanes transforms the answer the latter gave: it is not the other half of himself that the individual seeks in the other person; it is the truth to which his soul is related. Hence the ethical work he will have to do will be to discover and hold fast, without ever letting go, to that relation to truth which was the hidden medium of his love. And one thus sees how Platonic reflection tends to detach itself from a common problematization that revolved around the object and the status that ought to be given to him, in order to open a line of inquiry concerning love, which will revolve around the subject and the truth he is capable of.

Socratic erotics, in the form that Plato gives it, does deal with questions that were customary in discussions on love. But it does not undertake to define proper conduct, where the sufficiently long resistance of the beloved would counterbalance the sufficiently valuable services of the lover. It tries to determine the self-movement, the kind of effort and work upon oneself, which will enable the lover to elicit and establish his relation to true being. Instead of attempting once and for all to draw the line separating that which is honorable from that which brings disgrace, it endeavors to describe the progress of desire—with its difficulties, its ups and downs, and its setbacks—that leads to the point where it reencounters its own nature. The *Symposium* and the *Phaedrus* indicate a transition from an erotics structured in terms of "courtship" practice and recognition of the other's freedom, to an erotics centered on an ascesis of the subject and a common access to truth. The inquiry is thereby displaced: in reflection on the *chrēsis aphrodisiōn,* it dealt with pleasure and its dynamics, the just practice and the right distribution of which were to be ensured through self-mastery. In the Platonic reflection on love, the inquiry concerns the desire that must be led to its true object (which is truth) by recognizing it for what it truly is. The life of moderation, of *sōphrosynē,* as it is described in the *Laws,* is a life "that is mild in every way, with gentle pains and gentle pleasures, a life characterized by desires that are mild [*ēremaiai hēdonai, malakai epithumiai*] and loves that are not mad [*erōtes ouk emmaneis*]";[33] this statement speaks of an economy of pleasures ensured by the control that is exercised by oneself over oneself. To the soul whose voyage and amorous strivings are described by the *Phaedrus,* it is also recommended, if she is to receive her reward beyond the heavens, to practice "an orderly regimen" *(tetagmenē diaitē)* that is possible because she is "mistress of herself" and she is "heedful of measure," she has "subjected the power of evil" and "liberated the power of virtue."[34] But the struggle she has been able to sustain against the violence of her appetites, she would not have been able to conduct it without a twofold relation to truth: a relation to her own desire questioned in its being, and a relation to the object of her desire recognized as a true being.

Thus, we see where ground is broken for a future inquiry into desiring man. Which does not mean that Platonic erotics has suddenly and permanently taken leave of the ethics of pleasures and their use. We shall see on the contrary that the latter continued to develop and transform itself. But the tradition of thought that stems from Plato was to play an important role when, much later, the problematization of sexual behavior would be reworked in terms of the concupiscent soul and the deciphering of its arcana.

This philosophical reflection concerning boys suggests a historical paradox. To this male love, and more precisely to this love of young boys and adolescents—a love that was later to be so severely condemned for such a long time—the Greeks granted a legitimacy, which we are fond of seeing as proof of the freedom they granted themselves in this domain. And yet it was in connection with this love, much more than with health (which also preoccupied them) and much more than with women and marriage (the orderliness of which they nevertheless sought to maintain), that they spoke of the need to practice the strictest austerities. To be sure, except in a few instances, they did not condemn it or prohibit it. And yet it is in the reflection on love of boys that one sees the principle of "indefinite abstention" formulated; the ideal of a renunciation, which Socrates exemplifies by his faultless resistance of temptation; and the theme that this renunciation has a high spiritual value by itself. In a way that may be surprising at first, one sees the formation, in Greek culture and in connection with the love of boys, of some of the major elements of a sexual ethics that will renounce that love by appealing to the above principle: the requirement of a symmetry and reciprocity in the love relationship; the necessity of a long and arduous struggle with oneself; the gradual purification of a love that is addressed only to being per se, in its truth; and man's inquiry into himself as a subject of desire.

One would be missing the crucial point if one imagined that the love of boys gave rise to its own interdiction, or that an ambiguity peculiar to philosophy accepted its reality only by demanding its supercession. One should keep in mind that this "asceticism" was not a means of disqualifying the love of boys; on the contrary, it was a means of stylizing it and hence, by giving it shape and form, of valorizing it. The fact remains, however, that within this asceticism total abstention was posited as a standard and privilege was given to the question of desire, so that elements were introduced that could not easily be accommodated in an ethics organized around a search for the right use of pleasures.

Conclusion

Thus, in the field of practices that they singled out for special attention (regimen, household management, the "courting" of young men) and in the context of the discourses that tended to elaborate these practices, the Greeks questioned themselves about sexual behavior as an ethical problem, and they sought to define the form of moderation that it required.

This does not mean that the Greeks in general concerned themselves with sexual pleasure only from these three points of view. One would find in the literature that they have left us much evidence of other themes and preoccupations. But restricting oneself, as I have tried to do here, to the prescriptive discourses by which they attempted to reflect on and regulate their sexual conduct, these three focuses of problematization appear to have been the most important ones by far. Around them, the Greeks developed arts of living, of conducting themselves, and of "using pleasures" according to austere and demanding principles.

At first glance, one can have the impression that these three different forms of reflection bear a close resemblance to the forms of austerity that will be found later, in the Western, Christian societies. In any case, one may be tempted to correct the still rather commonly accepted notion of an opposition between a pagan thought that "tolerated" the practice of "sexual freedom" and the gloomy and restrictive moralities that succeeded it. In fact, though, it is important to recognize that the principle of a rigorous and diligently practiced sexual moderation is a precept that does not date either from Christian times, obviously, or from late antiquity, or even from the rigorist movements—such as were associated with the Stoics, for example—of the Hellenistic and Roman age. As early as the fourth century, one finds very clearly formulated the idea that sexual activity is sufficiently hazardous and costly in itself, and sufficiently linked to the loss of the vital substance, to require a meticulous economy that would discourage unnecessary indulgence. One also finds the model of a matrimonial relationship that would demand a similar abstention from all "extramarital" pleasure by either spouse. Furthermore, one finds the theme of the man's renunciation of all physical relations with a boy. A general principle of moderation, a suspicion that sexual pleasure might be an evil, the schema of a strict monogamous fidelity, the ideal of an absolute chastity: obviously it was not according to such a model that the Greeks lived; but isn't it the case that the philosophical, moral, and medical thought that formed in their midst formulated some of the basic principles that later ethics—and particularly those found in the Christian societies—seem to have only had to revive? We cannot stop there, however; the prescriptions may be formally alike, but this actually shows only the poverty and monotony of interdictions. The way in which sexual activity was constituted, recognized, and organized as a moral issue is not identical from the mere fact that what was allowed or prohibited, recommended or discouraged is identical.

We have seen how sexual behavior was constituted, in Greek thought, as a domain of ethical practice in the form of the *aphrodisia,* of pleasurable acts situated in an agonistic field of forces difficult to control. In order to take the form of a conduct that was rationally and morally admissible, these acts required a strategy of moderation and timing, of quantity and opportunity; and this strategy aimed at an exact self-mastery —as its culmination and consummation—whereby the subject would be "stronger than himself" even in the power that he exercised over others. Now, the requirement of austerity that was implied by the constitution of this self-disciplined subject was not presented in the form of a universal law, which each and every individual would have to obey, but rather as a principle of stylization of conduct for those who wished to give their existence the most graceful and accomplished form possible. If one wanted to assign an origin to those few great themes that shaped our sexual morality (the idea that pleasure belongs to the dangerous domain of evil, the obligation to practice monogamous fidelity, the exclusion of partners of the same sex), not only would it be a mistake to attribute them to that fiction called "Judeo-Christian" morality, it would be a bigger mistake to look behind them for the timeless operation of prohibition, or the permanent form of law. The sexual austerity that was prematurely recommended by Greek philosophy is not rooted in the timelessness of a law that would take the historically diverse forms of repression, one after the other. It belongs to a history that is more decisive for comprehending the transformations of moral experience than the history of codes: a history of "ethics," understood as the elaboration of a form of relation to self that enables an individual to fashion himself into a subject of ethical conduct.

Further, each of the three great arts of self-conduct, the three major techniques of the self, that were developed in Greek thought—dietetics, economics, and erotics—proposed, if not a particular sexual ethics, then at least a singular modulation of sexual conduct. In this elaboration of the demands of austerity, not only did the Greeks not seek to define a code of conducts binding everyone, neither did they seek to organize sexual behavior as a domain governed in all its aspects by one and the same set of principles.

In dietetics, one finds a form of moderation defined by the measured and timely use of the *aphrodisia;* the practice of this moderation called for an attention centered mainly on the question of "the right time" and on the correlation between the variable states of the body and the changing proprieties of the seasons. And at the core of this preoccupation there was manifested a fear of violence, a dread of exhaustion, and a twofold anxiety about the survival of the individual and the maintenance of the species. In economics, one finds a form of moderation defined not by the mutual faithfulness of marriage partners, but by a certain privilege, which the husband upholds on behalf of the lawful wife over whom he exercises his authority; the temporal objective in this case is not to seize the opportune moment, but to maintain, throughout life, a certain hierarchical structure appropriate to the household; it is with a view to ensuring this permanence that the man must fear all excess and practice self-control in the control he exercises over others. Lastly, the moderation that is required by erotics is of another type still, for even though it does not call for pure and simple abstention, we have seen that it tends in that direction and that it carries with it the ideal of a renunciation of all physical relations with boys. This erotics is linked to a perception of time that is very different from that found in connection with the body and with marriage: it experiences a fleeting time that leads ineluctably to an end that is near. As for the concern that animates it, it is that of the respect that is owing to the virility of the adolescent and to his future status as a free man. It is no longer simply the problem of a man's becoming the master of his pleasure; it is a problem of knowing how one can make allowance for the other's freedom in the mastery that one exercises over oneself and in the true love that one bears for him. And finally, it is in this reflection concerning the love of boys that Platonic erotics raises the question of the complex relations between love, the renunciation of pleasures, and access to truth.

It may be useful to recall something that K. J. Dover has written: "The Greeks neither inherited nor developed a belief that a divine power had revealed to mankind a code of laws for the regulation of sexual behavior; they had no religious institution possessed of the authority to enforce sexual prohibitions. Confronted by cultures older and richer and more elaborate than theirs, cultures which nonetheless differed greatly from each other, the Greeks felt free to select, adapt, develop and—above all—innovate."[1] For them, reflection on sexual behavior as a moral domain was not a means of internalizing, justifying, or formalizing general interdictions imposed on everyone; rather, it was a means of developing—for the smallest minority of the population, made up of free, adult males—an aesthetics of existence, the purposeful art of a freedom perceived as a power game. Their sexual ethics, from which our own derives in part, rested on a very harsh system of inequalities and constraints (particularly in connection with women and slaves); but it was problematized in thought as the relationship, for a free man, between the exercise of his freedom, the forms of his power, and his access to truth.

Taking a very schematic, bird's-eye view of the history of this ethics and its transformations over a long period of time, one notes first of all a shift of emphasis. It is clear that in classical Greek thought it was the relationship with boys that constituted the most delicate point, and the most active focus of reflection and elaboration; it was here that the problematization called for the most subtle forms of austerity. Now, surveying the course of a very slow evolution, we can see this focus move elsewhere: it is around women that, little by little, the problems come to be centered. This does not mean that the love of boys will no longer be practiced, nor that it will cease to be expressed, nor that people will no longer raise questions about it. But it is women and the relation to women that will be stressed in moral reflection on sexual pleasures, whether in the form of the theme of virginity, of the importance assumed by marital conduct, or of the value attributed to relations of symmetry and reciprocity between husband and wife. And we can see a new shift of the focus of problematization (this time from women to the body) in the interest that was shown, starting in the seventeenth and eighteenth centuries, in the sexuality of children, and, generally speaking, in the relationships between sexual behavior, normality, and health.

But at the same time as these shifts, a certain unification occurred between the elements that were distributed among the different "arts" of using the pleasures. There was a doctrinal unification—brought about in part by Saint Augustine— that made it possible to conceptualize, as parts of the same theoretical ensemble, the game of death and immortality, the institution of marriage, and the conditions of access to truth. But there was also a "practical" unification that recentered the different arts of existence around the decipherment of the self, purification procedures, and struggles against concupiscence. So that what was now at the core of the problematization of sexual conduct was no longer pleasure and the aesthetics of its use, but desire and its purifying hermeneutics.

This change was the result of a whole series of transformations. We have evidence of the beginnings of these transformations, even before the development of Christianity, in the reflection of the moralists, philosophers, and doctors of the first two centuries of our era.

Notes

For titles briefly cited here, fuller references are given in the Bibliography.

INTRODUCTION

Chapter 2: Forms of Problematization

1. Aretaeus, *On the Causes and Signs of Chronic Diseases,* II, 5.
2. L. Renaud, in ibid, French trans., p. 163.
3. Saint Francis of Sales, *Introduction to the Devout Life,* III, 39.
4. Pliny, *Natural History,* VIII, 5, 13.
5. Plutarch, *Life of Cato the Younger,* VII.
6. Isocrates, *To Nicocles,* 36.
7. Aristotle, *Politics,* VII, 14, 1335b.
8. H. Dauvergne, *Les Forçats,* p. 289.
9. Apuleius, *The Golden Ass,* VIII, 26ff.; Dio Chrysostom, *Fourth Discourse, On Kingship,* 101–115; Epictetus, *Discourses,* III, 1.
10. Seneca the Elder, *Controversiae,* I, Preface, 8.
11. Plato, *Phaedrus,* 239c–d.
12. Aristophanes, *The Thesmophoriazusae,* v. 130ff.
13. Philostratus, *The Life of Apollonius of Tyana,* I, 13.
14. Xenophon, *Agesilaus,* 5.
15. Plato, *Symposium,* 217a–219e.
16. See G. Duby, *Le Chevalier, la femme et le prêtre.*

PART ONE: THE MORAL PROBLEMATIZATION OF PLEASURES

Introduction

1. E. Leski, "Die Zeugungslehre der Antike," p. 1248.
2. See K. J. Dover, "Classical Greek Attitudes to Sexual Behavior," p. 59; *Greek Popular Morality,* p. 205; and *Greek Homosexuality,* p. 63.

Chapter 1: *Aphrodisia*

1. Xenophon, *Memorabilia,* I, 3, 13.
2. K. J. Dover, *Greek Popular Morality,* pp. 206–207.
3. See K. J. Dover, *Greek Homosexuality,* p. 4ff.
4. Saint Augustine, *Confessions,* IV, chap. 8–10.
5. Aristotle, *Nicomachean Ethics,* III, 10, 1118a–b.
6. Aristotle, *Eudemian Ethics,* III, 2, 8–9, 1230b.
7. Aristotle, *Nicomachean Ethics,* III, 10, 1118a–b. See also Aristotle (attributed), *Problems,* XXVIII, 2.
8. Xenophon, *Memorabilia,* I, 3, 12–13.
9. On the dangers of music, see Plato, *Republic,* III, 398e (the Lydian modes are harmful even to women, let alone men). On the mnemonic role of odors and of the visual image, see Aristotle, *Nicomachean Ethics,* III, 10, 1118a.
10. One finds a reproach of this kind repeated much later in the *Affairs of the Heart* (attributed to Lucian), 53.
11. Aristotle, *History of Animals,* V, 2, 539b.
12. Ibid., VI, 18, 571b and 572b.
13. Aristotle, *Parts of Animals,* 660b.
14. Plato, *Philebus,* 44ff.
15. Plato, *Gorgias,* 484d and 491d; *Symposium,* 196c; *Phaedrus,* 237d; *Republic,* IV, 430e and 431 c–d; IX, 571b; *Laws,* I, 647e; IV, 714a; VI, 782e; VII, 802e and 864b; X, 886b, etc. See also Aristotle, *Nicomachean Ethics,* VII, 4, 1148a.
16. Xenophon, *Memorabilia,* I, 2, 23; I, 4, 14; I, 8; IV, 5, 3, etc.
17. On Episthenes, see Xenophon, *Anabasis,* VII, 4; on Menon, ibid., II, 6.
18. On Agesilaus, see Xenophon, *Agesilaus,* V; on Arcesilaus, see Diogenes Laertius, *Lives of Eminent Philosophers,* IV, 6. Plu-

tarch notes, similarly, that Hypereides was given over to the *aphrodisia*.

19. Plato, *Laws*, I, 636c.
20. One finds a similar explanation for the emergence of love for boys through excessive self-indulgence in Dio Chrysostom, *Discourses*, VII, 150.
21. Plato, *Timaeus*, 86c–e.
22. Aristotle, *Nicomachean Ethics*, III, 11, 1118b.
23. Ibid., VII, 5, 1148b; X, 3, 1173b. On the question of desire, its natural objects, and its variations, see Plato, *Republic*, IV, 437c–d.
24. Aristotle, *History of Animals*, VIII, 1, 581a. Plato, in the *Republic* (IV, 426a–b), talks about sick individuals who, instead of following a regimen, continue to eat, drink, and *aphrodisiazein*.
25. Xenophon, *Symposium*, IV, 38; Aristotle (attributed), *On Sterility*, V, 636b.
26. Aristotle, *History of Animals*, IX, 5, 637a; VII, 1, 581b.
27. Xenophon, *Hiero*, III, 4.
28. Aristotle (attributed), *Problems*, IV, 26.
29. P. Manuli, "Fisiologia e patologia del feminile negli scritti hippocratici," p. 393ff.
30. Aristotle, *Generation of Animals*, I, 21, 729b.
31. Hippocrates, *Oath*, I, p. 300.
32. Plato, *Symposium*, 189d–193d. Regarding a mythical time when there was no sexual generation, see Plato, *Politics*, 271a–272b.
33. Aristotle, *Generation of Animals*, II, 1, 731b; cf. *On the Soul*, II, 4, 415a–b.
34. Plato, *Republic*, VIII, 559c; Aristotle, *Nicomachean Ethics*, VII, 4, 1147b.
35. Rufus of Ephesus, *Oeuvres*, p. 318.
36. Diogenes Laertius, *Lives of Eminent Philosophers*, IV, chap. 6.
37. On this sort of pleasure as a characteristic held in common with animals, see Xenophon, *Hiero*, VII; on the mixed character of physical pleasure, see Plato, *Republic*, IX, 538b ff; on pleasure accompanying the restoration of a previous bodily state, see Plato, *Timaeus*, 64d–65a; Aristotle, *Nicomachean Ethics*, VII, 4, 1147b.
38. Plato, *Laws*, I, 636c.
39. Ibid., VI, 783a–b.

40. Plato, *Republic*, III, 403a.
41. On hyperbole *(hyperbolē, hyperballein)* of pleasures, see, for example, Plato, *Republic*, III, 402e; *Timaeus*, 86b; Aristotle, *Nicomachean Ethics*, III, 11, 1118b; VII, 4, 1148a; VII, 7, 1150b. On revolt *(epanastasis, stasiazein)*, see Plato, *Republic*, IV, 442d; IV, 444b; IX, 586e; *Phaedrus*, 237d.
42. Plato, *Laws*, VI, 783a; Aristotle, *Nicomachean Ethics*, III, 12, 1119b; Diogenes Laertius, *Lives of Eminent Philosophers*, II, 8.
43. Xenophon, *Memorabilia*, I, 3, 15.
44. Plato, *Republic*, 111, 389e; see also IX, 580e.
45. Aristotle, *Nicomachean Ethics*, III, 11, 1118b.
46. Ibid., III, 9–10, 118a.
47. Plato, *Symposium*, 187e.
48. Aristotle, *Nicomachean Ethics*, VII, 14, 1154a.

Chapter 2: *Chrēsis*

1. Aristotle, *History of Animals*, VII, 1, 581b; *Generation of Animals*, II, 7, 747a.
2. Plato, *Republic*, V, 451c.
3. Polybius, *The Histories*, VI, 7.
4. Aristotle, *Rhetoric*, I, 9. On the notion of *nomos*, see J. de Romilly, *La Loi dans la pensée grecque*.
5. Diogenes Laertius, *Lives of Eminent Philosophers*, VI, 2, 46. See also Dio Chrysostom, *Discourses*, VI, 17–20; Galen, *On the Affected Parts*, VI, 5.
6. Diogenes Laertius, *Lives of Eminent Philosophers*, VI, 2, 69.
7. Xenophon, *Symposium*, IV, 38.
8. Xenophon, *Memorabilia*, I, 3, 14.
9. Ibid., II, 1, 33.
10. Ibid., IV, 5, 9.
11. See Plato, *Gorgias*, 492a–b, 494c, 507e; *Republic*, VIII, 561b.
12. Xenophon, *Memorabilia*, II, 1, 30.
13. Ibid., IV, 5, 9.
14. Ibid., I, 3, 5.
15. Plato, *Laws*, I, 636d–e. On the notion of *kairos* and its importance in Greek ethics, see P. Aubenque, *La Prudence chez Aristotle*, p. 95ff.

16. Aristotle, *History of Animals,* VII, 1, 582a.

17. Plutarch, *Table-Talks,* III, 6.

18. Xenophon, *Cyropaedia,* VIII.

19. Xenophon, *Memorabilia,* IV, 4, 21–23.

20. Plato, *Symposium,* 180c–181a, 183d; Demosthenes, *Erotic Essay,* 4.

21. Ibid., 34–35.

22. Xenophon, *Hiero,* VII.

23. Xenophon, *Agesilaus,* V.

24. Xenophon, *Memorabilia,* II, 6, 1–5.

25. Ibid., II, 1, 1–4.

26. Ibid., I, 5, 1.

27. Plato, *Republic,* IV, 431c–d.

Chapter 3: *Enkrateia*

1. Xenophon, *Cyropaedia,* VIII, 1, 30. On the notion of *sōphrosynē* and its evolution, see H. North, *Sōphrosynē;* the author emphasizes the proximity of the two words *sōphrosynē* and *enkrateia* in Xenophon (pp. 123–132).

2. Plato, *Gorgias,,* 491d.

3. Plato, *Republic,* IV, 430e.

4. Plato, *Gorgias,* 507a–b.

5. Plato, *Laws,* III, 697b.

6. H. North, *Sōphrosynē,* pp. 202–203.

7. Aristotle, *Nicomachean Ethics,* III, 11 and 12, 1118b–1119a; VII, 7, 1150a–1152a.

8. Plato, *Laws,* I, 647d.

9. Antiphon, in Stobaeus, *Florilegium,* V, 33. This is fragment no. 16.

10. Xenophon, *Hiero,* VII; Aristotle, *Nicomachean Ethics,* III, 10, 1117b.

11. One thus finds a whole series of words like *agein, ageisthai* ("to lead; to be led"): Plato, *Protagoras,* 355a; *Republic,* IV, 431e; Aristotle, *Nicomachean Ethics,* VII, 7, 3, 1150a. On *kolazein* ("to hold in check, keep in"): Plato, *Gorgias,* 491e; *Republic,* VIII, 559b; IX, 571b. On *antiteinein* ("to oppose"): Aristotle, *Nicomachean Ethics,* VII, 2, 4, 1146a; VII, 7, 5, and 6, 1150b.

On *ephrassein* ("to obstruct"): Antiphon, fragments no. 15 and 16. On *antechein* ("to resist"): Aristotle, *Nicomachean Ethics*, VII, 7, 4, and 6, 1150a–b.

12. On *nikan* ("to defeat"): Plato, *Phaedrus*, 238c; *Laws*, I, 634b; VIII, 634b; Aristotle, *Nicomachean Ethics*, VII, 7, 1150a: VII, 9, 1151a; Antiphon, fragment no. 15. On *kratein* ("to rule"): Plato, *Protagoras*, 353c; *Phaedrus*, 237a–238a; *Republic*, IV, 431a–c; *Laws*, 840c; Xenophon, *Memorabilia*, I, 2, 24; Antiphon, fragments no. 15 and 16; Aristotle, *Nicomachean Ethics*, VII, 4c, 1148a. On *hēttasthai* ("to be defeated"): Plato, *Protagoras*, 352e; *Phaedrus*, 233c; *Laws*, VII, 840c; *Letter VII*, 351a; Aristotle, *Nicomachean Ethics*, VII, 6, 1, 1149b; VII, 7, 4, 1150a; VII, 7, 6, 1150b; Isocrates, *Nicocles*, 39.

13. Xenophon, *Memorabilia*, I, 3, 14.

14. Xenophon, *Oeconomicus*, I, 23; Plato, *Republic*, VIII, 560b; IX, 572d–573b.

15. Ibid., IX, 571d.

16. Plato, *Laws*, VI, 783a–b.

17. Plato, *Phaedrus*, 232a; *Republic*, IV, 430c; *Laws*, I, 626e, 636e, 633e; VIII, 840c; *Letter VI*, 337a.

18. Plato, *Republic*, IV, 431a.

19. Plato, *Laws*, I, 626d–e.

20. Ibid., VIII, 840c.

21. Plato, *Republic*, IX, 571b.

22. Aristotle, *Nicomachean Ethics*, II, 9, 1109a.

23. Diogenes Laertius, *Lives of Eminent Philosophers*, IV, 7, 49.

24. Aristotle, *Nicomachean Ethics*, VII, 2, 1146a.

25. Ibid., III, 11, 1119a.

26. Diogenes Laertius, *Lives of Eminent Philosophers*, II, 8, 75.

27. Aristotle, *Nicomachean Ethics*, III, 12, 1119b.

28. Xenophon, *Oeconomicus*, I, 22–23.

29. Plato, *Laws*, III, 689a–b.

30. Plato, *Republic*, IX, 592b.

31. Ibid., IX, 592b.

32. Plato, *Laws*, I, 647d.

33. Xenophon, *Memorabilia*, I, 2, 19.

34. Ibid., I, 2, 24.

35. Plato, *Gorgias,* 527d.
36. On the connection between exercises and care of the self, see Plato, *Alcibiades,* 123d.
37. Diogenes Laertius, *Lives of Eminent Philosophers,* VI, 2, 70.
38. Plato, *Republic,* IX, 571c–572b.
39. Plato, *Laws,* I, 643.
40. Xenophon, *Constitution of the Lacedaemonians,* 2 and 3.
41. Plato, *Republic,* 413d ff.
42. Plato, *Laws,* I, 647e–648c.
43. Aristotle, *Nicomachean Ethics,* II, 2, 1104a.
44. Plato, *Republic,* III, 413e.
45. Plato, *Laws,* I, 643e.

Chapter 4: Freedom and Truth

1. Xenophon, *Memorabilia,* IV, 5, 2–3.
2. Aristotle, *Politics,* VII, 13, 1132a.
3. Diogenes Laertius, *Lives of Eminent Philosophers,* VI, 2, 66. Enslavement to pleasures is a very frequent expression: see Xenophon, *Oeconomicus,* I, 22; *Memorabilia,* IV, 5; Plato, *Republic,* IX, 577d.
4. Xenophon *Oeconomicus,* I, i, 17ff; *Memorabilia,* IV, 5, 2–11.
5. Plato, *Republic,* IX, 590c.
6. Ibid., IX, 580c.
7. Aristotle, *Politics,* V, 10.
8. Xenophon, *Cyropaedia,* VIII, 1.
9. Isocrates, *Nicocles,* 37–38.
10. Aristotle, *Politics,* V, 9, 1315a.
11. Plato, *Gorgias,* 491d.
12. Xenophon, *Oeconomicus,* X, 1.
13. Aristotle, *Politics,* I, 1260a.
14. Diogenes Laertius, *Lives of Eminent Philosophers,* VI, 54.
15. Aristotle, *Nicomachean Ethics,* III, 12, 1119b.
16. Xenophon, *Memorabilia,* III, 9, 4.
17. Plato, *Republic,* IV, 441e–442b.
18. Ibid.
19. Aristotle, *Nicomachean Ethics,* III, 12, 1119b.
20. Plato, *Laws,* I, 636d–e.

21. Xenophon, *Memorabilia*, IV, 5, 11.
22. Plato, *Phaedrus*, 254b.
23. Plato, *Gorgias*, 506d–507d.
24. Plato, *Republic*, 402d–403b.
25. Xenophon, *Cyropaedia*, VIII, 1, 33.

PART TWO: DIETETICS

Chapter 1: Regimen in General

1. Hippocrates, *Ancient Medicine*, III.
2. Plato, *Republic*, III, 405e–408d.
3. Homer, *Illiad*, 624 and 833.
4. Plato, *Republic*, III, 407c.
5. On the necessity of regimen for the cure of illnesses, see Plato, *Timaeus*, 89d.
6. Hippocrates, *Epidemics*, VI, 6, 1. On the different interpretation of this text in antiquity, see Hippocrates, *Oeuvres* (trans. Littre), vol. V, pp. 323–324.
7. Plato (attributed), *The Lovers*, 134a–d.
8. See R. Joly, "Notice," in Hippocrates, *Regimen*, French trans., p. xi.
9. Porphyry, *Life of Pythagoras*, 34; see also 15.
10. Xenophon, *Memorabilia*, III, 12.
11. Plato, *Republic*, IX, 591c–d.
12. See ibid., III, 404a; Aristotle, *Politics*, VIII, 16, 1335b; VIII, 4, 1338b–1339a.
13. Plato, *Republic*, III, 406a–407.
14. See ibid., 407c–e; *Timaeus*, 89b–c.
15. Plato, *Republic*, III, 404a–b.
16. Hippocrates, *Regimen*, III, 69, 1; cf. R. Joly's note in Hippocrates, *Regimen*, French trans., p. 71.
17. Plato, *Laws*, IV, 720b–e.
18. Plato, *Timaeus*, 89d.
19. Xenophon, *Memorabilia*, IV, 7.

Chapter 2: The Diet of Pleasures

1. See W. H. S. Jones, "Introduction" to works of Hippocrates (Loeb Classical Library ed.), vol. IV.

2. Oribasius, *Collection des médecins*, vol. III, pp. 168–182.

3. Paul of Aegina, *Chirurgie*, trans. R. Briau. On dietetics in the classical period, see W. D. Smith, "The Development of Classical Dietetic Theory," pp. 439–448.

4. Hippocrates, *Regimen*, I, 2, 1.

5. Ibid., II, 58, 2.

6. Ibid., III, 67, 1–2.

7. Ibid., III, 68, 10. In the same sense, see Hippocrates, *The Nature of Man*, 9, and *Aphorisms*, 51. The same theme is found in Aristotle (attributed), *Problems*, XXVIII, 1, and in Diocles' *Regimen*, in Oribasius, *Collection des médecins*, III, p. 181.

8. Hippocrates, *Regimen*, III, 68, 6 and 9.

9. Ibid., III, 68, 5.

10. Ibid., III, 68, 11.

11. Oribasius, *Collection des médecins*, III, pp. 168–178.

12. Ibid., p. 181.

13. Paul of Aegina, *Chirurgie*.

14. Oribasius, *Collection des médecins*, III, p. 177.

15. Aristotle (attributed), *Problems*, IV, 26 and 29. Cf. Hippocrates, *Regimen*, I, 24, 1.

Chapter 3: Risks and Dangers

1. Hippocrates, *Regimen*, III, 80, 2.

2. Ibid., III, 73, 2.

3. Diogenes Laertius, *Lives of Eminent Philosophers*, VIII, 1, 9.

4. Oribasius, *Collection des médecins*, III, 181; Aristotle (attributed), *Problems*, IV, 9, 877b.

5. Aristotle, *Generation of Animals*, V, 3, 783b.

6. Oribasius, *Collection des médecins*, III, p. 181.

7. Aristotle (attributed), *Problems*, IV, 2, 876a–b.

8. Ibid., IV, 30.

9. Hippocrates, *Diseases*, II, 51.

10. Hippocrates, *Epidemics*, III, 17, case 10; III, 18, case 16.

11. Plato, *Laws*, VII, 840a.

12. Ibid., VI, 775d–e.

13. Ibid., IV, 721a–b; VI, 785b.

14. Plato, *Republic*, V, 460e.

15. Aristotle, *Politics*, VII, 16, 1335a. On the ages for marriage in Athens, see W. K. Lacey, *The Family in Classical Greece*, pp. 106–107, 162.
16. Xenophon, *Constitution of the Lacedaemonians*, I, 4.
17. Plato, *Laws*, VI, 775c–d.
18. Aristotle, *Politics*, VII, 14, 1335b.
19. Xenophon, *Constitution of the Lacedaemonians*, I, 5.
20. Plato, *Laws*, VI, 784a–b.
21. Aristotle, *Politics*, VII, 16, 1335a.
22. Plato, *Laws*, VI, 783d–e.
23. Aristotle (attributed), *Problems*, X, 10.
24. Plato, *Laws*, VII, 792d–e.

Chapter 4: Act, Expenditure, Death

1. Plato, *Philebus*, 47b.
2. Aulus Gellius, *Attic Nights*, XIX, 2.
3. Clement of Alexandria, *Pedagogue*, I, 6, 48. Cf. R. Joly, "Notice," in his edition of Hippocrates, *Oeuvres* (C.U.F.), vol. XI.
4. Hippocrates, *The Seed*, 1–3.
5. Ibid., 3.
6. Ibid., 4.
7. Ibid., 1.
8. Ibid., 4.
9. Ibid.
10. Diogenes Laertius, *Lives of Eminent Philosophers*, VIII, 1, 28.
11. Hippocrates, *The Seed*, 2.
12. Ibid., 1 and 3.
13. Ibid., 4 and 2.
14. Ibid., 1.
15. Plato, *Timaeus*, 73b.
16. Aristotle, *Generation of Animals*, 724a–725b.
17. Ibid., 725b.
18. Ibid. See also Aristotle (attributed), *Problems*, IV, 22, 879a.
19. Aristotle (attributed), *Problems*, IV, 11, 877b.
20. Ibid., IV, 4 and 22.
21. Plato, *Laws*, IV, 721c.
22. Plato *Symposium*, 206e.
23. Ibid., 207a–b.
24. Plato, *Laws*, IV, 721b–c.

25. Plato, *Symposium*, 209b.
26. Aristotle, *On the Soul*, II, 4, 415a–b.
27. Aristotle, *Generation of Animals*, II, 1, 731b–732a.
28. Plato, *Laws*, IV, 721b–c.
29. Ibid., 723a.
30. R. Van Gulik, *La Vie sexuelle dans la Chine ancienne*.

PART THREE: ECONOMICS

Chapter 1: The Wisdom of Marriage

1. Demosthenes, *Against Neaera*, 122.
2. R. Van Gulik, *La Vie sexuelle dans la Chine ancienne*, pp. 144–154.
3. See the treatise *On Sterility* attributed to Aristotle and long considered to be Book X of *History of Animals*.
4. See above, Part Two.
5. As in Xenophon, *Oeconomicus*, VII, 11; Plato, *Laws*, 772d–773e.
6. Demosthenes, *Against Neaera*, 122.
7. Plutarch, *Life of Solon*, XX.
8. Diogenes Laertius, *Lives of Eminent Philosophers*, VIII, 1, 21.
9. Lysias, *On the Murder of Eratosthenes*, 33. Cf. S. Pomeroy, *Goddesses, Whores, Wives, and Slaves*, pp. 86–92.
10. Ibid., 12. See also in Xenophon's *Symposium* (IV, 8) the allusion to the ruses a husband might employ to conceal the sexual pleasures he intended to seek elsewhere.
11. W. K. Lacey, *The Family in Classical Greece*, p. 113.
12. Xenophon, *Symposium*, VIII, 3.
13. G. Mathieu, "Note," in Isocrates, *Nicocles*, p. 130.

Chapter 2: Ischomachus' Household

1. Xenophon, *Oeconomicus*, IV, 2–3.
2. Ibid., I, 5.
3. Regarding this praise of agriculture and enumeration of its beneficial effects, see all of Chapter 5 of Xenophon's *Oeconomicus*.
4. Xenophon, *Memorabilia*, III, 4.
5. Xenophon, *Oeconomicus*, IV, 18–25.
6. Ibid., XXI, 4–6.
7. Ibid., III, 15.
8. Ibid., III, 12–13.

9. Ibid., III, 11.
10. Ibid., VII, 5.
11. Ibid., VII, 11.
12. Ibid., VII, 12.
13. Ibid., VII, 13.
14. Ibid., VII, 15.
15. Ibid., VII, 19–35. On the importance of spatial factors in domestic organization, see J.-P. Vernant, "Hestia-Hermès: Sur l'expression religieuse de l'espace chez les Grecs," *Mythe et pensée chez les Grecs*, I, pp. 124–170.
16. Xenophon, *Oeconomicus*, VII, 39–40.
17. Ibid., VII, 22.
18. Ibid., VII, 26.
19. Ibid., VII, 31.
20. Ibid., VII, 30.
21. Ibid., VII, 23 and 12.
22. Ibid., I, 22–23.
23. Ibid., II, 1.
24. Ibid., VII, 27.
25. Ibid., X, 1–8.
26. Ibid., X, 7.
27. Ibid., X, 9.
28. Ibid., X, 10.
29. Ibid., X, 11.
30. See Xenophon, *Hiero*, I.
31. Euripides, *Medea*, v. 465ff.
32. Euripides, *Ion*, v. 836ff.
33. Xenophon, *Oeconomicus*, VII, 41–42.

Chapter 3: Three Policies of Moderation

1. Plato, *Laws*, VI, 773c and e.
2. Ibid., VI 783e; cf. IV, 721a; VI, 773b.
3. Ibid., VI, 773a–e.
4. Ibid., VI, 784a–c.
5. Ibid., VI, 784d–e.
6. Ibid., VI, 784e.
7. Ibid., VIII, 835e.
8. Ibid., VIII, 838a–839e.

9. Ibid., VIII, 840a–c.

10. Ibid., VIII, 840d–e.

11. Ibid., VIII, 841a–b.

12. Ibid., VIII, 841c–d.

13. Isocrates, *Nicocles,* 31–35.

14. Ibid., 42.

15. Ibid., 40.

16. Ibid., 41.

17. Isocrates, *To Nicocles,* 29.

18. Isocrates, *Nicocles,* 36. Regarding this frequent theme, see Aristotle, *Politics,* V, 1311a–b.

19. Isocrates, *Nicocles,* 37.

20. Ibid., 36.

21. Ibid., 37.

22. Isocrates, *To Nicocles,* 31.

23. Isocrates, *Nicocles,* 39.

24. Ibid., 45.

25. Ibid., 47.

26. Isocrates, *To Nicocles,* 11.

27. Aristotle (attributed), *Economics,* I, 1, 1, 1343.

28. Aristotle, *Politics,* I, 13, 1259b.

29. Aristotle (attributed), *Economics,* I, 3, 1, 1343b.

30. Ibid., I, 2, 1–3, 1343a–b.

31. Ibid., I, 3, 1, 1343b.

32. Aristotle, *Politics,* I, 2, 1252a; *Nicomachean Ethics,* VIII, 12, 7, 1162a.

33. Aristotle (attributed), *Economics,* I, 3, 1, 1343b.

34. Ibid., I, 3, 3, 1343b.

35. Ibid., I, 4, 1, 1344a.

36. Aristotle, *Politics,* I, 12, 1259. In the *Nicomachean Ethics* (VIII, 10, 5, 1161a), Aristotle alludes to the authority of heiress wives.

37. Aristotle, *Politics,* I, 12, 1259b.

38. Aristotle, *Nicomachean Ethics,* VIII, 10, 5, 1161a.

39. Aristotle, *Magna Moralia,* I, 33, 18.

40. Aristotle, *Nicomachean Ethics,* VIII, 11, 4, 1161a.

41. Ibid., VIII, 12, 8, 1162a. On the relations between *philia* and marriage in Aristotle, see J.-C. Fraisse, *Philia, la notion d'amitié dans la philosophie antique.*

42. Aristotle, *Politics,* VII, 16, 1335b–1336a.

PART FOUR: EROTICS

Chapter 1: A Problematic Relation

1. Plato, *Republic,* IX, 573d.
2. Ibid., IX, 574b–c.
3. Diogenes Laertius, *Lives of Eminent Philosophers,* IV, 7, 49.
4. Plato, *Laws,* VIII, 840a.
5. Xenophon, *Cyropaedia,* VII, 5.
6. On this point, cf. K. J. Dover, *Greek Homosexuality,* pp. 60–63.
7. Plato, *Symposium,* 181b–d.
8. Xenophon, *Symposium,* I, 9.
9. Ibid., II, 3.
10. Ibid., IX, 5–6.
11. Cf. Xenophon, *Anabasis,* VII, 4, 7.
12. See F. Buffière, *Éros adolescent,* pp. 90–91.
13. Plato, *Gorgias,* 494e.
14. Plato, *Symposium,* 182a–183d.
15. Cf. F. Buffière, *Éros adolescent,* pp. 605–607.
16. Regarding these two boys and their very slight age difference, see Plato, *Euthydemus,* 271b.
17. Plato, *Charmides,* 154c.
18. F. Buffière, *Éros adolescent,* p. 613, n. 33; Aelian, *Varia Historia,* XIII, 5.
19. Homer, *Illiad,* XI, 786. On the discussion about their respective roles, see Plato, *Symposium,* 180a–b; Aeschines, *Against Timarchus,* 143.
20. K. J. Dover, *Greek Homosexuality,* pp. 87–97.
21. Cf. what Aeschines says about the schools and the precautions the schoolmaster had to take in *Against Timarchus,* 9–10. On the meeting places, see F. Buffière, *Éros adolescent,* p. 561ff.
22. Xenophon, *Hiero,* I.
23. Plato, *Protagoras,* 309a.
24. Cf. the criticism of Meno in Xenophon, *Anabasis,* II, 6, 28.
25. Plato, *Symposium,* 181d–e.
26. Xenophon, *Symposium,* IV, 17.
27. On the opposition between the sturdy boy and the weakling, see Plato, *Phaedrus,* 239c–d, and *The Lovers.* Regarding the erotic

value of the masculine boy and the evolution of taste toward a more effeminate physique, perhaps already under way in the fourth century, see K. J. Dover, *Greek Homosexuality*, pp. 69–73. In any case, the notion that the charm of a young boy was connected with a femininity that inhabited him would become a common theme later.

28. On the definition of *philia,* see J.-C. Fraisse, *Philia, la notion d'amitié dans la philosophie antique.*
29. Xenophon, *Symposium,* VIII, 13–18.
30. Ibid., VIII, 3.

Chapter 2: A Boy's Honor

1. Xenophon, *Symposium,* VIII, 12. On the relationships between eulogy and precept, see also Aristotle, *Rhetoric,* I, 9.
2. Demosthenes, *Erotic Essay,* 1.
3. Ibid., 5.
4. Ibid., 53.
5. Aristotle, *Rhetoric,* I, 9.
6. Plato, *Symposium,* 182a–d.
7. Ibid., 178d.
8. Aeschines, *Against Timarchus,* 39–73.
9. Demosthenes, *Erotic Essay,* 17–19.
10. Ibid., 55.
11. Ibid., 53.
12. Ibid., 55.
13. Ibid., 3.
14. Ibid., 5.
15. Ibid., 4.
16. Plato, *Symposium,* 183d; see also 181a.
17. Demosthenes, *Erotic Essay,* 20.
18. Ibid., 7, 33, and 16; 8 and 14; 21; 23 and 25; 30.
19. Ibid., 31.
20. Ibid., 17.
21. On the importance of not being dominated and on the misgivings that were felt apropos of sodomy and passive fellation in homosexual relations, see K. J. Dover, *Greek Homosexuality,* pp. 100–109.

22. Demosthenes, *Erotic Essay*, 39–43.
23. Ibid., 38.
24. Ibid., 37.
25. Ibid., 28–29.

Chapter 3: The Object of Pleasure

1. Aristotle, *Politics*, I, 5, 1259a–b.
2. Ibid., I, 5, 1260b.
3. Cf. the laws cited by Aeschines, *Against Timarchus*, 9–18.
4. Ibid., 19–20.
5. K. J. Dover, *Greek Homosexuality*, pp. 19–20.
6. Aeschines, *Against Timarchus*, 52.
7. Aristophanes, *Knights*, v. 428ff; *Assemblywomen*, v. 112ff. Cf. F. Buffière, *Éros adolescent*, pp. 185–186.
8. Diogenes Laertius, *Lives of Eminent Philosophers*, VI, 34.
9. Ibid., VI, 2, 59 (see also 54 and 46).
10. Plato, *Laws*, I, 636b–c.
11. Ibid., VIII, 836c–d.
12. Plato, *Phaedrus*, 250e.
13. Or *diaprettesthai*, cf. ibid., 256c.
14. Xenophon, *Symposium*, IV, 15.
15. Xenophon, *Hiero*, I and VII; Plato, *Symposium*, 184c–d. See K. J. Dover, *Greek Homosexuality*, pp. 44–45.
16. Xenophon, *Symposium*, VIII, 21.
17. Plato, *Symposium*, 184e.
18. Ibid., 184a.

PART FIVE: TRUE LOVE

1. See J. Boswell, *Christianity, Social Tolerance, and Homosexuality*.
2. Plato, *Symposium*, 178d. On the speeches of the *Symposium*, see L. Brisson, "Eros," *Dictionnaire des mythologies*.
3. Plato, *Symposium*, 181b–d.
4. Ibid., 183d–e; *Phaedrus*, 231a–233a.
5. Plato, *Symposium*, 182a; *Phaedrus*, 239a.
6. Plato, *Phaedrus*, 231e–232a; 239e–240a.
7. Ibid., 240d.
8. Ibid., 239c–d.

9. Ibid., 241a–c.
10. Plato, *Symposium*, 191e.
11. Ibid., 192a.
12. Ibid., 192b.
13. On Socrates' reply to Aristophanes, see Plato, *Symposium*, 205e.
14. Xenophon, *Symposium*, VIII, 12; VIII, 25; VIII, 13.
15. Ibid., VIII, 14.
16. Ibid., IV, 26; see also *Memorabilia*, I, 3.
17. Xenophon, *Symposium*, VIII, 18.
18. Xenophon, *Constitution of the Lacedaemonians*, II, 12–15.
19. Xenophon, *Symposium*, VIII, 18.
20. Plato, *Phaedrus*, 244a.
21. Plato, *Symposium*, 184e, 185b.
22. Ibid., 196c.
23. Plato, *Phaedrus*, 244a.
24. Plato, *Symposium*, 201d.
25. Plato, *Phaedrus*, 259e.
26. Ibid., 204e.
27. Ibid., 210c–d.
28. Ibid., 256c–d.
29. Ibid., 255b–c.
30. Ibid., 255e–256a.
31. Plato, *Symposium*, 222b. Regarding the relations of Socrates and Eros, see P. Hadot, *Exercices spirituels et philosophie antique*, pp. 69–82.
32. H. Joly, *Le Renversement platonicien*, pp. 61–70.
33. Plato, *Laws*, V, 734a.
34. Plato, *Phaedrus*, 256a–b.

Conclusion

1. K. J. Dover, *Greek Homosexuality*, p. 203.

Bibliography

Classical authors' names and works are given in the form familiar in English, with the edition Foucault used listed first and that used by the translator (if different) cited in brackets. Modern sources are given in the language Foucault consulted.

Aeschines. *Against Timarchus.* French ed. & trans. V. Martin & G. de Budé. Collection des universités de France. [English trans. C. D. Adams. Loeb Classical Library.]

Antiphon. *Discourses.* French ed. & trans. L. Gernet. Collection des universités de France.

Apuleius. *Metamorphoses* (or *The Golden Ass*). French trans. P. Grimal. Paris: Gallimard, La Pléiade, 1963.

Aretaeus. *On the Causes and Signs of Chronic Diseases.* Text in *Corpus Medicorum Graecorum,* II. Berlin, 1958. French trans. L. Renaud. Paris, 1834. [English trans. T. F. Reynolds. Philadelphia: Haswell, Barrington, & Haswell, 1841.]

Aristophanes. *The Acharnians.* French ed. V. Coulon, trans. H. Van Daele. Collection des universités de France.

———. *The Assemblywomen.* French ed. V. Coulon, trans. H. Van Daele. Collection des universités de France.

———. *The Knights.* French ed. V. Coulon, trans. H. Van Daele. Collection des universités de France.

———. *The Thesmophoriazusae.* French ed. V. Coulon, trans. H. Van Daele. Collection des universités de France.

Aristotle. *The Eudemian Ethics.* English ed. and trans. H. Rackhan. Loeb Classical Library.

————. *Generation of Animals.* French ed. and trans. P. Louis. Collection des universités de France. [English trans. A. Platt. In *Complete Works of Aristotle,* Rev. Oxford Trans., ed. J. Barnes. Princeton: Princeton University Press, 1984.]

————. *History of Animals.* French ed. and trans. P. Louis. Collection des universités de France. [English trans. d'A. W. Thompson. In *Complete Works of Aristotle,* Rev. Oxford Trans., ed. J. Barnes. Princeton: Princeton University Press, 1984.]

————. *Magna Moralia.* English trans. G.C. Armstrong. Loeb Classical Library.

————. *The Nicomachean Ethics.* English ed. and trans. H. Rackman. Loeb Classical Library. French trans. R.-A. Gauthier and J.-Y. Jolif. Louvain-Paris, 1970. [English trans. D. Ross, Rev. J. L. Ackrill and J. O. Urmson. New York: Oxford University Press, 1980.]

————. *On the Soul.* French ed. A. Jannone, trans. E. Barbotin. Collection des universités de France.

————. *Parts of Animals.* French ed. and trans. P. Louis. Collection des universités de France.

————. *The Politics of Aristotle.* English ed. and trans. H. Rackman. Loeb Classical Library. [English trans. E. Barker. New York: Oxford University Press, 1958.]

————. *Rhetoric.* French ed. & trans. J. Voilquin and J. Capelle. Paris, 1944.

Aristotle (attributed). *Economics.* French ed. and trans. A. Wartelle. Collection des universités de France. [English trans. E. S. Forster. In *Complete Works of Aristotle,* Rev. Oxford Trans., ed. J. Barnes. Princeton: Princeton University Press, 1984.]

————. *On Sterility.* French ed. and trans. P. Louis. In *History of Animals,* Book III. Collection des universités de France. [English trans. J. Barnes. In *History of Animals,* Book X, in *Complete Works of Aristotle,* Rev. Oxford Trans., ed. J. Barnes. Princeton: Princeton University Press, 1984.]

————. *Problems.* English ed. and trans. W. S. Hett. Loeb Classical Library.

Aubenque, P. *La Prudence chez Aristote.* Paris: Presses Universitaires de France, 1963.

Augustine, Saint. *Confessions.* French ed. M. Skutella, trans. E. Trehorel an G. Bouisson. In *Oeuvres,* vol. XIII. Paris, 1962.

Aulus Gellius. *Attic Nights.* French ed. and trans. R. Macache. Collection des universités de France. [English trans. J. C. Rolfe. Loeb Classical Library.]

Boswell, J. *Christianity, Social Tolerance, and Homosexuality.* Chicago: University of Chicago Press, 1980.

Brisson, L. "Eros." In *Dictionnaire des mythologies.* Paris: Flammarion, 1981.

Buffière, F. *Éros adolescent: La Pédérastie dans la Grèce antique.* Paris: Les Belles Lettres, 1980.

Clement of Alexandria. *The Pedagogue.* French ed. and trans. M. Harl. Paris: Éditions du Cerf, 1960. [English trans. Rev. G. W. Butterworth. Loeb Classical Library.]

Dauvergne, H. *Les Forçats.* Paris, 1841.

Demosthenes. *Against Neaera.* French ed. and trans. L. Gernet. Collection des universités de France. [English trans. A. T. Murray. Loeb Classical Library.]

———. *The Erotic Essay.* French ed. and trans. R. Clavaud. Collection des universités de France. [English trans. N. W. Dewitt and N. J. Dewitt. Loeb Classical Library.]

Dio Chrysostom. *Discourses.* English ed. and trans. J. W. Cohoon. Loeb Classical Library.

Diocles. *Regimen.* In Oribasius, *Collection des médecins,* vol. III. French ed. and trans. U. Bussemaker and C. Daremberg. Paris, 1858.

Diogenes Laertius. *Lives of Eminent Philosophers.* English ed. and trans. R. D. Hicks. Loeb Classical Library. French trans. R. Genaille. Paris: Garnier-Flammarion, 1965.

Dover, K. J. "Classical Greek Attitudes to Sexual Behavior." *Arethusa* 6 (1973).

———. *Greek Homosexuality.* London, 1978. French trans. S. Saïd. Grenoble, 1982.

———. *Greek Popular Morality in the Time of Plato and Aristotle.* Oxford, 1974.

Duby, G. *Le Chevalier, la femme et le prêtre.* Paris: Hachette, 1981. [English trans. B. Bray. *The Knight, the Lady, and the Priest.* New York: Pantheon Books, 1983.]

Epictetus. *Discourses.* French ed. and trans. J. Souilhé. Collection des universités de France.

Euripides. *Ion.* French ed. and trans. P. Parmentier and H. Grégoire. Collection des universités de France. [English trans. M. Hadas and J. H. McLean. New York: Dial Press, 1936.]

———. *Medea.* French ed. and trans. L. Méridier. Collection des universités de France.

Flandrin, J.-L. *Un Temps pour embrasser.* Paris: Éditions du Seuil, 1983.

Fraisse, J.-C. *Philia, la notion d'amitié dans la philosophie antique.* Paris: Vrin, 1974.

Francis of Sales, Saint. *Introduction to the Devout Life.* French ed. C. Florisoone. Collection des universités de France. [English trans. M. Day. London: J. M. Dent, 1961.]

Galen, *On the Affected Parts.* French trans. C. Daremberg. Paris, 1856. [English trans. R. E. Siegel. Basel: Karger, 1976.]

Hadot, P. *Exercices spirituels et philosophie antique.* Paris: Études augustiniennes, 1981.

Hippocrates. *Ancient Medicine.* French ed. and trans. A.-J. Festugière. Paris, 1948. [English trans. W. H. S. Jones. Loeb Classical Library.]

———. *Aphorisms.* English ed. and trans. W. H. S. Jones. Loeb Classical Library.

———. *Diseases II.* French ed. and trans. J. Jouanna. Collection des universités de France.

———. *Epidemics.* English ed. and trans. W. H. S. Jones. Loeb Classical Library. [English trans. J. Chadwick and W. N. Mann. In *Hippocratic Writings.* Penguin Classics, 1983.]

———. *The Nature of Man.* English ed. and trans. W. H. S. Jones. Loeb Classical Library.

———. *Oath.* English ed. and trans. W. H. S. Jones. Loeb Classical Library.

———. *Regimen in Acute Diseases.* French ed. and trans. R. Joly. Collection des universités de France. [English trans. W. H. S. Jones. Loeb Classical Library.]

———. *Regimen in Health.* English ed. and trans. W. H. S. Jones. Loeb Classical Library.

———. *The Seed.* French ed. and trans. R. Joly. Collection des universités de France. [English trans. I. M. Lonie. In *Hippocratic Writings.* Penguin Classics, 1983.]

Isocrates. *Nicocles.* French ed. and trans. G. Mathieu and E. Brémond. Collection des universités de France. [English trans. G. Norlin. Loeb Classical Library.]

————. *To Nicocles.* French ed. and trans. G. Mathieu and E. Brémond. Collection des universités de France. [English trans. G. Norlin. Loeb Classical Library.]

Joly, H. *Le Renversement platonicien, logos, epistēmē, polis.* Paris: Vrin, 1974.

Lacey, W. K. *The Family in Classical Greece.* Ithaca: Cornell University Press, 1968.

Leski, E. "Die Zeugungskehre der Antike." *Abhandlungen der Akademie der Wissenschaften und Literatur* 19 (Mayence, 1950).

Lucian (attributed). *Affairs of the Heart.* English ed. and trans. M. D. MacLeod. Loeb Classical Library.

Lysias. *On the Murder of Eratosthenes.* French ed. and trans. L. Gernet and M. Bizos. Collection des universités de France. [English trans. W. R. M. Lamb. Loeb Classical Library.]

Manuli, P. "Fisiologia e patologia del feminile negli scritti hippocratici." *Hippocratica.* Paris, 1980.

North, H. *Sōphrosynē: Self-Knowledge and Self-Restraint in Greek Literature.* In *Cornell Studies in Classical Philology,* vol. 35. Ithaca: Cornell University Press, 1966.

Oribasius. *Collection des médecins latins et grecs.* French ed. and trans. U. Bussemaker and C. Daremberg. Paris, 1851–1876.

Paul of Aegina. *Chirurgie.* French trans. R. Briau. Paris, 1855.

Philostratus. *The Life of Apollonius of Tyana.* French trans. P. Grimal. Paris: Gallimard, La Pléiade, 1963.

Plato. *Alcibiades.* French ed. and trans. M. Croiset. Collection des universités de France.

————. *Charmides.* French ed. and trans. A. Croiset. Collection des universités de France.

————. *Euthydemus.* French ed. and trans. L. Méridier. Collection des universités France.

————. *Gorgias.* French ed. and trans. A. Croiset. Collection des universités de France. [English trans. T. Irwin. New York: Oxford University Press, 1979.]

————. *Laws.* French ed. and trans. É. des Places and A. Diès. Collection des universités de France. [English trans. T. L. Pangle. New York: Basic Books, 1980.]

————. *Letters.* French ed. and trans. J. Souilhé. Collection des universités de France.

————. *Phaedrus.* French ed. and trans. L. Robin. Collection des universités de France. [English trans. W. Hamilton. Penguin Classics, 1973.]

————. *Philebus.* French ed. and trans. A. Diès. Collection des universités de France. [English trans. J. C. B. Gosling. New York: Oxford University Press, 1975.]

————. *Politics.* French ed. and trans. A. Diès. Collection des universités de France.

————. *Protagoras.* French ed. and trans. A. Croiset. Collection des universités de France.

————. *Republic.* French ed. and trans. E. Chambry. Collection des universités de France. [English trans. G. M. A. Grube. Indianapolis: Hackett Publishing Company, 1974.]

————. *Symposium.* French ed. and trans. L. Robin. Collection des universités de France. [English trans. W. Hamilton. Penguin Classics, 1980.]

————. *Timaeus.* French ed. and trans. A. Rivaud. Collection des universités de France. [English trans. F. M. Cornford. Indianapolis: Bobbs-Merrill, 1959.]

Plato (attributed). *The Lovers.* French ed. and trans. J. Souilhé. Collection des universités de France.

Pliny the Elder. *Natural History.* French ed. and trans. J. Beaujeu. Collection des universités de France. [English trans. W. H. S. Jones. Loeb Classical Library.]

Plutarch. *Life of Cato the Younger.* French ed. and trans. R. Flacelière and E. Chambry. Collection des universités de France.

————. *Life of Solon.* French ed. and trans. E. Chambry, R. Flacelière, and M. Juneaux. Collection des universités de France.

————. *Table-Talks.* French ed. and trans. F. Fuhrmann. Collection des universités de France.

Polybius. *The Histories.* French ed. and trans. R. Weil and C. Nicolet. Collection des universités de France.

Pomeroy, S. *Goddesses, Whores, Wives and Slaves: Women in Classical Antiquity.* New York: Schocken, 1975.

Porphyry. *Life of Pythagoras.* French ed. and trans. É. des Places. Collection des universités de France.

Romilly, J. de. *La Loi dans la pensée grecque des origines à Aristote.* Paris: Les Belles Lettres, 1971.

Rufus of Ephesus. *Oeuvres.* French ed. and trans. C. Daremberg and C.-E. Ruelle. Paris, 1878.

Seneca the Elder. *Controversiae.* French trans. H. Bornecque. Paris: Garnier, 1932. [English trans. M. Winterbottom. Loeb Classical Library.]

Smith, W. D. "The Development of Classical Dietetic Theory." *Hippocratica.* Paris, 1980.

Stobaeus. *Florilegium.* Ed. A. Meineke. Leipzig, 1860–1864.

Van Gulik, R. *La Vie sexuelle dans la Chine ancienne.* French trans. L. Évrard. Paris: Gallimard, 1971.

Vernant, J.-P. *Mythe et pensée chez les Grecs.* Paris: Maspero, 1966.

Xenophon. *Agesilaus.* English ed. and trans. E. C. Marchant. Loeb Classical Library. French trans. P. Chambry. Paris: Garnier-Flammarion, 1967.

———. *Anabasis.* English ed. and trans. C. L. Brownson and O. J. Todd. Loeb Classical Library. French trans. P. Chambry. Paris: Garnier-Flammarion, 1967.

———. *The Constitution of the Lacedaemonions.* French trans. P. Chambry. Paris: Garnier-Flammarion, 1967. [English trans. E. C. Marchant. In *Scripta Minora.* Loeb Classical Library.]

———. *Cyropaedia.* French ed. and trans. M. Bizos and É. Delebecque. Collection des universités de France. [English trans. W. Miller. Loeb Classical Library.]

———. *Hiero.* English ed. and trans. E. C. Marchant and G. W. Bowersock. Loeb Classical Library. French trans. P. Chambry. Paris: Garnier-Flammarion, 1967.

———. *Memorabilia.* English ed. and trans. E. C. Marchant. Loeb Classical Library. French trans. P. Chambry. Paris: Garnier-Flammarion, 1967.

———. *Oeconomicus.* French ed. and trans. P. Chantraine. Collection des universités de France. [English trans. C. Lord. In *Xenophon's Socratic Discourse,* by L. Strauss. Ithaca: Cornell University Press, 1971.]

———. *Symposium.* English ed. and trans. C. L. Brownson and O. J. Todd. Loeb Classical Library. French trans. P. Chambry. Paris: Garnier-Flammarion, 1967.

Index